THE AMERICAN PIPE DREAM:
CRACK COCAINE AND THE INNER CITY

THE AMERICAN PIPE DREAM: CRACK COCAINE AND THE INNER CITY

Dale D. Chitwood

James E. Rivers

James A. Inciardi

The South Florida AIDS Research Consortium

Harcourt Brace College Publishers

Fort Worth   Philadelphia   San Diego   New York   Orlando   Austin   San Antonio
Toronto   Montreal   London   Sydney   Tokyo

Publisher	Ted Buchholz
Senior Acquisitions Editor	Stephen T. Jordan
Developmental Editor	Margaret McAndrew Beasley
Project Editor	Deanna Johnson
Production Manager	Lois West
Art Director	Garry Harman
Digital Compositor	Kim Standish

Cover image: Justus Hardin & Associates—Steve Turner

ISBN: 0-15-503093-0

Library of Congress Catalog Card Number: 95-81633

Address for Editorial Correspondence: Harcourt Brace College Publishers, 301 Commerce Street, Suite 3700, Fort Worth, TX 76102.

Address for Orders: Harcourt Brace & Company, 6277 Sea Harbor Drive, Orlando, FL 32887-6777. 1-800-782-4479, or 1-800-433-0001 (in Florida).

Excerpt from *Crack Cocaine: A Practical Treatment Approach for the Chemically Dependent* by Barbara Wallace (New York: Brunner/Mazel, 1991; pp. 143-159) is reprinted with permission from Brunner/Mazel, Inc. and the author.

Printed in the United States of America

6 7 8 9 0 1 2 3 4 5   066   9 8 7 6 5 4 3 2 1

CONTENTS

PREFACE

We have taught courses on criminology, drug abuse, and social problems for a cumulative total of several decades, and every year it is clear that the course to be taught this semester differs from preceding ones. New problems create new questions. Yet through the years specific themes have endured to form the backbone of these courses.

This book has two distinct qualities. First, we examine themes germane to these substantive areas from a contemporary perspective by enmeshing them within the context of the major drug problem of the 1990s, the distribution and use of crack. More than ten years have passed since crack became a household word. This is recent enough to permit a contemporary assessment of its origins and the recurring myths that accompany the rise of new illicit drugs, and distant enough to provide important perspectives on enduring problems such as the connection between crime and drugs.

Second, each chapter addresses a specific social issue. Crack is a metaphor for myriad social problems that exist in the inner city and are spreading to other regions of America. An exploration of the crack phenomenon is an exploration of many problems which intertwine to bring misery and despair to residents of inner cities. The issues addressed follow.

- The interrelatedness of street pharmacology, international drug trafficking, media responses to emergent drug use patterns, and the entrepreneurial nature of drug distribution
- The subculture of social institutions such as opium dens, speakeasies, and shooting galleries from which new settings like the crack house have emerged
- The validity, extent and nature of crack-crime relationships as they relate to drug legalization, courts, treatment, and public health
- The popular myth that crack use is solely the domain of African American inner city residents
- The role of gender in the crack culture and the degradation of women in many drug use settings

- The dual nature of the AIDS and the crack epidemics related to the diversity of sexual activity by crack users
- The relationship of crack use to homelessness
- The treatment needs and barriers to treatment that women experience
- Effective models for the treatment of crack users

This book is the work of the South Florida AIDS Research Consortium, an interdisciplinary organization of investigators and institutions who have combined their experience and expertise to address these social problems from the context of crack use.

INTRODUCTION

Crack is not a particularly new drug to the United States, although it did not become a household word until 1986. Even though crack had been known for a number of years, it was first reported in the literature during the early 1970s. At that time, however, awareness of crack seemed to be restricted to segments of cocaine's freebasing subculture. Crack often was referred to as "garbage freebase" by cocaine aficionados who quickly discarded the drug because it contained many impurities. It was rediscovered at the beginning of the 1980s, and by the middle of the decade it had taken on a life of its own.

For the inner cities, the introduction of crack could not have happened at a worse time. The economic base of the working poor had been shrinking for years, the result of a number of factors, including the loss of many skilled and unskilled jobs to cheaper labor markets, the movement of many businesses to the suburbs and sunbelt states, and competition from foreign manufacturers. Standards of living, health, and overall quality of life also were in a downward spiral, the negative consequences of suburbanization and the shrinking tax bases of central cities, combined with changing economic policies at the federal level that shifted the responsibility for many social supports to the local and private sectors. Without question, by the early to mid-1980s there was a growing and pervasive climate of hopelessness in ghetto America. At the same time, funding for drug abuse treatment declined, HIV and AIDS was spreading rapidly through inner city populations of injection drug users and their sex partners, and high purity cocaine was abundant at a low price on the streets of urban America because the production of coca and cocaine in South America had reached an all-time high.

The next chapter in the story of crack is fairly well-known, having been reported (and perhaps over-reported) in the media since early in 1986—the "highs", binges, and "crashes" that induce addicts to sell their belongings and their bodies in pursuit of more crack; the high addiction liability of the drug that instigates users to commit any manner and variety of crimes to support their habits; the rivalries in crack distribution networks that have turned some inner-city communities into urban "dead zones" where homicide rates are so high that police have written them off as anarchic badlands; the involvement of inner-city youths in the crack business, including the "peewees" and "wannabees" (want-to-be's), those street-gang acolytes in grade school and junior-high who patrol the streets with two-way radios and cellular phones in the vicinity of crack houses, serving in networks of look-outs, spotters, and steerers, and aspiring to be "rollers" (short for high-rollers) in the drug distribution business; the child abuse, child neglect, and child abandonment by crack-addicted mothers; and finally, the growing cohort of crack-exposed infants that are troubled not only physically, but emotionally and behaviorally as well.

Crack is not just another drug-of-the-month type of substance. The continual presence of crack since its emergence in the 1980s establishes this stimulant as an enduring drug of use. Crack use is endemic in the inner-city communities of many metropolitan areas of America and is becoming endemic in some inner-city-type areas of rural America. This is not surprising since it is but one form of cocaine, and cocaine—whether snorted, injected, or smoked—has been a major drug of abuse for the past two decades. In several communities cocaine is the primary drug of abuse, and crack is the primary form of cocaine that is used.

Will crack remain endemic in our society? Its presence during the last decade indicates the potential exists. Will the problems associated with crack use continue to harass our society? They undoubtedly will persist if the knowledge obtained through the study of crack is ignored by policy makers.

The chapters of this book have been written with these facts in mind. Crack is a recent enough phenomenon to permit a contemporary review of its origins and has been enduring enough to permit the examination of chronic societal problems such as the crime and drug connection that are associated with major illicit drugs.

Chapter 1 describes the evolution of crack from its origins as "garbage freebase," to its reintroduction to the United States by Caribbean immigrants and its emergence as the media-riveting drug event of the 1980s. The authors demonstrate the interrelatedness of street pharmacology, drug trafficking, media treatment of emergent drug use patterns, and the entrepreneurial foundations and organizational structure of drug distribution. This chapter debunks popular myths about crack that typically circulate whenever a psychoactive drug catches the attention and imagination of the media and the public.

The discussion of inner-city crack houses in Chapter 2 reveals the crack house as but the latest manifestation in a series of similar social institutions, such as opium dens, speakeasies, and shooting galleries, that have always existed within the subculture of drug use. Far from being a monolithic structure, there are many types of crack houses that can be cataloged by the different functions they perform within the subculture. This chapter examines various typologies which describe crack houses and the behaviors which occur in different user settings. The social, economic, and health issues associated with crack houses that are discussed in subsequent chapters are introduced in this section.

Chapter 3 examines several issues about crime and drugs in the specific context of the crack phenomenon. The authors critically examine the validity, extent, and nature of crack-crime relationships among both adult and juvenile populations of crack users. This chapter discusses the problem of causal inference in the crack-crime relationship and gives special attention to public policy about drug legalization, drug courts, drug treatment, and public health.

A widespread perception exists, rooted in television news, news magazines, and other media presentations that there is an overwhelming relationship between race/ethnicity and crack use. In the public mind, crack use is regarded as almost exclusively an African American activity. Chapter 4 debunks this popular myth that crack use is the domain solely of African American inner-city residents and demonstrates that crack is a multi-ethnic problem.

The role of gender in the crack subculture and resultant degradation of women is discussed in Chapter 5, where the implications of the use of crack on the health and status of women are explored. While women historically have been relegated to subservient roles in virtually all drug cultures, the sex for crack exchange is a defining phenomenon of the crack epidemic in most inner cities. Prostitution has reached a new level of degradation as a crack-generated activity, and women who engage in sex for crack are debased to a greater extent than the non-crack-driven traditional street prostitute.

The AIDS epidemic and the crack epidemic exploded upon the American scene at approximately the same time. Chapter 6 addresses this important issue. While early in the AIDS epidemic injection drug users were known to be at high risk for HIV infection, recognition of crack use as a major risk factor came later. The unparalleled frequency and diversity of sexual activity by crack users place them at high risk not only for AIDS but also for other sexually transmitted diseases.

Homelessness has become a major problem in many metropolitan areas. Chapter 7 is a presentation of an ethnographic component of a larger project studying the homeless in Miami, Florida in which the complex interaction between crack use and homelessness is explored. Not all people who are homeless are crack users, yet crack plays a role both in the cause of homelessness and as a constant threat to the vulnerable members of the homeless population. Verbatim ethnographic reports from the participants in the study are included. As well as providing a picture of crack use among the homeless, this chapter provides an example of the contribution of ethnography in the study of social issues.

Chapter 8 discusses the deficiency in drug treatment and related barriers to treatment access experienced by women. Historically, drug abuse treatment programs have been aimed toward the needs of male drug users. The particular needs of female drug users are often unrecognized and not addressed in treatment services. The authors present the results of a study among women at high risk for drug use that examine the social service needs and barriers to service for women.

Chapter 9 is a discussion of the current state of knowledge of the treatment of cocaine addiction. Currently, there is little information available on treatment focusing on crack addiction. Through a review of outcome-evaluation studies, the author explores various treatment modalities and the successes and failures of each type of treatment. Suggestions and implications for designing cost-effective treatments are addressed.

The chemistry and psychopharmacology of crack, combined with the tangle of socioeconomic and psychocultural strains that exist in the inner-city communities where the drug is concentrated, have brought a substantial level of human suffering to the American drug scene. This book addresses the major criminal, social, and public health problems associated with the use of crack.

The American Pipe Dream:
Crack Cocaine and the Inner City

Chapter 1

THE ORIGINS OF CRACK[*]

James A. Inciardi
Hilary L. Surratt
Dale D. Chitwood
Clyde B. McCoy

The first mention of crack cocaine in the major media occurred on November 17, 1985.[1] Buried within the pages of that Monday edition of the prestigious *New York Times,* journalist Donna Boundy, in writing about a local drug abuse treatment program, unceremoniously commented, "Three teenagers have sought this treatment already this year . . . for cocaine dependence resulting from the use of a new form of the drug called 'crack' or rock-like pieces of prepared 'freebase' (concentrated) cocaine" (*New York Times,* 17 Nov. 1985, p. B12).

Although Boundy, like so many after her, had erred in describing crack as "freebase" or "concentrated" cocaine,[2] her mere mentioning of what was ostensibly an old drug initiated a major media event. Crack suddenly took on a life of its own, and in less than 11 months the *New York Times,*[3] the *Washington Post,*

---

[*] Portions of this chapter were adapted from "Hurricane Crack," in James A. Inciardi, *The War on Drugs II* (Mountain View, CA: Mayfield, 1992).

[1] The media story of crack can actually be traced to the latter part of 1984 when the Los Angeles dailies began reporting on local "rock houses" where small pellets of cocaine could be had for as little as $25 (for example, *Los Angeles Times,* 25 Nov. 1984, pp. CC1, CC8. *Newsweek* (11 Feb. 1985, p. 33) later gave a half page to the Los Angeles item, but the term *crack* was never used, and little attention was given to the matter.

[2] Rather than "concentrated" or "purified" cocaine, crack might be better described as the "fast-food" analogue of cocaine.

[3] Following Boundy's brief mention of crack earlier in November, it was likely that the front-page story in the November 29, 1985, issue of the *Times,* headlined "A New Purified Form of Cocaine Causes Alarm as Abuse Increases," represented the beginning of the drug's concentrated media attention.

the *Los Angeles Times,* the wire services, *Time, Newsweek,* and *U.S. News & World Report* collectively had served the nation with more than 1,000 stories in which crack had figured prominently. Or as social critic Malcolm Gladwell (1986, p. 11) recalled the episode, ". . . coverage feeding coverage, stories of addiction and squalor multiplying across the land."

And then CBS capped their reporting with "48 Hours on Crack Street," a prime-time presentation that reached 15 million viewers and became one of the highest rated documentaries in the history of television. Not to be outdone, NBC offered "Cocaine Country," culminating a 6-month stretch in which the network had broadcast more than 400 reports on drug abuse.

As the crack frenzy was mounting during the summer of 1986, a number of researchers in the drug community were somewhat perplexed. Although *Newsweek* (Smith, 1986) claimed crack was the biggest story since Vietnam and the fall of the Nixon presidency, and other media giants compared the spread of crack with the plagues of medieval Europe, researchers were finding crack to be not a national epidemic, but a phenomenon isolated to but a few inner-city neighborhoods in less than a dozen urban areas. By late August, crack hysteria had reached such proportions that the Drug Enforcement Administration (DEA) felt compelled to respond. Based on reports from its field agents and informants in cities throughout the country, a DEA (1986) report concluded,

> Crack is readily available in Atlanta, Boston, Detroit, Houston, Kansas City, Miami, New York City, Newark, San Diego, San Francisco, Seattle, and St. Louis. Availability at some level has also been reported in Dallas, Denver, Los Angeles, Minneapolis, Phoenix, and Washington, D.C. Crack generally is not available in Chicago, New Orleans, and Philadelphia.
>
> Crack is currently the subject of considerable media attention. The result has been a distortion of the public perception of the extent of crack use as compared to the use of other drugs. With multi-kilogram quantities of cocaine hydrochloride available and with snorting continuing to be the primary route of cocaine administration, crack presently appears to be a secondary rather than primary problem in most areas.

Curiously, most of the major newspapers, networks, and weekly magazines ignored the DEA report. It was not until the revelations about Lt. Col. Oliver L. North and the Iran-contra connection toward the close of 1986 that the media coverage concerning crack declined significantly.

In contrast with the media contention that crack was "everywhere," observations during the summer of 1986 tended to concur with DEA's position (see Inciardi, 1987). Additional support in this regard came from New York City. Throughout 1986, crack seemed to be concentrated in the city's Washington Heights section, an inner-city neighborhood at the northern end of Manhattan. Many of the streets in Washington Heights had been transformed into outdoor drug marketplaces. One of the more curious aspects of the situation was that the streets frequently were clogged with cars from other parts of New York City, its suburbs, its neighboring states, and other locations (*New York Times,*

21 Jan. 1987, p. B1). But outside of Washington Heights at that time, crack was generally unavailable. Elsewhere, as Dr. Sidney H. Schnoll, at the time affiliated with the Northwestern University Medical School, commented about Chicago late in the summer of 1986: "It's a hoax! There's just no crack in Chicago!" (personal communication, August 1986).

Nevertheless, *Newsweek* (Morganthou, Greenberg-Fink, Murr, Miller, & Raine, 1986) described the crack scene as "an inferno of craving and despair." *Time* (Lamar, 1986, p. 16) stated it somewhat differently: "In minutes the flash high is followed by a crashing low that can leave a user craving another hit."

On the same day, this story appeared in *USA Today:* "Katrina Linton was 17 when she first walked into a crack house in the Bronx. By then she was selling her body to crack dealers just to support her $900-a-day habit" (16 June, 1986, p. 1A).

In these and other media stories the implication was clear: Crack plunged the user almost immediately into the nightmare worlds of Charles Adams, Stephen King, and Rod Serling, from which there was little chance of return. But to researchers and clinicians in the drug field who remembered the media's portrayal of the so-called PCP epidemic a decade earlier, reports of the pervasiveness of crack were regarded with skepticism. Interestingly, the media and the drug professionals were at the same time both right and wrong about what they were saying. During the summer and fall of 1986, contrary to media claims, crack indeed had *not* been an epidemic drug problem in the United States. Crack was there, but it was not until the beginning of 1987 that it really began to assert itself, eventually becoming perhaps the most degrading drug of the century.

UNRAVELING CRACK COCAINE

The history of crack dates back to at least the early 1970s, but to fully understand its evolution, a short diversion into a few other products of the coca leaf is warranted. More specifically, "freebase" and "coca paste" are prominent players in the story of crack.

Powder Cocaine and Freebase Cocaine

During the late 1960s, when cocaine had begun its contemporary trek from the underground to mainstream society, most users viewed it as a relatively "safe" drug. They snorted it in relatively small quantities, and use typically occurred within a social-recreational context (Siegel, 1977). But as the availability of cocaine increased in subsequent years, so too did the number of users and the ways of ingesting it. Some began sprinkling street cocaine on tobacco or marijuana and smoking it as a cigarette or in a pipe, but this method did not produce effects distinctly different from snorting (Grinspoon & Bakalar, 1985).

But a new alternative soon became available called *freebasing,* the smoking of "freebase cocaine."

Freebase cocaine is actually a different chemical product than cocaine itself. In the process of freebasing, cocaine hydrochloride is transformed to the base state in a crystalline form. The crystals are then crushed and heated in a special glass pipe. By 1977 some 4 million people were estimated to be users of cocaine in the United States (Abelson, Cohen, Schrayer, & Rappaport, 1978), with as many as 10% of these freebasing the drug exclusively (Siegel, 1982). Yet few outside of the drug-using and drug research and treatment communities were even aware of the existence of the freebase culture, and even fewer had an understanding of the additional complications that freebasing had introduced to the cocaine scene.

The complications are several. First, cocaine in any of its forms is highly seductive. With freebasing, the euphoria is more intense than when the drug is snorted. Moreover, this profound euphoria subsides into intense craving after only a few minutes, thus influencing many users to continue freebasing for days at a time—until either they, or their drug supplies, are fully exhausted. Second, freebasing is expensive. When snorting cocaine, a single gram can last the social user an entire weekend or longer. With street cocaine ranging in price anywhere from $40 to $120 a gram depending on availability and purity, even this method of ingestion can be an expensive recreational pursuit. Yet with freebasing, the cost can undergo a geometric increase. Habitual users have been known to freebase continuously for 3 or 4 days without sleep, using up to 150 grams of cocaine in a 72-hour period. Third, a special danger of freebasing is the proximity of highly flammable ether (or rum when it is used instead of water as a coolant in the pipe) to an open flame. This problem is enhanced because the user generally is suffering from a loss of coordination produced by cocaine or a combination of cocaine and alcohol. As such, there have been many freebasing situations where the volatile concoction has exploded in the face of the user.

By 1980 reports of major problems associated with freebasing had begun to reach a national audience, crystallized by the near death by explosion of comedian-actor Richard Pryor, presumably the result of freebasing.[4]

Coca Paste – Pasta Basica de Cocaina

Common in the drug-using communities of Colombia, Bolivia, Venezuela, Ecuador, Peru, and Brazil is the use of coca paste, known to most South Americans as *basuco, susuko, pasta basica de cocaina,* or just simply *pasta* (Jeri, 1984). Perhaps best known as *basuco,* coca paste is one of the intermediate

---

[4] Although Pryor denied he had been using cocaine at the time of the June 1980 explosion, he later admitted he had been freebasing for three days prior to the event (see *Time,* July 6, 1981, p. 63). In a 1986 interview with Barbara Walters, Pryor once again changed his story, claiming the fire was the result of a suicide attempt because he couldn't overcome his dependence on freebase.

products in the processing of the coca leaf into cocaine. It is typically smoked straight or in cigarettes mixed with either tobacco or marijuana.

The smoking of coca paste became popular in South America beginning in the early 1970s. It was readily available, inexpensive, had a high cocaine content, and was absorbed quickly. As researchers studied the phenomenon, however, they quickly realized that paste smoking was far more dangerous than any other form of cocaine use. In addition to cocaine, paste contains traces of all the chemicals used initially to process the coca leaves—kerosene, sulfuric acid, methanol, benzoic acid, and the oxidized products of these solvents, plus any number of other alkaloids that are present in the coca leaf (Almeida, 1978). One analysis undertaken in Colombia in 1986 found all of these chemicals, plus traces of brick dust, leaded gasoline, ether, and various talcs (Bogota *El Tiempo,* 19 June 1986, p. 2-D).

When the smoking of paste was first noted in South America, it seemed to be restricted to the coca-processing regions of Bolivia, Colombia, Ecuador, and Peru, appealing primarily to low-income groups because of its cheap price when compared with that of refined cocaine (Jeri, Sanchez, & Del Pozo, 1976). By the early 1980s, however, it had spread to other South American nations, to various segments of the social strata, and throughout the decade paste smoking further expanded to become a major drug problem for much of South America.[5] At the same time, coca paste made its way to the United States–first to Miami, its initial smuggling port of entry, and then elsewhere.[6] Interestingly, the paste quickly became known to young North American users as "bubble gum," likely due to the phonetic association of the South American *basuco* with the American Bazooka brand bubble gum.[7]

---

[5] See Caracus (Venezuela) *El Universal,* October 4, 1985, pp. 4, 30; Caracus *Zeta,* September 12–23, 1985, pp. 39–46; Manaus (Brazil) *Jornal Do Comercio,* May 20, 1986, p. 16; Bogota *El Tiempo,* June 1, 1986, p. 3-A; Medellin *El Colombiano,* July 22, 1986, p. 16-A; Bogota *El Tiempo,* October 6, 1986, p. 7-A; Lima (Peru) *El Nacional,* November 14, 1986, p. 13; La Paz (Bolivia) *Presencia,* March 3, 1988, Sec. 2, p. 1; Sao Paulo (Brazil) *Folha de Sao Paulo,* June 11, 1987, p. A29; Buenos Aires (Argentina) *La Prensa,* June 20, 1987, p. 9; Sao Paulo *O Estado de Sao Paulo,* March 8, 1988, p. 18; Bogota *El Espectador,* April 2, 1988, pp. 1A, 10A; La Paz *El Diario,* October 21, 1988, p. 3; Cochabamba (Bolivia) *Los Tiempos,* June 13, 1989, p. B5; Sao Paulo *O Estado de Sao Paulo,* June 18, 1989, p. 32; Rio de Janiero (Brazil) *Manchete,* October 28, 1989, pp. 20–29; Philadelphia *Inquirer,* September 21, 1986, p. 25A; Timothy Ross, "Bolivian Paste Fuels Basuco Boom," *WorldAIDS,* September 1989, p. 9.

[6] Curiously, coca paste was reportedly available in Italy during 1987. See Milan *Corriere Della Sera,* October 26, 1987, p. 8.

[7] During the latter part of the 1980s, a new form of coca paste smoking was noticed, principally in Brazil. For years in the nations of Peru, Bolivia, Ecuador, Argentina, and Brazil, the term *pitillo* (also "petilho," and "pitilio" in Portuguese) had referred to a marijuana cigarette, or marijuana laced with coca paste. The new "pitillo," however, also referred to in parts of Brazil as "Bolivian crack," was marijuana and coca paste residue—the dregs left in the processing drum after coca paste precipitate had been removed. Although no analyses of this residue have been reported in the literature, it is suspected the product has even higher concentrations of sulfuric acid and petroleum products than does coca paste. See Sao Paulo *Folha de Sao Paulo,* July 30, 1986, p. 15; Cochabamba *Los Tiempos,* October 13, 1986, p. 5; Sao Paulo *O Estado de Sao Paulo,* November 10, 1990, p. 5, Rio de Janiero *O Globo,* November 30, 1986, p. 18; Buenos Aires *La Prensa,* June 20, 1987, p. 9; Sao Paulo *Veja,* December 12, 1990, pp. 22–23.

The Coca Paste/Crack Cocaine Connection

Contrary to popular belief, crack is not a new substance, having been first reported in the literature during the early 1970s (*The Gourmet Cokebook,* 1972). At that time, however, knowledge of crack, known then as "base" or "rock" (not to be confused with "rock cocaine," a cocaine hydrochloride product for intranasal snorting), seemed to be restricted to segments of cocaine's freebasing subculture. Crack is processed from cocaine hydrochloride by adding ammonia or baking soda and water and heating this mixture to remove the hydrochloride. The result is a pebble-sized crystalline form of cocaine base.

Contrary to another popular belief, crack is neither "freebase cocaine" nor "purified cocaine." Part of the confusion about what crack actually is comes from the different ways the word *freebase* is used in the drug community. Freebase (the noun) is a drug, a cocaine product converted to the base state from cocaine hydrochloride after adulterants have been chemically removed. Crack is converted to the base state *without* removing the adulterants. Freebasing (the act) means to inhale vapors of cocaine base, of which crack is but one form. Finally, crack is not purified cocaine because during its processing, the baking soda remains as a salt, thus reducing its homogeneity somewhat. Informants in the Miami drug subculture indicate that the purity of crack ranges as high as 80%, but generally contains much of the filler and impurities found in the original cocaine hydrochloride, along with some of the baking soda (sodium bicarbonate) and cuts (expanders, for increasing bulk) from the processing. And interestingly, crack gets its name from the fact that the residue of sodium bicarbonate often causes a crackling sound when the substance is smoked.[8]

As to the presence of crack in the drug communities of the early 1970s, it was available for only a short period of time before it was discarded by freebase cocaine aficionados as an inferior product. Many of them referred to it as "garbage freebase" because of the many impurities it contained. In this regard, a 42-year-old Miami cocaine user commented in 1986,

> Of course crack is nothing new. The only thing that's new is the name. Years ago it was called *rock, base,* or *freebase,* although it really isn't *true* "freebase." It was just an easier way to get something that gave a more potent rush, done the same way as now with baking soda. It never got too popular among the 1970s cokeheads because it was just not as pure a product as conventional freebase.

---

[8] Some comment seems warranted on the practice of referring to crack as "smokable cocaine." Technically, crack is not really smoked. "Smoking" implies combustion, burning, and the inhalation of smoke. Tobacco is smoked. Marijuana is smoked. Crack, on the contrary, is actually inhaled. The small pebbles or rocks, having a relatively low melting point, are placed in a special glass pipe or other smoking device and heated. Rather than burning, crack vaporizes and the fumes are inhaled.

The rediscovery of crack seemed to occur simultaneously on the East and West coasts early in the 1980s. As a result of the Colombian government's attempts to reduce the amount of illicit cocaine production within its borders, it apparently, at least for a time, successfully restricted the amount of ether available for transforming coca paste into cocaine hydrochloride. The result was the diversion of coca paste from Colombia, through Central America and the Caribbean, into South Florida for conversion into cocaine. Spillage from shipments through the Caribbean corridor introduced the smoking of coca paste to local island populations, who in turn developed the forerunner of crack cocaine in 1980 (Hall, 1986). Known as *baking-soda base, base-rock, gravel,* and *roxanne,* the prototype was a smokable product composed of coca paste, baking soda, water, and rum. Migrants from Jamaica, Haiti, Trinidad, and locations along the Leeward and Windward islands chain introduced the crack prototype to Caribbean inner-city populations in Miami's immigrant undergrounds, where it was ultimately produced from powder cocaine rather than paste. As a Miami-based immigrant from Barbados commented in 1986 about the diffusion of what he referred to as "baking-soda paste,"

> Basuco and baking-soda paste seemed to come both at the same time. There was always a little cocaine here and there in the islands, but not too much, and it wasn't cheap. Then 'bout five, maybe six, years ago, the paste hit all of the islands. It seemed to happen overnight—Barbados, Saint Lucia, Dominica, and [Saint] Vincent and [Saint] Kitts—all at the same time.[9]
>   . . . Then I guess someone started to experiment, and we got the rum-soda-paste concoction. We brought it to Miami when we came in '82, and we saw that the Haitians too were into the same combination.

Apparently, at about the same time, a Los Angeles basement chemist rediscovered the rock variety of baking soda cocaine, and it was initially referred to as "cocaine rock" (Inciardi, 1988, p. 470). It was an immediate success, as was the East Coast type, for a variety of reasons. First, it could be "smoked" rather than snorted. When cocaine is smoked, it is more rapidly absorbed and crosses the blood-brain barrier within 6 seconds. Hence it creates an almost instantaneous high. Second, it was cheap. Although a gram of cocaine for snorting may cost $60 or more depending on its purity, the same gram can be transformed into anywhere from 5 to 30 "rocks." For the user, this meant that individual rocks could be purchased for as little as $2, $5 (*nickel rocks*), $10 (*dime rocks*), or $20. For the seller, $60 worth of cocaine hydrochloride (purchased

---

For those unfamiliar with the geography of the Caribbean, the locations spoken of by this informant are part of the Leeward and Windward islands. The Leeward Islands are the northern segment of the Lesser Antilles and stretch some 400 miles in a southerly arc from the Virgin Islands to Dominica. The Windward Islands are the southern part of the Lesser Antilles, stretching some 200 miles from Martinique south to Grenada. Barbados is located just west of the southern half of the Windward chain, but is not geographically part of it.

wholesale for $30) could generate as much as $100 to $150 when sold as wholesale for $30) could generate as much as $100 to $150 when sold as rocks. Third, it was easily hidden and transportable, and when hawked in small glass vials, it could be readily scrutinized by potential buyers. As a South Miami narcotics detective described it during the summer of 1986,[9]

> Crack has been a real boon to both buyer and seller. It's cheap, real cheap. Anybody can come up with $5 or $10 for a trip to the stars. But most important, it's easy to get rid of in a pinch. Drop it on the ground and it's almost impossible to find; step on it and the damn thing is history. All of a sudden your evidence ceases to exist.

By the close of 1985 when crack had finally come to the attention of the national media, it was predicted to be the "wave of the future" among the users of illegal drugs (*New York Times,* 29 Nov. 1985, p. A1). Media stories also reported that crack was responsible for rising rates of street crime. As a cover story in *USA Today* put it,

> Addicts spend thousands of dollars on binges, smoking the contents of vial after vial in crack or "base" houses—modern-day opium dens—for days at a time without food or sleep. They will do anything to repeat the high, including robbing their families and friends, selling their possessions and bodies. (*USA Today,* 16 June 1986, p. 1A)

As the media blitzed the American people with lurid stories depicting the hazards of crack, Congress and the White House began drawing plans for a more concerted war on crack and other drugs. At the same time, crack use was reported in Canada, most European nations, Hong Kong, South Africa, Egypt, India, Mexico, Belize, Bermuda, Barbados, Colombia, Brazil, and the Philippines.[10]

---

[10] Windsor (Canada) *Windsor Star,* June 26, 1986, p. A13; Toronto *Globe and Mail,* September 2, 1987, p. A5; Ottawa *Citizen,* Febrary 13, 1988, p. A15; Belfast (Ireland) *News Letter,* July 9, 1986, p. 3; Helsinki (Finland) *Uusi Suomi,* July 28, 1986, p. 8; Rio de Janeiro *O Globo,* May 24, 1986, p. 6; Hong Kong *South China Morning Post,* August 2, 1986, p. 16; Johannesburg (South Africa) *Star,* September 23, 1986, p. 1M; Cape Town (South Africa) *Argus,* March 10, 1987, p. 13; Johannesburg *City Press,* January 7, 1990, p. 5; Milan (Italy) *Panorama,* May 3, 1987, pp. 58–59; Oslo (Norway) *Arbeiderbladet,* June 4, 1987, p. 13; Madrid (Spain) *El Alcazar,* September 14, 1986, p. 11; Nuevo Laredo (Mexico) *El Diario de Nuevo Laredo,* October 12, 1986, Sec. 4, p. 1; Calcutta (India) *Statesman,* October 16, 1986, p. 1; Belize City (Belize) *Beacon,* October 25, 1986, pp. 1, 14; London *Al-Fursan,* September 13, 1986, pp. 51–53; London *Sunday Telegraph,* April 12, 1987, p. 1; Geneva (Switzerland) *Journal de Geneve,* December 26, 1986, p. 1; Brussels (Belgium) *Le Soir,* November 10/11, 1986, p. 3; Munich (West Germany) *Sueddeutsche Zeitung,* October 18/19, 1986, p. 12; Lisbon (Portugal) *O Jornal,* January 30–February 5, 1987, p. 40; Hamburg (West Germany) *Die Zeit,* April 24, 1987, p. 77; Hamilton (Bermuda) *Royale Gazette,* December 3, 1987, p. 3; Bridgetown (Barbados) *Weekend Nation,* January 15–16, 1988, p. 32; Stockholm (Sweden) *Dagens Nyheter,* January 2, 1988, p. 6; Grand Cayman (Bahamas) *Caymanian Compass,* January 20, 1988, pp. 1–2; Paris *Liberation,* January 12, 1990, p. 33; Bangkok (Thailand) *Siam Rat,* August 13, 1988, p. 12.

CRACK IN THE MIAMI INNER CITY

Although the use of crack cocaine became evident in most major cities across the United States during the latter half of the 1980s, cocaine and crack tend to be associated more often with Miami than most other urban areas. In part, this is due to Miami's association with the cocaine wars of the late 1970s and early 1980s, and with South Florida's reputation for cocaine importation and distribution (see Allman, 1987; Buchanan, 1987; Carr, 1990; Rieff, 1987; Rothchild, 1985). No doubt the image of the city as America's Casablanca, or the Casablanca on the Caribbean, presented in TV's *Miami Vice* contributed as well. In reality, crack is indeed a significant facet of Miami street life, and the Miami experience is targeted in much of this book to illustrate the players, the situations, the adventures, the degradation, and the tragedies associated with crack use.

Crack was already part of the street scene in Miami by 1980. A report in 1980 to the National Institute on Drug Abuse noted that many of the 55 cocaine "freebasers" who were enrolled in an exploratory study of patterns of cocaine use in Miami, Florida, were already using baking soda to transform cocaine hydrochloride into smokable cocaine (Chitwood, 1980; Martinez, 1980). According to several informants, the drug could be purchased at inner-city *get-off houses* (shooting galleries)[11] by 1981. A longtime heroin user and resident of Miami's Overtown community recalled:

> I remember it clear like it was yesterday, 'cause I remember my brother Freddie and me were out celebrating. He had just finished doin' eighteen months for a B & E [breaking and entering] and this was the first I had seen him since he was out. That was the last time he done any hard time, and he got out in May of '81.
>
> Anyway, there was this place on 17th Street, near a little park. It was a get-off house, you know, a shooting gallery. Freddie wanted some white boy [heroin], so since he was just out an' all that I told him it was on me. So we go to this place on 17th. After we're there a few minutes the house man [shooting gallery owner] shows me these small cocaine rocks. I forget exactly what he called them, but later on we know'd it as crack. Said they were comin' down every day from Little Haiti and he'd been dealin' them out of his place for three months for the smokin' cokeys [cocaine users]. I remember Freddie laughin' about it, that with there bein' coke there and the kind of people it attracted the place wouldn't be respectable much longer.

The use of crack and the existence of crack houses proliferated in Miami and elsewhere throughout the 1980s. Subsequent to the initial media sensationalism, press coverage targeted the involvement of youths in crack distribution,

---

[11] Get-off houses and shooting galleries are places where many injection drug users go to use drugs and rent injection equipment.

the violence associated with struggles to control the crack marketplace in inner-city neighborhoods, and the child abuse, child neglect, and child abandonment by crack-addicted mothers.[12] In Miami, although the violence associated with crack distribution never reached the proportions apparent in other urban centers (Inciardi, 1990), crack use was nevertheless a major drug problem. By 1989 the Drug Enforcement Administration had estimated there were no fewer than 700 operating crack houses in the greater Miami area (DEA, 1989). As in other urban locales, the production, sale, and use of crack (Bourgois, 1989; Fagen & Chin, 1989; Hall, 1988/1989; Massing, 1989; Mieczkowski, 1990; Wallace, 1989), as well as prostitution and sex for drugs exchanges,[13] became prominent features of the Miami crack scene.

In addition to the media coverage of crack in Miami, empirical data also document its presence in Miami well before the drug's so-called discovery by the *New York Times.* A large-scale study of cocaine use and related criminality was conducted between April 1988 and March 1990 in the Miami (Dade County), Florida, metropolitan area (Inciardi & Pottieger, 1994). Of the 699 cocaine users interviewed, 94.1% had used crack. Twenty-six (4.0%) of the crack-using respondents had used crack prior to 1980, with the earliest report of crack use in 1973. Of the remaining respondents, most (66.9%) first used crack between 1984 and 1986.

A subsequent study of seriously delinquent youths in Miami observed that crack use existed in the early 1980s. By the mid-1980s, it was not uncommon for delinquent youths to be established users of crack since their early teens (Inciardi & Pottieger, 1991).

DOING CRACK

Crack is known by many pseudonyms. Most commonly, it might be *cracks, hard white, white,* or *flavor.* Furthermore, there are *bricks, boulders,* and *eight-ball* (large rocks or slabs of crack), *doo-wap* (two rocks), as well as *crumbs, shake,*

---

[12] See Ron Rosenbaum, "Crack Murder: A Detective Story," *New York Times Magazine,* February 15, 1987, pp. 29–33, 57, 60; *Newsweek,* February 22, 1988, pp. 24–25; *Time,* March 7, 1988, p. 24; *Newsweek,* March 28, 1988, pp. 20–29; *Newsweek,* April 27, 1988, pp. 35–36; *Time,* May 9, 1988, pp. 20–33; *New York Times,* June 23, 1988, pp. A1, B4; *Time,* December 5, 1988, p. 32; *New York Doctor,* April 10, 1989, pp. 1, 22; *U.S. News & World Report,* April 10, 1989, pp. 20–32; *New York Times,* June 1, 1989, pp. A1, B4; *New York Times* (National Edition), August 11, 1989, pp. 1, 10; Andrew C. Revkin, "Crack in the Cradle," *Discover,* September 1989, pp. 62–69.

[13] See "Sex for Crack: How the New Prostitution Affects Drug Abuse Treatment," *Substance Abuse Report,* 19 (November 15, 1988), pp. 1–4; "Syphilis and Gonorrhea on the Rise Among Inner-City Drug Addicts," *Substance Abuse Report,* 20 (June 1, 1989), pp. 1–2; "Syphilis and Crack Linked in Connecticut," *Substance Abuse Report,* 20 (August 1, 1989), pp. 1–2; *New York Times,* August 20, 1989, pp. 1, 36; *New York Times,* October 9, 1989, pp. A1, A30; *U.S. News & World Report,* October 23, 1989, pp. 29–30; *Newsweek,* September 25, 1989, p. 59; *Miami Herald,* October 22, 1989, pp. 1G, 6G.

and *kibbles and bits* (small rocks or crack shavings). The *dope man* or *bond man* (crack dealer) can deliver a *cookie* (a large quantity of crack, sometimes as much as 90 rocks), which he carries in his *bomb bag* (any bag in which drugs are conveyed for delivery) to any crack house in his neighborhood territory. The *dope man* may also *deal* (sell) or *juggle* (sell, for double what it is worth) his crack on the street.

In many crack houses (Chapter 2), the drug might be displayed on *boards* (tables, mirrors, or bulletin boards), whereas in the street crack is hawked in small glass vials or plastic bags. In a few locales, these bags are sealed or stamped with a brand name. Such a practice affords the illusion of quality control and gives the buyer a specific name to ask for. In New York City, crack labeling has included such brands as "White Cloud," "Conan," and "Handball," and in Miami, the better known labels of the early 1990s included "Cigarette" (named after the high-performance racing boat), "Biscayne Babe" (an epithet for prostitutes who *stroll* Miami's Biscayne Boulevard), "Olympus" (perhaps from Greek mythology), "Bogey" (of *Key Largo* fame), "Noriega's Holiday" (after the former Panamanian dictator), "Bush" (after the former president, who escalated a "war on drugs in Miami"), and "Pablo" (after the late head of the Medellin cartel, Pablo Escobar).

"Beaming Up"

Many crack users are uncertain about what crack actually is. Some know it as cocaine that has been "cooked" into a hard solid form called a "rock." Exactly what is in crack, in addition to street cocaine, is also debated: Some say baking soda; others say ether. Actually, most users don't know or care. A few argue that crack is the purest form of cocaine, but others hold that "freebase" is. Still others believe crack *is* freebase.

The *rocking up* (preparation) of crack is done in a variety of ways, all of which require baking soda that binds with cocaine and frees it from hydrochloride salt. In most instances a *cut* (expander) of some sort is also added to increase the volume and weight of the crack, and hence, the profits. Typical in this behalf are *comeback, swell up, blow up,* and *rush,* all of which are cocaine analogues (novocaine, lidocaine, and benzocaine) that bind with the cocaine when cooked. Crack is easy to cook, regardless of whether the recipe calls for a serving for 2 or 200 or the heat source is a hand-held cigarette lighter or a microwave.

Crack is "smoked" in a variety of ways—special glass pipes, makeshift smoking devices fabricated from beer and soda cans, jars, bottles, and other containers known as *stems, straight shooters, skillets, tools, ouzies,* or more directly, the *devil's dick.* A *beam* (from "Beam me up, Scotty" of TV's original *Star Trek*) is a hit of crack, as is a *bubb, backs* (a single hit), and *back up* (a second hit). Crack is also smoked with marijuana in cigarettes, called *geek joints, lace joints,* and *pin joints.* Some users get high from a *shotgun*—secondary smoke exhaled from one crack user into the mouth of another.

Users typically smoke for as long as they have crack or the means to purchase it—money or sex, stolen goods, furniture, or other drugs. It is rare that smokers have but a single hit. More likely they spend $50 to $500 during a *mission*—a 3- or 4-day binge, smoking almost constantly, 3 to 50 rocks per day. During these cycles, crack users rarely eat or sleep. And once crack is tried, for many users it is not long before it becomes a daily habit. For example, a recovering crack user commented,

> I smoked it Thursday, Friday, Saturday, Monday, Tuesday, Wednesday, Thursday, Friday, Saturday on that cycle. I was working at that time. I would spend my whole $300 check. Everyday was a crack day for me. My day was not made without a hit. I could smoke it before breakfast, don't even have breakfast or I don't eat for three days.

And a crack user/dealer reported:

> For the past five months I've been wearing the same pants. And sneakers are new but with all the money you make a day at least $500/$600 a day you don't want to spend a $100 in clothes. Everything is rocks, rocks, rocks, rocks, rocks. And to tell you the truth I don't even eat well for having all that money. You don't even want to have patience to sit down and have a good dinner. I could tell you rock is . . . I don't know what to say. I just feel sorry for anyone who falls into it.

As a final note here, crack has been called the fast-food variety of cocaine. It is cheap, easy to conceal, vaporizes with practically no odor, and the gratification is swift: an intense, almost sexual euphoria that lasts less than 5 minutes. Given these attributes, it would appear that crack cocaine might be a safer alternative to powder cocaine. But such a conclusion is far from accurate. There are many problems associated with cocaine use, including a high addiction potential, hyperstimulation, digestive disorders, nausea, loss of appetite, weight loss, tooth erosion, brain abscess, stroke, cardiac irregularities, occasional convulsions, and sometimes paranoid psychoses and delusions of persecution. Smoking crack as opposed to snorting cocaine results in a more immediate and direct absorption of the drug. Smoking produces a quicker and more compelling high that greatly increases the potential for dependence. Moreover, there is increased risk of acute toxic reactions, including brain seizure, cardiac irregularities, respiratory paralysis, paranoid psychosis, and pulmonary dysfunction.

The tendency to binge on crack for days at a time, neglecting food, sleep, and basic hygiene, severely compromises physical health. As such, crack users often appear emaciated. They lose interest in their physical appearance. Many have scabs on their faces, arms, and legs, the results of burns and picking on the skin (to remove bugs and other insects believed to be crawling *under* the skin). Crack users may have burned facial hair from carelessly lighting their smoking paraphernalia, they may have burned lips and tongues from the hot stems of their pipes, and many seem to cough constantly. The tendency of both male and female crack users to engage in high-frequency unprotected sex with numerous anonymous partners increases their risk for sexually transmitted diseases, including AIDS.

According to national surveys, crack has not become prevalent in the general population. But for reasons difficult to understand, crack's appeal in the majority of the nation's inner cities has endured. Perhaps the best explanation of crack's appeal in the inner city comes from anthropologist Philippe Bourgois (1989):

> Substance abuse in general, and crack in particular, offers . . . [a] metamorphosis. Users are instantaneously transformed from being unemployed, depressed high school dropouts, despised by the world . . . into being a mass of heart-palpitating pleasure, followed . . . by a jaw-gnashing crash and wide-awake alertness that provides their lives with concrete purpose: Get more crack—fast! (642–643)

REFERENCES

Abelson, H., Cohen, R., Schrayer, R., & Rappaport, M. (1978). Drug experience, attitudes and related behavior among adolescents and adults. In *Annual Report.* Washington, DC: Office of Drug Abuse Policy.

Allman, T. D. (1987). *Miami: City of the future.* New York: Atlantic Monthly Press.

Almeida, M. (1978). Contrabucion al estudio de la historia natural de la dependencia a la pasta basica de cocaina. *Revista de Neuro-Psiquiatria, 41,* 44–45.

Bourgois, P. (1989). In search of Horatio Alger: Culture and ideology in the crack economy. *Contemporary Drug Problems, 16,* 619–649.

Bogota El Tiempo, (1986, June 19). p. 2D.

Buchanan, E. (1987). *The corpse had a familiar face: Covering Miami, America's hottest beat.* New York: Random House.

Carr, P. (1990). *Sunshine states.* New York: Doubleday.

Chitwood, D. D. (1980). Patterns of cocaine use: Preliminary Observations. *Local Drug Abuse: Trends, Patterns and Issues* (pp. 156–166). Rockville, MD: National Institute on Drug Abuse.

Drug Enforcement Administration. (1986, August 22). *Special report: The crack situation in the United States.* Unpublished release from the Strategic Intelligence Section, Drug Enforcement Administration, Washington, DC.

Drug Enforcement Administration. (1989). *Crack/cocaine: Overview 1989.* Washington, DC: Author.

Fagen, J., & Chin, K. (1989). Initiation into crack and cocaine: A tale of two epidemics. *Contemporary Drug Problems, 16,* 579–617.

Gladwell, M. (1986, October 27). A new addiction to an old story. *Insight,* pp. 8–12.

The gourmet cokebook: A complete guide to cocaine. (1972). Sonoma, CA: White Mountain Press.

Grinspoon, L., & Bakalar, J. B. (1985). *Cocaine: A drug and its social evolution.* New York: Basic Books.

Hall, J. N. (1986). Hurricane crack. *Street Pharmacologist, 10,* 1–2.

Hall, J. N. (1988/1989, Fall/Winter). Cocaine smoking ignites America. *Street Pharmacologist,* pp. 28–30.

Inciardi, J. A. (1987). Beyond cocaine: Basuco, crack, and other coca products. *Contemporary Drug Problems, 14,* 461–492.

Inciardi, J. A. (1990). The crack/violence connection within a population of hard-core adolescent offenders. In M. DeLaRosa, E. Y. Lambert, & B. Gropper (Eds.), *Drugs and violence: Causes, correlates, and consequences* (pp. 92–111). Rockville, MD: National Institute on Drug Abuse.

Inciardi, J. A., & Pottieger, A. E. (1991). Kids, crack and crime. *Journal of Drug Issues 21,* 257–270.

Inciardi, J. A., & Pottieger, A. E. (1994). Crack cocaine use and street crime. *Journal of Drug Issues, 24,* 273–292.

Jeri, F. R. (1984, April–June). Coca-paste smoking in some Latin American countries: A severe and unabated form of addiction. *Bulletin on Narcotics,* pp. 15–31.

Jeri, F. R., Sanchez, C., & Del Pozo, T. (1976). Consumo de drogas peligrosas por miembros familiares de la fuerza armada y fuerza policial peruana. *Revista de la Sanidad de las Fuerzas Policiales, 37,* 104–112.

Lamar, J. V., Jr. (1986). Crack, a cheap and deadly cocaine is spreading menace. *Time,* June 2, pp. 16–18.

Martinez, R. (1980). Freebase cocaine. *Local Drug Abuse; Trends, Patterns, and Issues* (pp. I-67–I-70). Rockville, MD: National Institute on Drug Abuse.

Massing, M. (1989, October 1). Crack's destructive sprint across America. *New York Times Magazine,* pp. 38–41, 58–59, 62.

Mieczkowski, T. (1990). Crack distribution in Detroit. *Contemporary Drug Problems, 18,* 9–30.

Morganthou, T., Greenberg-Fink, V., Murr, A., Miller, M., & Raine, G. (1986). *Newsweek,* June 16, pp. 16–22.

New York Times, (1985). Nov. 17, p. B12.

New York Times, (1985). Nov. 29, p. A1

New York Times, (1987). Jan. 21, p. B1.

Rieff, D. (1987). *Going to Miami: Exiles, tourists, and refugees in the new America.* Boston: Little, Brown.

Rothchild, J. (1985). *Up for grabs: A trip through time and space in the sunshine state.* New York: Viking Press.

Siegel, R. K. (1977). Cocaine: Recreational use and intoxication. In R. C. Petersen & R. Stillman (Eds.), *Cocaine: 1977* (pp. 119–136. Rockville, MD: National Institute on Drug Abuse.

Siegel, R. K. (1982). Cocaine smoking. *Journal of Psychoactive Drugs, 14,* 271–359.

Smith, R. M. (1986, June 16). The drug crisis. *Newsweek,* p. 15.

(1986, June 16). *USA Today,* p. 1A.

Wallace, B. (1989). Psychological and environmental determinants of relapse in crack cocaine smokers. *Journal of Substance Treatment, 6,* 95–106.

Chapter 2

INNER-CITY CRACK HOUSES

Mary Comerford
Dale D. Chitwood
James A. Inciardi
David K. Griffin

What are the origins and the characteristics of the crack house? Is the crack house a totally new entity unique to the phenomenon of crack use, or are its roots embedded in earlier settings that were part of the drug use subculture? Are crack houses identical in form and function or are there a variety of types? This chapter addresses these questions.

HISTORICAL ANTECEDENTS OF THE CRACK HOUSE

A historical overview identifies the crack house as the latest manifestation of drug use locations where subcultures of drug users have evolved and thrived for years. Although the types of drugs and their forms of use have changed over time, the gathering places for consumption of drugs have a common ancestry with drug use establishments that have existed since the early Aztec, Egyptian, and Roman civilizations (Knipe, 1995).

The modern era of drug use in Europe and the United States is linked with the opium smoking behaviors of the 1880s. Immediate predecessors of the crack house have included opium dens of the late 19th century, speakeasies of the American Prohibition era, shooting galleries of the mid- to late 20th century, after-hours clubs that developed with the reemergence of cocaine in the late 1970s, and most recently, base houses that produced free-base cocaine.

The Opium Den

In Sir Arthur Conan Doyle's story "The Man with the Twisted Lip," Sherlock Holmes's biographer, Dr. Watson, describes the location of an opium den in Victorian London where Holmes is conducting an undercover investigation while disguised as an opiate addict (Conan Doyle, 1988, pp. 230–231).

> Upper Swandam Lane is a vile alley lurking behind the high wharves which line the northside of the river to the east of London Bridge. Between a slop-shop and a gin-shop, approached by a steep flight of steps leading down to a black gap like the mouth of a cave, I found the den of which I was in search.

Watson describes the opium den as ". . . a long low room, thick and heavy with the brown opium smoke, and terraced with wooden berths. . . ." He continues,

> Through the gloom one could dimly catch a glimpse of bodies lying in strange fantastic poses, bowed shoulders, bent knees, heads thrown back, and chins pointing upward, with here and there a dark, lack-lustre eye turned on the newcomer. Out of the black shadows there glimmered little red circles of light, now bright, now faint, as the burning poison waxed or waned in the bowls of the metal pipes. . . . As I entered, a sallow Malay attendant had hurried up with a pipe for me and a supply of the drug, beckoning me to an empty berth.

The opium den of Conan Doyle's fictional Sherlock Holmes had real counterparts in the opium dens that emerged in the United States in the closing decades of the 19th century, although such fictionalized accounts exaggerated the evils of opium dens (Knipe, 1995). Originally associated with the smoking of opium that was imported by the Chinese into the United States, the patterns of behavior that developed at these dens quickly spread to white members of the underworld (Courtwright, 1982). Many gamblers, prostitutes, professional criminals, and others who lived life in the proverbial fast lane soon became attracted to smoking opium. Courtwright (1982) and Stephens (1991) suggest that a user subculture developed in the opium den that functioned as a sanctuary and meeting place for smokers. Customers and visitors of these dens not only were taught the techniques of use but also learned a set of behaviors and rules. "In virtually all particulars [including] peer enforcement, exclusive membership, common argot, and shared rules of appropriate behavior," writes Courtwright, "opium smoking anticipated the pattern of the various [subsequent] drug subcultures" (Courtwright, 1982, p. 74).

Opium dens, also referred to as hash houses, were popular in the 19th century. They not only existed in the cellars described by Conan Doyle, but also in the wealthiest neighborhoods. In upper-class hash houses, customers had to receive an invitation to enter. An opium smoker in 1883 described the inner chambers of a hash house that contained a public room for males and females where any member could indulge in smoking or eating hash. Opium and cocaine also were available in various forms. Several rooms were located off the public room for the use of persons who required more privacy or who wished to avoid detection. One author estimated that over 600 hash houses existed in New York (Kane, 1983).

Speakeasy Establishments

The speakeasies of the 1920s and 1930s were gathering places for the sale and consumption of illegal alcohol and, in many cases, for cocaine as well. Cocaine users found the substance to be increasingly difficult to obtain after the 1914 Harrison Narcotic Act suppressed the sale of cocaine (Musto, 1989). However, speakeasy establishments were known to either sell the substance or condone its use among members. Speakeasies frequently combined the sale of illegal alcohol and other illicit drugs with the availability of gambling and prostitution.

Shooting Galleries/Dope Houses

The decline in availability of cocaine and the increased availability of heroin from the 1950s to the 1970s stimulated the proliferation of "dope houses," "shooting galleries," or "get-off houses" where users and addicts readily could buy and inject narcotics and obtain drug paraphernalia. Although some dealers maintained a decent pad, as they called it, where narcotics could be sold to a more discriminating clientele, many street junkies were reduced to using shooting galleries sometimes located in rat-infested abandoned buildings. Unknown customers, if admitted, might be forced to shoot up in front of the house man in an effort to ferret out police undercover agents. Almost any bar, barbershop, or dwelling was a potential dope house during that time. Some addicts would make their own home a place in which other addicts could inject in relative safety. Someone was always in attendance to help the addicts inject the drugs. A menu of services was provided. Generally $1 or $2 or a small amount of drugs were charged for each of the following services: use of the facility, rental of injection equipment, and having the house "doctor" administer the injection to customers who were unwilling or unable to inject themselves. Many addicts moved from one shooting gallery to another within the neighborhood (Agar, 1973). As cocaine has become more available in the last quarter of the 20th century, the opportunistic shooting galleries increasingly have become centers for the injection of this stimulant.

After-Hours Clubs

With the reemergence of cocaine use in the late 1970s and early 1980s among nonheroin drug users, other forms of dope houses evolved. In New York, cocaine users and dealers met in "after-hours clubs" (Williams, 1978, 1978–1989; Williams & Kornblum, 1985), places where alcohol was illegally sold after club closing time and cocaine was snorted or sold. Initially, cocaine users brought the drug with them to these clubs. When cocaine dealers realized the financial benefits of these clubs, they became regular patrons and promoted their business on the premises. These clubs advocated moderation in cocaine snorting and controlled those patrons who were inclined to overindulge.

Base Houses

Many after-hours clubs, following the introduction of freebase cocaine in the early 1980s, converted to base houses, where someone was available on the premises to "base" the cocaine (Williams, 1978, 1978–1989; Williams & Kornblum, 1985). In many instances the controlled moderate use of freebase cocaine gave way to compulsive use that fostered paranoia and distrust. Cocaine snorters began to refuse to associate with the basers and the ambience of the after-hours clubs changed dramatically. Most of the converted clubs were located in the low-income areas of major cities and were run by minority dealers.

Crack Houses

Crack use in the latter part of the 1980s introduced another type of house: the crack house. Although crack was mass marketed to inner-city neighborhoods, it initially was favorably received in more affluent communities. Crack houses were found in the homes of wealthy suburbanites or "uptown" condominiums (Hopkins, 1989). Different forms of crack houses rapidly emerged in poorer marginal communities where crack was being mass marketed. Many houses soon operated as for-profit businesses. The vast majority of crack houses today, like base houses, are located in minority, low-income, inner-city neighborhoods. The operations of these crack houses have much in common with the inner-city street shooting galleries and base houses of the past three to four decades.

A crack house may be located in a house, an apartment, a small shack on an empty lot, rooms in a vacant or abandoned building, or any other location where users can congregate to smoke crack. Crack houses, in addition to providing a place to smoke, may offer a variety of services and perform other functions for the crack smoker. Crack may be made or sold on the premises. Crack paraphernalia are available for use or rent in many houses. The procurement of sex for drugs (or money) is an integral part of many crack houses. As the services and functions of the houses differ, so do the rules. Some crack houses maintain a strict set of rules to limit violence and provide a "safe" environment for smoking. Other houses have few or no rules and behavior in these houses can become dangerous and violent.

Ethnographies (Geter, 1994; Mieczkowski, 1992, 1994; Ratner, 1993; Williams, 1992) and descriptions (Kailhla, 1989; Minerbrook, 1989; Stone, 1989) of crack houses have been reported from many major metropolitan areas in the United States. Although differences exist between geographical areas, the variations between areas often are no greater than the variations between crack houses within a given city. Regional terminology and the organization and functions of the crack houses may differ, but the crack house culture is remarkably similar across the country.

TYPOLOGIES OF CRACK HOUSES

Typologies have been developed to delineate categories of establishments based on variations in the physical conditions, functions, and social relationships of different crack houses. Inciardi (1993) identifies seven types of crack houses in Miami: (1) the castle, (2) the resort, (3) the base house, (4) the brothel, (5) the residence house, (6) the abandoned building, and (7) the organized crack house.

Castles

Castles are fortified structures in which large amounts of crack are manufactured, packaged, and sold. Crack users are not permitted inside. Castles typically are fortified with barred windows, steel doors with heavy bolts, reinforced walls, and other devices to hamper police raids. Workers usually are well armed. Crack sales usually occur with little or no interaction, sometimes through a slot or hole in the door. An informant described a castle this way:

> The whole idea [of the fortification] is to keep the cops off yer backs long enough to dump the stuff [crack] before they get in. This one rock castle I was in had all the doors and walls braced with steel bars drilled into the floor and ceiling. It had TV [security system] cameras lookin' up and down the street. Nothin' could go down without them knowin' about it. The only time the DEA [Drug Enforcement Agency] got in was when they came with a tow truck to pull down the door and a battering ram to get past a concrete barrier. It took them fifteen minutes to get in, and by then we had the place clean [free of drugs]. (Inciardi, 1993, p. 40)

Base Houses

The base/crack houses are similar to the traditional shooting galleries commonly used by injection drug users, and in some instances are shooting galleries that have expanded to include the smoking of crack. A variety of drugs are used in these houses, including but not limited to crack cocaine. Injection drug use is more common and more accepted in this type of crack house than it is in other houses. Some users inject drugs and smoke crack during the same visit. The establishments are shooting galleries that sell crack at times and keep crack pipes and related paraphernalia available for customers.

Sex for drug exchanges are rare and usually not permitted in base houses. A Miami crack user explains:

> You can go there and shoot drugs and she [the owner] shoot, but she didn't smoke crack. She'll let you smoke there as long as you . . . give her two dollars. If you was a smoker, a rock smoker, you can give her two dollars to smoke. If you was a cocaine shooter you give her cocaine to shoot or buy her some wine or something. The only thing she didn't let us do there is bring johns [customers]. (Inciardi, 1993, p. 41)

Resorts

The resorts are the "typical" crack houses where crack is sold and smoked, where sex is traded, and where violence and chaos are standard. The physical layout is similar to any apartment or house but has been adapted for crack use. The kitchen is used for cooking rock, at least one bedroom is used for sex, and the living space is used for selling and smoking. The owners of these crack houses are concerned about two things: money and crack. Many of these owners are long-term crack users whose primary reason for owning a crack house is to support their habit. Payment to use the house is often in the form of crack as well as money.

The customers may vary by race, gender, age, and ethnic origin. However, due to the rules of entree, customers tend to be representative of the demographics of the area in which the crack house is located. The houses are described as filthy, chaotic, and crowded. The crack smokers tend to get into fights, attempt to steal crack, and are very paranoid. A great deal of violence ranging from assault to rape and homicide occurs in this kind of crack house.

Sex for drug exchanges are common in resorts. A room (freak room) is usually set aside for sex. Women will perform various sex acts with anyone who will give them a "hit." The male customers pay the owner of the house a fee for use of the freak room.

Although these crack houses have workers with designated tasks, the hierarchy is not as extensive or structured as it is in the organized crack houses (described later). Procedures for purchasing crack differ depending on the house. Some charge an entrance fee and customers are free to smoke and have sex as they wish. In these houses, the crack is usually on the table and purchases are informal.

> It was just an apartment house where a lot of people that smoke crack come inside and just do drugs and smoke. One of them [the apartment rooms of the house man] . . . was his main room and the other two he would rent out, one for sexuals and one for just smoking and they just come to have sex in both of them. Inside, candles burning, pillows on the floor, it wouldn't be very good for a person in his right mind. (Inciardi, 1993, pp. 41–42)

Brothels

Some crack houses are owned and run by pimps. Although prostitution and trading sex for crack are primary activities of other crack houses, the exchange system is different in the brothel. In other crack houses the bartering of sex and crack occurs between the prostitute and the customer, and the owner of the crack house receives a fee of either crack or money from the customer for use of the room. The customer pays both the owner of the house and the prostitute. In the brothel the prostitutes are not involved in the payment process. They receive their payment, usually crack and boarding, from the owner after services have been rendered. These prostitutes also live in the crack house. One prostitute explained,

> Bein' that I been workin' the streets since I was eleven and don't really mind sexin' a lot of different guys, I thought it would be a real easy way for getting all the cracks that I needed. So this bond man [drug dealer] that I's know real well takes me in. He says all it is is givin' a lotta brains [oral sex] . . . I really got myself into somethin' bad. It wasn't just brains like he said. It was everything. . . . And I tried to leave but I was a prisoner there. (Inciardi, 1993, p. 45)

The extremely degraded status of prostitutes in brothel type crack houses is discussed in more detail in Chapter 5.

Residence Houses

Residence houses are conventional apartments or houses where numerous people gather regularly to smoke crack. Many owners are reluctant to call these places crack houses; however, the primary activities are the same as those in the crack house, including sex for drug exchange. The major differences are the payment system, the fact that crack is not sold in these houses (only smoked), and the social relationship between crack users because they usually knew the owner of the house prior to smoking crack there. In a crack house, payment can be made either with money or crack, money being preferred. In a friend/crack house, payment is made only with crack. The users give crack or share pipes (give hits) with the owner of the house or apartment in return for having a place to smoke or turn a trick. There usually are fewer people in this type of house: 5 or 6 compared to 15 or 20 in a regular crack house. These customers tend to be the same 5 or 6 people, whereas the typical crack house has a greater turnover of individuals who are not otherwise known to each other. An operator of a residence house in Miami described this situation:

> Thursday and Friday nights I would take my kids next door to the neighbor. As long as they [crack smokers] gonna use the house [we live in] they give me drugs. It was like we all hit together, you make one hit you pass around, all around. You share the shit, we were friends. It's my house and I keep my house secure. (Inciardi, Lockwood, & Pottieger, 1993, p. 73)

Abandoned Buildings

Some abandoned buildings are commonly known as places to smoke crack. No one who uses them actually owns these places, but there seem to be turf issues associated with them that are based on squatters' rights. Users bring their own crack.

> It's an empty house, empty rooms. So somebody like go into this room, the first one there. They might put a board you know, you have a cloth, you know, a bucket of water to bathe and shit. I did it myself. Put up those boards and shit, sometimes curtains hanging over the door, this room had no doors, no windows, nothing like that. (Inciardi, 1993, p. 45)

Organized Crack Houses

The organized crack house is very controlled and is run purely as a for-profit business. The owners are generally present and monitor the activities more closely than do operators of other kinds of houses. Violence and chaos are not as common; the atmosphere is calm. Children are not permitted inside the premises. Workers who rotate on shifts are employed by the owner; most of them are lookouts who watch for the police.

Purchasing crack in these houses is a structured process. Some of the houses may have regular hours of operation. Once in the crack house, customers are sold crack and seated with pipes. Thereafter, individuals are left alone and order is maintained. Sex for drugs exchanges do not occur in this type of house.

> They would have people outside, lookouts. Way up and down the street like on the corner. And another guy sitting in the yard like he was cleaning the yard or something. There would be like a bouncer at the door with a gun to watch to make sure no cops or anything would walk in. Or to make sure that there were no problems within the place itself. Just to make it secure for their sake. (Inciardi, 1993, p. 46)

Additional typologies have been developed by researchers in other metropolitan areas. Mieczkowski (1994) classifies Detroit crack house styles along a continuum ranging from "austere" to "open" or "tavern culture" houses. At the austere end are houses that manufacture and sell crack but are off-limits to customers except for the purchase of crack. Little or no social interaction occurs. These would be analogous to the castles described by Inciardi. At the other end are the "open" houses in which anything goes, with considerable social interaction among the users including sex and violence. Inciardi's categories of the brothel and the resort would fall at this open end of the continuum.

Geter (1994) characterizes four general types of crack houses in Philadelphia according to function: (1) the crack house, (2) the cop house, (3) drug house III, and (4) drug house IV. Of these four types, the crack house is used by addicts for the consumption of crack cocaine; the other three types of houses are for the sale (cop house), production (drug house III), and storage of crack and money (drug house IV). He further partitions crack houses into four distinct types based in descending order on the economic and social status of the house person and clientele: (1) the party house, (2) the hit house, (3) the smoke house, and (4) the bandominium.

The party house is located in the home of an addict and caters to "working-class men." This type of house is the elite of crack houses and is usually well maintained. Both crack and sex are available. In return for use of the house, the operator, usually a woman, receives crack or money for various services she provides. One of Geter's informants who ran a party house explained her fee schedule:

> So in order for you to go up my steps [use a bedroom], that's $5 every half hour for the room. Then you got me runnin' [buying drugs]. I've gone to the cop man gettin' $10 caps. Plus you gonna give me three out of the ten. Plus the $5 for the half hour for the room. And what you do with that bitch, I ain't got nothin' to do with that. But it's about me gettin' my money. (Geter, 1994, p. 1022)

The hit house is similar to the party house except the patrons tend to be members of the "poverty class," and order is not well maintained. Party houses deteriorate into hit houses as the clientele changes from working-class men to unemployed crack addicts. The operator loses the incentive to keep things "nice," and conflicts and violence arise. Hit houses then can deteriorate into "smoke houses." In smoke houses, the operator has little or no control over the activities that take place. These houses are often filthy as the description by one informant reported by Geter depicts:

> No runnin' water. No place to relieve yourself. Filth, you come in there smellin' good and leave out of there with that house odor. . . . Toilet wasn't workin'—the sink was all broke up. . . . Roaches everywhere. A little mouse runnin' around here or there. (Geter, 1994, p. 1024)

Bandominiums are located in abandoned buildings that have been taken over by addicts. There is usually no house person and the environment is of the "anything goes" variety.

> You have to be careful who's comin in, who's comin' out. You know. And you don't have to pay a door charge but when you walk in they on you [begging, conning, and stealing]. And you never let nobody know how much you got. . . . 'Cause you'll sit right there and . . . you'll get robbed. (Geter, 1994, p. 1025)

Although regional variations do occur, the types of crack houses are remarkably similar throughout the country. In each city several types of crack houses can be found that would easily fit into one of the typographies just mentioned. For example, a 28-year-old woman in San Francisco described such a setting this way:

> Everybody who comes through the door they'll shoot the dope [heroin] and then go to where the table is and smoke [crack]. [This shooting gallery] had like six little smoking tables–pipes, matches, broken pipes, whole outfits—a lot of them [customers] still speedball. . . . (McDonnell, Irwin, & Rosenbaum, 1990, p. 148–149)

This well describes the base house in the typography of Inciardi.

Crack houses in Chicago have been described as ranging from dictatorial to near anarchy. One of the more dictatorial houses (which appears to be similar to Inciardi's organized crack houses) was depicted in the following manner:

> You can't talk to anyone you didn't come in with. . . . [The owner] goes by my rules to be left alone [by others in the house]. . . . You can't bring anything in with you; he has it all. . . . You can't move around from room to room. . . . You can't give a hit to someone you didn't come in with. . . . There's no hangin' around when you're done . . . no sex. (Ouellet, Wiebel, Jimenez, & Johnson, 1993, p. 81)

A description from Detroit could describe a crack house in any city:

> The scene in the crack houses was a place that stolen TVs were brought to get crack. People would come in and sometimes be a dollar short and maybe the dealer would let him go. There would be three or four that hung there all the time walking around with guns on, busted toilets, and so forth. Women would come in there and go in separate rooms and give johns $4 or $5 worth. I have been in there when some have pulled guns on guys. . . . (Mieczkowski, 1990, p. 76)

THE CRACK HOUSE: SOCIAL INSTITUTION

Crack houses are social institutions within the subculture of crack users, and specific social roles are common and essential to their conduct. Although social roles differ according to type of crack house, four of the most common roles have been described by John French (1993).

1. The house man.   The house man (or woman) is the person in charge of the crack house. He or she makes the rules and determines what type of order will be maintained. The crack house frequently is located in the home of the house man. In some circumstances the house man will cook his own supply of cocaine hydrochloride with baking soda to produce crack that he then sells to his clientele. He alternatively may process the customer's cocaine into crack. In other situations, this person may cop the crack at other locations, transport the drug to the house, and supply it to the customer. In exchange for the use of the facilities and equipment, the house man may receive money or, more likely, either a percentage of the crack or "hits" from the user's pipe.

2. The runner.   The runner assists the house man. He (the runner is usually male) runs errands, may help cook the crack, and helps maintain order. In houses that do not sell crack, the runner will purchase crack for the customers. Runners are customarily paid by "hits" on the pipe either by the house man or the customer.

3. The skeezers.   The skeezers are women who exchange sex for crack. Skeezers perform sex usually for "hits" on the customer's pipe. In some houses, the skeezer may be employed by the house man and live in the house. The woman is expected to perform sex with any customer who wishes it and is paid by the house man rather than the customer. The customer in return pays the house man.

4. The customer.   Most customers want a "safe" place to smoke and in some cases obtain crack. Both men and women may be customers. Female customers are more likely than male customers to be willing to exchange sex for crack. Customers come from all age and ethnic groups but because the tendency is to utilize a crack house in the immediate neighborhood, the ethnic makeup of the neighborhood usually determines the ethnic mix of the customers. Customers must either be known to the house man or come with someone known who can vouch for the new customer.

SEX IN THE CRACK HOUSE

Sex is an integral part of the crack house scene. Although a few crack houses may discourage or prohibit sexual activity, the vast majority not only tolerate sex but encourage it. Prostitution in the houses is in the form of sex for crack exchange and is looked down on by the traditional street prostitutes. The customers for sex (johns) look down on the "crack whores" who, depending on the region, are called "skeezers," "tosses," "chicken heads," "strawberries," and a variety of other derogatory terms. One man in San Francisco explained why the term *tosses* was used: "'Cause everybody havin' sex with her. Everybody has sex and she just toss. . . . It's like I can toss her and I guess I call her a toss 'cause I toss her to my buddy . . ." (Lown, Winkler, Fullilove, & Fullilove, 1993, p. 93).

Women who exchange sex for crack are degraded as crack whores because of their willingness to perform almost any type of sexual activity in order to get a hit from the pipe or a piece of rock. Bourgois describes how one crack dealer at a crack house degrades women who regularly service him with oral sex by calling them "my moufs [mouths]." He often underpays them by baiting them with a $3 vial of crack and subsequently only giving them a hit on his pipe (Bourgois & Dunlap, 1993).

Two types of prostitutes work the crack houses. The first type is the woman who goes to the crack house to obtain crack and either has no money or runs out of money. In order to meet the desire for crack, the woman will perform sex for anyone who has crack to offer. These women are paid by the johns with crack. Oral sex appears to be the most frequent form of sex; however, vaginal and anal sex will be performed if required. Many crack houses have a "freak room" dedicated for sex, but in more uncontrolled houses sex may be carried out in any part of the house in view of anyone else present.

> In the house there's usually a few people around and a lotta guys just don't want to be droppin' their pants. But they don't seem to have much qualms about a quick blow job, when people can see them, so long as they can keep their pants up. . . . (Inciardi, 1989, p. 696)

Heterosexual women also have reported performing sex with other women because a john enjoyed watching this type of sex. Group sex with more than one male having sex with the same woman at the same time is not uncommon in some houses.

The second type of prostitute is the house girl. The house girl lives in the house and is supplied crack by the proprietor in exchange for performing sex with the customers. The customers then pay the house man rather than the woman for her services.

Because the high produced by crack lasts for only a few minutes, women who desire to maintain a crack high and have no resources except their bodies must perform multiple sex acts with different partners. It is not uncommon for crack whores to report having sex with more than 100 different partners within a 30-day period (Inciardi, Lockwood, & Pottieger, 1993; Siegal, Carlson, Falck, Forney, Wang, & Li, 1992). Some have reported up to 40 different men a day (Inciardi, Lockwood, & Pottieger, 1993). Most, if not all, of these encounters occur in the crack house.

> I probably had sex maybe 10,000 times in the last two years. A lot of blow jobs, and I did a lot of it with the same mens over an' over. But I bet I sexed with couple of thousand different guys, an' a few dozen ladies. (Inciardi, Lockwood, & Pottieger, 1993, p. 95)

Researchers have associated crack use with hypersexuality (Washton & Gold, 1987) and sexual dysfunction (Macdonald, Waldorf, Reinarman, & Murphy, 1988; Weatherby et al., 1992). This contradiction results in situations in which men demand sex for crack yet cannot reach orgasm. Some prostitutes in crack houses report giving oral sex for prolonged periods of an hour or more without the male reaching climax (Inciardi, Lockwood, & Pottieger, 1993). Such an experience was described by one of Bourgois and Dunlap's informants in Harlem:

> The place it was in had no door there, and the curtain was sheer so you could see through, like beige or something. And we watchin' in the next room and

the girl was tellin' him that she didn't want to. She was sayin' she been here for about two hours and he could have his money back 'cause she don't want to have sex with him because . . . she was gettin' tired. . . . And then he punched her in the mouth, started slappin' her and she cried for a little while and attempted to leave. He made her sit down. (Bourgois & Dunlap, 1993, pp. 123–124)

A man in Denver explains the frustration with this dysfunction:

It take me so long sometimes that I just get frustrated. Like I had this one broad I was telling you about. I was smoking with her and I thought in my mind that I wanted to get down. . . . I told her, "I will give you some [crack] to turn you on but I want some [oral sex]." So she starts . . . and it took me about two hours before I could cum. (Koester & Schwartz, 1993, p. 199)

Some women have learned to use this phenomenon to their own advantage. A woman in Chicago explains it this way:

A man buy himself a rock, he think he got to come . . . and then he can't. . . . Every time a man buy himself some rocks, he got to find himself a female, he got to find himself any kind of female just so he can get his nut off. . . . And then women get hip to that shit, that if they take more than three bumps [hits], ain't nothing goin' on. So they make sure the man, you know, "Here, baby, take another bump" . . . so he can't get it up, he can't come. (Goldstein, Ouellet, & Fendrich, 1992, p. 357)

Sex in crack houses tends to be of the anything goes variety. So determined to maintain a high, the crack whores will perform almost any type of sex act to receive hits on the pipe. Multiple anonymous partners are the rule. This sex for crack exchange is a main characteristic of the crack house and differentiates it from earlier types of drug houses.

SOCIAL IMPLICATIONS OF CRACK HOUSES

The crack house serves as a major component of the crack culture, and all activity in a crack house centers around the drug. As sociologist Terry Williams states (Stone, 1989, p. 107), "Everything that's happening has to do with the drug. Every word, every gesture is connected with one of four rituals of crack: copping it, cooking it, smoking it, and having sex on it." The house serves as a social center for crack users, and all of the social deviance displayed by crack users is seen in the crack house. Although some crack houses may be well maintained, most houses can become frantic activity centers for "crack heads." A common sight in the crack house is that of "tweaking" or "chasing ghosts"— users compulsively searching every inch of a room over and over again looking for bits of crack (Rosse, Fay-McCarthy, Collins, Risher-Flowers, Alim, & Deutsch, 1993).

Paranoia and suspicion are common and violence can occur at any time. Fagin and Chin found a higher degree of violence associated with crack selling than with other illicit drugs (Fagan & Chin, 1990).

Most of the violence that occurs in the crack house centers around crack. Although there are multiple sources of violence, Mieczkowski (1990) concludes that the more frequent instances of violence are the result of crack distribution, the personal disorganization inherent in the crack culture, and distortions of character caused by crack binges. Mieczkowski studied crack house violence in Detroit, but the causes of violence he identified are prevalent in all areas of heavy crack use. Paranoid users may believe, whether or not true, that someone is stealing crack or seeking to harm them. Violence frequently occurs in these situations. Likewise, if the house man believes he is being ripped off by an employee or customer, disciplinary action often becomes violent. Customers of many crack houses are frisked at the door for guns and other weapons, and the house man or other employees usually are armed. Violence often is used to establish and maintain order and to enforce the repayment of a debt. A house man or customer who is perceived to be weak may be the victim of violence. Stronger individuals may steal crack from a newcomer through violence or the threat of violence.

Women are often subjected to abusive and violent behavior by men. A common complaint of crack whores is not being paid after performing sex. Many of the women describe this as rape (Inciardi, 1993; Inciardi, Lockwood, & Pottieger, 1993). Violent sexual acts also occur with or without the permission of the women involved.

Because of the flagrant sexual activity in the crack houses, these houses serve as vectors for sexually transmitted diseases (Bouknight, 1990; Fullilove, Fullilove, Bowser, & Gross, 1990; Needle, Su, & Gust, 1991) including HIV (Chiasson, Stoneburner, Hildebrandt, Ewing, Telzak, & Jaffe, 1991; McCoy & Inciardi, 1995). The houses themselves are often filthy, particularly those in vacant buildings. Often there is no running water and no attempt is made at personal hygiene. Safer sex practices are rarely used.

In many communities, the crack house is an important link in the sale and distribution of crack. Although in some communities, such as Philadelphia and Newark (French, 1993), it is rare for crack to be sold in the crack houses, in most areas crack houses are a major distribution point. In a survey done with crack users in Detroit, the crack house was reported to be the most popular method to purchase crack (Mieczkowski, 1990). The operational method of the sale of crack depends on the type of house. Some houses, such as the castles of Inciardi, the drug houses of Geter, and the austere houses of Mieczkowski, are in the business of distributing crack. They are not places where customers interact socially, and smoking is not permitted on the premises. These houses are usually heavily guarded and business transactions take place through a slot in the door or other such mechanism to ensure the safety of the sellers.

Many crack houses that are set up for users to smoke and spend time also have crack available for sale. In houses owned by a dealer, the customer is expected to purchase the crack at the house and not bring it in. In other houses, the crack is sold as a convenience to the customer; the crack smoker may smoke crack not purchased at the establishment if so desired. In the crack houses where crack is not sold, runners often are available who will go purchase crack for the customers, usually in return for some hits on the pipe.

In view of the socially undesirable characteristics of crack houses, it comes as no surprise that police and other municipal authorities frequently target these establishments. Although police raids regularly occur in some urban areas, many city police departments admit defeat. Crack houses are located in dangerous areas of the city and raiding crack houses has had limited success. Houses either reopen or move to new locations. Raids can also lead to violence and retaliation with innocent people drawn into the line of fire. Crack houses in vacant buildings often are bulldozed, but operators simply reopen in a new location, often within the same block. In some cities, tenants of public housing units who run crack houses have been systematically evicted. This, too, has resulted in limited success. Some dealer/managers of the crack houses conduct business at multiple sites. When one site is shut down, another opens nearby. Police often are aware of the location of crack houses, but lack the time and resources to take effective action (Bowser, 1989; Kailhla, 1989). Ineffective policing of crack houses has led to vigilante attacks by frustrated neighbors in some communities (Minerbrook, 1989).

SUMMARY

To the casual observer, there appears to be a proliferation of crack houses in the inner-city neighborhoods. Media attention has shifted from shooting galleries, which still exist in sufficient numbers to be of concern, to the newest phenomenon, crack houses. Pressure from community leaders and neighbors to force police to shut down crack houses has produced little success. As long as crack houses perform the social functions they do, this will be the case. Crack houses will continue to endure as long as they serve an important role in the drug use culture.

Although a number of different forms, organization, and management of crack houses have been identified, the basic purpose of these houses remains the same: a common meeting ground for drug users who have similar needs and habits. Crack houses are the latest manifestation of drug houses that have been in existence for decades. They combine common elements from earlier forms of drug use establishments with the particular features associated with crack cocaine use. Some houses are highly organized and well managed, resembling the hash house of the 1800s and the after-hours clubs of the 1970s where proceedings were kept under control. Some are like the street shooting galleries and base houses, where overindulgence of the substance, violence, chaos, and overcrowding are the norm. Some crack houses are located in homes and only invited guests are allowed entry, similar to the drug parties held in the basements of the well-to-do who indulged in opium, heroin, hash, and cocaine.

Each form of crack house serves a function in the crack culture and reflects the various aspects of that culture. Many crack houses attract those who are at the extreme end of the behavioral spectrum. Crime and violence, so prevalent among crack users, are exhibited in the crack house. Many houses also contribute to the degradation of women through their sexual exploitation. Crack houses can be instrumental in the transmission of sexually transmitted diseases, including HIV. Crack houses differ from previous forms of drug use houses in the amount and type of violence generated and in the extent of sexual activities that occur within them.

REFERENCES

Agar, M. (1973). *Ripping and running: A formal ethnography of heroin addicts.* New York: Seminar Press.

Bouknight, L. G. (1990). The public health consequences of crack cocaine. *New York State Journal of Medicine, 90,* 493–495.

Bourgois, P., & Dunlap, E. (1993). Exorcising sex-for-crack: An ethnographic perspective from Harlem. In M. S. Ratner (Ed.), *Crack pipe as pimp* (pp. 97–132). New York: Lexington Books.

Bowser, B. P. (1989). Crack and AIDS: An ethnographic impression. *Journal of the National Medical Association, 81,* 538–540.

Chiasson M. A., Stoneburner, R. L., Hildebrandt, D. S., Ewing, W. E., Telzak, E. E., & Jaffe, H. W. (1991). Heterosexual transmission of HIV-1 associated with the use of smokable freebase cocaine (crack). *AIDS, 5,* 1121–1126.

Conan Doyle, A. (1988). The man with the twisted lip. In *The Complete Sherlock Holmes* (pp. 229–244). Garden City: Doubleday.

Courtwright, D. T. (1982). *Dark paradise.* Cambridge, MA: Harvard University Press.

Fagan, J., & Chin, K. (1990). Violence as regulation and social control in the distribution of crack. In M. DeLaRosa, E. Y. Lambert, & B. Gropper (Eds.), *Drugs and violence: Causes, correlates, and consequences* (pp. 8–43). NIDA Monograph 103. Washington, DC: U.S. Government Printing Office.

French, J. F. (1993). Pipe dreams: Crack and life in Philadelphia and Newark. In M.S. Ratner (Ed.), *Crack pipe as pimp* (pp. 205–232). New York: Lexington Books.

Fullilove, R. E., Fullilove, M. T., Bowser, B. P., & Gross, S. A. (1990). Risk of sexually transmitted disease among black adolescent crack users in Oakland and San Francisco, Calif. *Journal of the American Medical Association, 263,* 851–855.

Geter, R. S. (1994). Drug user settings: A crack house typology. *The International Journal of the Addictions, 29,* 1015–1027.

Goldstein, P. J., Ouellet, L. J., & Fendrich, M. (1992). From bag brides to skeezers: A historical perspective on sex-for-drugs behavior. *Journal of Psychoactive Drugs, 24,* 349–361.

Hopkins, W. (1989, April 7). *Street perspectives on drug use.* Paper presented at the Conference on Drug Abuse Prevention, John Jay College of Criminal Justice, New York.

Inciardi, J. A. (1989). Trading sex for crack among juvenile drug users: A research note. *Contemporary Drug Problems, 16,* 689–700.

Inciardi, J. A. (1993). Kingrats, chicken heads, slow necks, freaks, and blood suckers: A glimpse at the Miami sex-for-crack market. In M.S. Ratner (Ed.), *Crack pipe as pimp* (pp. 37–68). New York: Lexington Books.

Inciardi, J. A., Lockwood, D., & Pottieger, A. E. (1993). *Women and crack-cocaine.* New York: Macmillan.

Kailhla, P. (1989, April 3). A journey into hell: The horrors of a dope den. *Maclean's,* p. 51.

Kane, H. H. (1883, Nov.). A hashish-house in New York. *Harper's Monthly,* 944–949.

Knipe, E. (1995). *Culture, society and drugs.* Prospect Heights, IL: Waveland Press.

Koester, S., & Schwartz, J. (1993). Crack, gangs, sex, and powerlessness: A view from Denver. In M.S. Ratner (Ed.), *Crack pipe as pimp* (pp. 187–204). New York: Lexington Books.

Lown, E. A, Winkler, K., Fullilove, R. E., & Fullilove, M. T. (1993).Tossin' and tweakin': Women's consciousness in the crack culture. In C. Squire (Ed.), *Women and AIDS* (pp. 90–105). Newbury Park, CA: Sage.

Macdonald, P. T., Waldorf, D., Reinarman, C., & Murphy, S. (1988). Heavy cocaine use and sexual behavior. *Journal of Drug Issues, 18,* 437–455.

McCoy, C. B., & Inciardi, J. A. (1995). *Sex, drugs, and the continuing spread of AIDS.* Los Angeles: Roxbury.

McDonnell, D., Irwin, J., & Rosenbaum, M. (1990). "Hops and hubbas": A tough new mix. A research note on cocaine use among methadone maintenance users. *Contemporary Drug Problems, 17,* 145–156.

Mieczkowski, T. (1990). The operational styles of crack houses in Detroit. In M. De-LaRosa, E. Y. Lambert, & B. Gropper (Eds.), NIDA Research Monograph 103. *Drugs and violence: Causes, correlates, and consequences* (pp. 60–91). Washington, DC: U.S. Government Printing Office.

Mieczkowski, T. (1992). Crack dealing on the street: The crew system and the crack house. *Justice Quarterly, 9,* 153–161.

Mieczkowski, T. (1994). The experiences of women who sell crack: Some descriptive data from the Detroit Crack Ethnography Project. *Journal of Drug Issues, 24,* 227–248.

Minerbrook, S. (1989, April 10). A night in a crack house. *U.S. News & World Report,* 29.

Musto, D. F. (1989). Evolution of American attitudes toward substance abuse. *Annals of the New York Academy of Sciences, 562,* 3–7.

Needle, R., Su, S. S., & Gust, L. (1991). *Use of crack and cocaine, sexually transmitted diseases, and HIV prevention.* Community-Based AIDS Prevention. Proceedings of the First Annual NADR National Meeting (pp. 353–366) (DHHS Publication No. ADM 91-2752). Washington, DC: U.S. Government Printing Office.

Ouellet, L. J., Wiebel, W. W., Jimenez, A. D., & Johnson, W. A. (1993) Crack cocaine and the transformation of prostitution in three Chicago neighborhoods. In M. S. Ratner (Ed.), *Crack pipe as pimp* (pp. 69–96). New York: Lexington Books.

Ratner, M. S. (Ed.). (1993). *Crack pipe as pimp.* New York: Lexington Books.

Rosse, R. B., Fay-McCarthy, M., Collins, J. P., Risher-Flowers, D., Alim, T. N., & Deutsch, S. I. (1993). Transient compulsive foraging behavior associated with crack cocaine use. *American Journal of Psychiatry, 150,* 151–155.

Siegal, H. A., Carlson, R. G., Falck, R., Forney, M. A., Wang, C., & Li, L. (1992). High-risk behaviors for transmission of syphilis and human immunodeficiency virus among crack cocaine-using women. *Sexually Transmitted Diseases, 19,* 266–271.

Stephens, R. C. (1991). *The street addict roll.* Albany: State University of New York Press.

Stone, M. (1989, April 25). *High Times,* pp. 107–108.

Washton, A. M., & Gold, M. S. (1987). *Cocaine: A clinician's handbook.* New York: Guilford Press.

Weatherby, N. L., Shultz, J. M., Chitwood, D. D., McCoy, H. V., McCoy, C. B., Ludwig, D. D., & Edlin, B. R. (1992). Crack cocaine use and sexual activity in Miami, Florida. *Journal of Psychoactive Drugs, 24,* 373–380.

Williams, T. (1978). *The cocaine culture in after-hours clubs.* Unpublished doctoral dissertation, City University of New York.

Williams, T. (1978–1989). *Field notes from ethnographic observations of cocaine dealers in New York City.* New York: Narcotic and Drug Research, Inc.

Williams, T. (1992). *Crack house: Notes from the end of the line.* Reading, MA: Addison-Wesley.

Williams, T., & Kornblum, W. (1985). *Growing up poor.* Lexington, MA: Lexington Books.

Chapter 3

CRACK AND CRIME

Duane C. McBride
James E. Rivers

Extensive crack cocaine use in many cities has had significant consequences in contemporary society. Crack use negatively affects our economy through lower productivity and money diverted from legitimate uses. Major health and social consequences from crack use include malnutrition, infectious diseases, fetal damage, personality disorders, and broad effects on social interaction and relationships. All of these consequences affect daily life in U.S. cities today, not only for crack users but also for all citizens. The consequences that produce the highest degree of public concern, however, are the criminal behaviors perceived to result from crack use.

Since the mid-1980s, frequent media reports have attributed crimes to crack use. These reports have included gun fights between dealers for the control of street corner distribution points, violence resulting from crack-induced paranoia, crimes committed by crack users to get money to buy the drug, and violence as a regular part of the cultural behavioral patterns of crack users (e.g., see Adler, 1988; Salholz, 1989). Crack is frequently portrayed as causing users to do anything or harm anyone for access to it or for a lucrative place to sell it.

Because there is a widespread popular perception about the strength of the crack-crime relationship and because so much of current drug policy is premised on that perception, it is important to examine critically the existence, extent, and nature of the relationship between crack cocaine use and criminal behavior. This chapter looks at the following issues:

1. The statistical association between crack cocaine use and criminal behavior. Here the extent of crime among crack users, the extent of crack use in criminal populations, and the association in the general population are examined.
2. The types of criminal behavior coincident with crack use.

3. Causal inferences in the crack-crime relationship. For example, does crack use emerge following or prior to extensive criminal behavior and what is the evidence regarding the existence of a causal effect of crack on criminal behavior?
4. The policy issues that face our society as it responds to the extensive crack use and its presumed criminal consequences.

THE STATISTICAL ASSOCIATION

The basic rationale for the perceived causal relationship between crack use and crime is the extensive crack use among criminal populations and the high levels of crime among crack users. The statistical correlation between drug use in general and crime has been examined extensively. Over the past few decades, studies have shown extensive illegal drug use in many types of populations of criminals and extensive criminal behavior among all types of illegal drug users (for a general overview of this issue see McBride & McCoy, 1993). The correlation between crack use and crime has been a consistent research focus since the emergence of the crack phenomena (see Fagan, 1994; Inciardi, Horowitz, & Pottieger, 1993; McBride & Swartz, 1990).

Crack Use among Criminal Justice Populations

An extensive surveillance project that attempts to address this issue is the Drug Use Forecasting program (DUF). This project samples arrestees four times a year in 23 cities across the United States from the larger cities such as New York, Chicago, and Los Angeles to smaller cities like Indianapolis, Indiana, and Portland, Oregon. Arrestees are approached at booking facilities and asked to participate in this research project. Volunteers are interviewed at the booking facility and asked to provide a urine sample. All data are anonymous and have no impact on the arrest charge or the subjects processing through the criminal justice system. The DUF project reports that about 90% of those approached agree to be interviewed with about 80% of those participants agreeing to provide a urine specimen. The specimens are tested for 10 types of drugs including cocaine, opiates, marijuana, and PCP. Although the DUF project has some methodological problems of representation and consistent methodology, the project sponsors argue their data likely underestimates the extent of drug use among arrestees (for a brief methodological discussion of the DUF project, see Drug Use Forecasting Program, 1994a, p. 2).

DUF data have documented the extent of illegal drug use in arrested populations since 1990. Generally, in all study sites, a majority of male and female arrestees have tested positive for at least one illegal drug. Since the beginning of the DUF project, in most study sites, cocaine has been more likely to be detected in the subjects' urine samples than marijuana or any other type of illegal drug. (The urinalysis method used can detect a metabolite of cocaine; it cannot detect the form in which it was ingested.) Evidence of cocaine has usually been found in over 50% of arrestees in the largest eastern cities such as New York, Chicago, and Miami. In study cities where female arrestees are sampled, they are more likely than males to have ingested cocaine (see Drug Use Forecasting Program, 1994a). The DUF adult report suggests a virtual saturation of illegal drug use in arrested populations, most of which involves cocaine use. In addition to the adult study, the DUF project also has a juvenile component in some of the same cities. These data generally show that about one-third of the juveniles arrested and studied have used an illegal drug. Cocaine was used by about 8%, with use more likely by females (see Drug Use Forecasting Program, 1994b). These juvenile data, however, do not control for seriousness of criminal behavior and may include juvenile status offenders.

Crack and Gangs

Although the DUF data indicate the extent of cocaine use among those arrested, similar information about the extent of crack use exists in studies of inner-city street delinquents and gang members who are not in jail or prison. For example, Inciardi, Horowitz, and Pottieger (1993) found that just under two-thirds of the street delinquents in their study in Miami were using crack at least once a week. Ethnographic observations and interviews with these street delinquents revealed that crack use was an integral part of their lives and was involved with their street delinquent lifestyle. Many observers have argued that juvenile delinquent gangs are heavily involved in the national distribution of crack (Skolnick, Correl, Navarro, & Rabb, 1988). Subsequent research in additional cities has produced a consensus that juveniles and adult inner-city gangs are not sufficiently nationally organized and disciplined to be a continuous major force in national crack distribution. Rather, inner-city street gangs appear to be primarily involved in local street distribution within their own communities. Researchers also have concluded that although inner-city gangs are involved in low-level street distribution and generally have high rates of use, they do not appear to control local distribution exclusively and many street distributors are not gang members (see Fagan, 1990; Inciardi, Horowitz, & Pottieger, 1993; Klein, Maxson, & Cunningham, 1991). Today, likely because of the popularity, positive effect, and addictive nature of crack, inner-city delinquents and gangs have very high rates of crack use. In addition, street-level crack distribution comprises a significant amount of their criminal activity and a significant amount of crime-derived income.

Criminal Behavior among Crack Users

Studies of criminal behavior among crack users have shown that the large majority of crack users are heavily engaged in criminal activity. In a study of about 700 crack users in Miami who were not incarcerated, Inciardi, McBride, McCoy, & Chitwood (1994) found that almost all users were frequently engaged in illegal behavior. About 90% had been arrested, two-thirds had been convicted, and a majority had served time in a jail or prison. Criminal activity and involvement in the criminal justice system was found to be an integral part of the daily lives of crack users. One of the consistent research findings in drugs and crime research is the association between increases in drug use and increases in criminal behavior (e.g., see Nurco, Ball, Shaffer, & Hanlon, 1985). Research has also shown a consistent correlation between frequency of crack use and the extent of criminal behavior. That is, those who use crack more frequently engage in more criminal activities. Further, this statistical relationship appears to be stronger for the crack-crime relationship than for the relationship between other types of drugs and criminal behavior (Inciardi & Pottieger, 1994).

The Crack-Crime Relationship in the General Population

Although research on crack-using and criminal populations shows a strong statistical association between crack use and crime, these studies have many inherent biases. They usually involve identified populations. That is, they are identified for their deviant behavior by the criminal justice system, the treatment system, or recruited by researchers because of their deviance. It is often very difficult to determine how representative they are of a general population or even of populations of crack users or criminals. However, recent general population studies examining the statistical association between crack cocaine use and criminal behavior also have shown a strong relationship. Fagan and his colleagues (1990) studying a population of inner-city students found that those males who committed the highest number of different types of crimes also were the most likely to have also used hard drugs such as cocaine. In an analysis of data from a statistically representative sample of all households in the United States, Harrison and Gfroerer (1992) found that cocaine use (usually in the form of crack) was more highly correlated with all types of criminal behavior than was the use of alcohol or other types of drugs. In the National Household Survey, crack use is the most statistically powerful predictor of property crime, violent crime, or being arrested for a crime.

CRACK USE AND TYPES OF CRIME

Some Considerations in Understanding the Crack and Type of Crime Relationship

In any discussion of the relationships between crack cocaine and types of criminal activities, it is wise to keep a few caveats in mind. First, it is important to know if the population under discussion is juvenile or adult. For studies that use official justice system data, this distinction is important because possession and sale of crack are officially criminal law violations in most jurisdictions regardless of age, but crack use by adolescents is typically considered to be *delinquent* behavior and a matter for the juvenile justice system in many urban areas in the United States. In fact, adolescents suspected of violating laws that prohibit the sale, manufacture, and distribution of crack also may be retained in juvenile courts because of overcrowded courts and jails. Thus, for juveniles, little official information is available on crack use and type of crime. Crack use is often just a part of a finding of delinquency.

Second, it should be noted whether the analysis is based on official police or justice system records. These systems are typically deficient in capturing drug involvement information (if the case did not involve explicit charges of drug law violations). This omission is particularly likely in juveniles' records where concerns about labeling and protection of confidentiality are traditional and often mandated by statute. Studies involving direct interviews with drug users outside the confines of justice systems—for example, anonymous surveys and street-based ethnographic studies—offer other perspectives on drug use-crime relationships, albeit ones that depend on investigators' skills in eliciting valid self-reports from study participants.

Time and place are also important factors to consider when discussing crack and type of crime relationships. Criminal activity is not uniformly distributed across the United States; it varies by area of the country, between urban-rural groups, by city size, and other location-related variables—for example, population demographics, economic conditions, and extent of drug importation/trafficking. Similarly, the availability or popularity of given illegal drugs varies by time and place. These factors change over time, as does the creation of state and local drug laws and enforcement policies. For example, the practice of using juveniles as lookouts, couriers, holders, and street-level sellers of drugs increased in the 1980s as crack dealers sought to reduce their personal risk of arrest. Many states passed new laws that imposed severe penalties for using juveniles in these ways. Similarly, media-fanned fears that dealers were targeting juveniles for illegal drug sales in the vicinity of schools increased in the late 1980s. In response, some states increased the penalty of such violations, including mandatory sanctions of additional years of incarceration. Police departments may emphasize "stings," "buy-bust operations," "crack-house raids," or demolitions and other tactics; special appropriations for "overtime" operations can dramatically affect arrest statistics in many crime categories, including drug dealing and possession. Therefore, local behavior patterns, laws, and enforcement policies play a major role in producing particular types of crimes that are committed by crack users.

However, despite the complexity of pertinent variables, the research literature does suggest that the use of crack influences the types of crimes users engage in and for which they are arrested.

Drug Law Violations

Possession of cocaine is probably the most common criminal charge reported for crack users. The likelihood for crack users to be arrested for possession is increased by crack's pharmacologic properties. The intense but short duration of crack's effect prompts users to seek additional supplies of crack. Frequently in their eagerness to use crack again quickly, users do not exercise due caution. The probability of being arrested for selling crack is related to the logistics of the sale and the nature of the dosage unit; crack rocks are small and relatively inexpensive per unit, and this requires many sellers and sales transactions to generate volume revenues. The sales portion of the crack distribution system is dominated by youth, who are available in numbers and who are attracted by the lure of income far beyond what they could ever hope to attain by legal means. Street dealers' interaction patterns with buyers are easy for police to detect and law enforcement agencies in many jurisdictions have emphasized street arrests of users and sellers and raids on houses where crack is sold and immediately used. These points are very clearly illustrated by Inciardi and his colleagues (1994). They found that over 90% of crack users' arrests involved drug law violations. Consequently, arrests of crack users (for possession) and dealers (for sales, manufacture, and distribution) have generated huge numbers in most urban jurisdictions, threatening to overwhelm overcrowded courtrooms, jails, and prisons in many areas of the United States.

Miscellaneous Charges

As already noted, crack users and sellers place themselves in jeopardy of police surveillance because they frequently are on the street in search of deals. It is not unusual, however, for the buyer or seller to be able to dispose of crack rocks in their possession just prior to police apprehension. In such cases, particularly when the officers feel the accused has "flunked the attitude test" or has become "obstinate" or "disrespectful," some police have been reported to file unofficial charges of "felony bad attitude" (Sheldon & Brown, 1991). These researchers attributed much of a noted increase in charges in one jurisdiction to this phenomenon; the most common charges were resisting arrest by a police officer and obstructing a police officer. In this same jurisdiction, the investigators found that police routinely "overcharged" when the cases involved drug law violations. For example, they filed separate counts for each piece of "paraphernalia" found and each count added $250 to the bail amount. Other charges in this general category of crime that may be added to drug charges or substituted for them when evidence is lacking are disorderly conduct, vagrancy, and loitering.

Crimes That Produce Income

Auto theft, breaking and entering, burglary, and buying, concealing, and receiving stolen property are income-producing crimes associated with crack use as well as with illegal drug use (especially by youth) and street drug users in general. The stereotypical perception of adult crack users is that they will sell all the furniture and food in the house, offer their spouses and children as prostitutes, and steal anything that opportunity brings their way in order to obtain crack. Such cases, when found, often generate a media frenzy, unlike another category of adult crack users whose members resort to more mundane property crimes to generate crack-purchasing dollars. Examples of this category are employees who pilfer company products, supplies, and receipts or who embezzle to finance their crack use. Other less assertive crack users may resort to the crimes of counterfeiting, forgery, or passing bad checks in order to obtain funds for their crack purchases.

Some crack users engage in another category of income-producing crime that sometimes is called "victimless crime"—for example, gambling, commercialized vice, and prostitution. Crack-using women are particularly susceptible to resorting eventually to prostitution or "sex for crack" as their addiction progresses and all other legitimate and illegal sources of income have been exhausted (Chapter 4). Inciardi and his colleagues have documented the extent to which even youthful female crack users engage in sex acts for crack (Inciardi, Horowitz, & Pottieger, 1993) and have graphically described the depths of degradation and risk of infection experienced by women who consent to serve as crack house prostitutes in return for a continuing supply of crack cocaine (Inciardi, 1993b; Inciardi, Lockwood, & Pottieger, 1993).

Crimes Against Persons or Violent Crime

Armed robbery could be considered a property crime committed by crack users to obtain funds to purchase their drugs, but because it involves a personal confrontation with a victim, it is classified as a more serious offense with more severe punishments by U.S. criminal codes. This is one of the crimes that is popularly perceived as prevalent among crack users, especially youthful ones. This perception would not seem to be supported by recent data from the Drug Use Forecasting program that focused on male juvenile arrestee/detainees in 12 cities throughout the United States (Drug Use Forecasting Annual Program, 1994b).

Inciardi, Horowitz, and Pottieger (1993) report a far different picture drawn from data from a Miami street study of youth. They studied a population of extremely hard-core adolescent criminal offenders still active on the street (in contrast to juveniles enmeshed in the juvenile justice system or adolescents representative of the general population). In this study, over 85% of the 611 youths interviewed were regular users of crack and almost two-thirds had participated in a robbery (see also Rivers, 1989).

As the 1980s progressed, researchers found increasingly that cocaine use was related to violent confrontational crime among men and women (Datesman, 1981; Simonds & Kashani, 1980; Spunt, Goldstein, Bellucci, & Miller, 1990). Research has also indicated that cocaine use may be related not only to committing a violent offense, but also to being a victim of violent crime. McBride and his colleagues (1986) found that cocaine was the most common illicit drug found in the bodies of homicide victims in Miami, Florida. In a New York study, Goldstein and others (1993) found that increased cocaine use was associated with being a victim of violent crime for women.

A "tripartite scheme" devised by Goldstein (1985) for interpreting the relationship between illegal drugs and violence seems particularly applicable for crack-associated violence. This scheme characterizes drug-related violence as involving psychopharmacological, economically compulsive, and systemic aspects.

Some of the violent behavior of crack cocaine users may be attributable to the drug's psychopharmacology. Crack use is reported to produce an intense but brief high. These characteristics, plus the relatively low cost of single dosage units ("rocks") contribute to the tendency for crack users to binge. Following a binge, for periods ranging from hours to several days, crack users are in a crash phase, characterized early by agitation, depression, anorexia, and high cocaine craving. These symptoms are followed by fatigue, depression, insomnia, paranoia, and exhaustion. If the crack user does not binge again soon, withdrawal symptoms often appear (as early as 1 week or as late as 10 weeks postbinge). These symptoms include anhedonia (inability to experience pleasure), anxiety, and high levels of craving for cocaine exacerbated by conditioned cues (Gawin, 1991). All of these effects could result in an increased willingness on the part of crack users to act aggressively and in ways that will bring violence upon themselves.

As discussed earlier, crack use tends to progress rapidly to addiction with progressively larger amounts being consumed. The ability and willingness to derive drug-purchasing funds from legitimate sources declines proportionately as the addiction progresses. As crack users' addictions progress, they often take more risks in the criminal acts they are willing to commit in order to obtain drug-purchasing funds. This may involve progression from economic crimes to crimes against property, to violent income-producing crimes against persons.

The systemic aspect of Goldstein's model refers to violence that is a subcultural behavior pattern endemic to street-drug use in general, but which may be particularly associated with the street distribution of crack cocaine. As shown by Inciardi, Horowitz, and Pottieger (1993), youth involved in the crack business in Miami are more heavily involved in other types of crime and specifically violent crime. Further, the more heavily involved the youth were in the crack business, the more crack they themselves consumed. Moreover, the lifestyle itself is seen as reinforcing. From the perspective of youth, all the dangers associated with potential death, overdose, arrest, and street violence were welcomed as intoxicating challenges. The elevated levels of violence associated with competition among higher level traffickers for control of given markets also can be classified as systemic. Violence against otherwise law-abiding crack-using citizens who become heavily indebted to or who rip off violent drug dealers can also be placed in this category.

CRACK USE AND CRIMINAL CAREERS

Longitudinal research evidence suggests that most delinquents cease their illegal activity by late adolescence or early adulthood (e.g., Kandel, Simcha-Fagan, & Davies, 1986). Normative age-related activities such as legitimate employment, marriage, and rearing children traditionally have been interpreted as activities signifying "maturation," increasing an individual's "stakes in conformity"—that is, they have something to lose. These factors have been seen as influential in age-related decreases in illegal behavior as reflected in official arrest rates that historically have dropped sharply beginning at about 25 years of age.

A considerable variety of research conducted before the widespread use of crack cocaine indicates that frequent drug use may dramatically retard the normative maturation process, with direct implications for consequent continuation of criminal careers initiated as youth and sustained through early adulthood (see Dembo et al., 1987; Elliott & Huizinga, 1985; Faupel & Klockars, 1987). Research evidence on this subject as it relates to crack cocaine users is scant and may not be widely generalizable but is worth noting nonetheless.

Inciardi, Horowitz, and Pottieger (1993) suggest that past research, particularly that which focused on drug-using juveniles and their careers, may not be highly applicable to youth who reach the level of serious delinquency and involvement in the crack business. They state,

> This analysis suggests that crack use and consequent crack-market participation have criminogenic effects not previously observed among adolescent drug users. Crack is cocaine that is (1) so cheap that teenagers can start using it with the money from their allowances, (2) so widely available that, in cities, 12-year-olds have no problem finding it, and (3) so powerful and short acting a euphoric drug that it is both rapidly addicting and unlimited in its potential financial requirements. As a result, adolescents can find themselves entangled in the kind of classic addictive drug cycle originally described only for adult heroin users: dealing finances use, use encourages more use, and more use requires more profit-making crimes of all sorts to support an ever-growing addictive use pattern. Until the 1980s, this cycle was simply not seen among adolescents for two reasons. First, they did not commonly use addictive drugs with potentially high financial obligations (i.e., heroin and cocaine). Second, adults severely limited the involvement of adolescents in drug-marketing networks. The advent of crack changed both these factors, with highly criminogenic consequences for street kids. (p. 178)

These investigators also note the importance of the strong attractiveness the crack business lifestyle holds for the youth involved in it, descriptions of which they recall as reminiscent of those applied more than a quarter century ago to the heroin users' subculture: the joys of hustling and "taking care of business," the thrills of a "cops and robbers" street life (see Preble & Casey, 1969; Sutter, 1969). Inciardi and his colleagues conclude that the serious delinquents in their Miami-based study:

will not automatically grow out of their law-breaking activities, as most youth who commit "deviant" acts tend to do. These adolescents are already well entrenched in a culture and lifestyle that include a profusion of illicit and drug-seeking behaviors. Moreover, they are heavily involved in a range of additional economic, violent, and other predatory crimes less directly associated with their acquisition of drugs. It appears that, for many, there may be no turning back from the criminal way of life. (Inciardi, Horowitz, & Pottieger, 1993, p. 189)

To the extent that youth in other communities in the United States are similarly involved in the crack business, these findings have ominous implications for the criminal careers of this age cohort and for the future public safety of America's urban areas unless effective intervention efforts can be mounted.

Concluding Comments on the Crack Type of Crime Relationship

A final caution is warranted in this discussion of crack cocaine and violent crime. Moore (1993) notes that the national concern regarding violent crime seems to have reached a point of near hysteria similar to the national attitude about the drug abuse epidemic in the 1980s. The statistics are not uniform across the country, but some 1993 crime statistics for the state of Florida are illustrative. As reported in a Miami newspaper, auto thefts reached a record number in Florida in 1993, rising by almost 9% from the previous year. Firearm crimes also increased, but only by 4.4%. But most other crimes dropped: burglaries and robberies were down by nearly 3%, homicides hit a 14-year low, and violent crime was down by almost 2%. Yet crime, or rather the fear of crime, was the lead issue for virtually all candidates for political office in 1994 "from the school board on up to the governor." A criminologist from a state university used the words "cynical," "disingenuous," "unjustified," and "moral panic." He felt the local and national media and the public had overreacted to a few sensationalized 1993 homicides involving European tourists. Other explanations offered in the newspaper report were "free-floating fear and rage of crime-weary Floridians crystallized by these murders" and a reality-based public reaction to "a real increase in gun-involved juvenile crime" (*Miami Herald,* Oct. 30, 1994, p. 1A).

Inciardi, Horowitz, and Pottieger (1993) specifically suggest that a good deal of the current concern about crack-related violence may be more the result of media creation than experiential reality. They analyzed annual city homicide rates from 1985 through 1990 for six cities that have high rates of crack availability and distribution and are known for their high rates of crime and violence. They concluded that higher homicide rates do not necessarily go hand in hand with higher rates of the distribution or use of crack.

However, existing research evidence that was accumulated via a variety of methodologies, including life histories, longitudinal, ethnographic, and survey studies, show the frequent use of crack cocaine is at least partially responsible for increases in criminal activities. This conclusion is most clearly evident for crimes committed to obtain funds for crack purchases or to otherwise acquire and use crack cocaine. Further, data strongly suggest that crack use is involved with sustaining criminal activities. Crack users appear to have particular difficulty in disengaging from their drug use patterns and its associated criminal activity.

CAUSAL ISSUES IN THE CRACK-CRIME RELATIONSHIP

Implicit in the concern about the relationship between crack use and crime is the assumed causal nature of the relationship. It is frequently assumed that the ingestion of crack causes criminal behavior. That argument is often explicit in the media portrayal of crack use. Traditionally, the arguments for the causal nature of the crack-crime relationship have focused on the psychopharmacological effects of crack and the economic costs of the drug. As we discussed in the preceding section, clinicians and researchers have documented that crack cocaine may cause increased states of excitement, paranoia, and aggressive behavior. Self-reports by crack users frequently describe feelings of being able to be faster, tougher, and stronger than anyone else and being highly suspicious about others' intent and behavior. These feelings of aggression and paranoia coupled with the effect of a central nervous system stimulant are often perceived to be involved with violent and other types of criminal behavior (see Waldorf, Reinarman, & Murphy, 1992).

Life history and longitudinal studies of crack users, however, do not portray a population of innocent youth driven into crime by the use of crack. Generally these types of studies document extensive criminal behavior for a few years before the initiation of crack use. For example, in an extensive study of crack users in Miami, Inciardi and his colleagues found that the average age for first crime, first drug sale, first theft, robbery, or prostitution was younger than the age for first use of crack cocaine (Inciardi, McBride, McCoy, & Chitwood, 1994). These data suggest that the relationship between crack use and crime is not a simple linear one of direct causation. That is, data do not suggest that crack use drives noncriminally involved youth into a life of violent, or nonviolent, crime.

The available data warrant the conclusions that crack use and other criminal activities may have common or similar etiologies, and their relationship is better characterized as autocorrelated, bidirectional, or recursive than as simply linear. For example, once initiated, crack use often becomes addictive and as use escalates, so does other criminal behavior associated with crack acquisition and use. Conversely, the initiation of criminal behavior can result in subcultural participation and subsequent initiation of crack use as a symbol of membership (see Clayton & Tuchfeld, 1982). This argument largely focuses on the drug or crack crime relationship existing within the framework of broader subcultural ecological patterns. As Goldstein (1985) well notes, much of the drugs-crime connection occurs within drug-using subcultural behavior patterns and within a street culture that values toughness. This may involve disputes about quality of drugs, street corner distribution of drugs, and dealing with police informers. Further, McBride and McCoy (1981) and McBride and Swartz (1990) have argued that crack use, other drug use, and crime statistically occur in the same environmental contexts characterized by poverty, high unemployment, and single parent households within a society with incredible access to very lethal weapons. These perspectives remind us that the crack-crime relationship is not easily documented as directly causal but rather is probably based on some direct effect plus broader subcultural behaviors and values and, to a significant extent, produced by common background causes.

Akers (1992) concludes that "drugs/alcohol and crime/delinquency are highly related but cannot be said to cause one another. Depending on the substance, setting, and group, first commission of illegal acts will sometimes precede and sometimes follow first drug use" (p. 69). He feels the best answer to the drugs-crime connection is that "the two are related through the association they hold in common with another set of social factors and processes." More specifically, drug abuse is "related to the same social correlates and in the same direction as are delinquency and crime—age, sex, race, socioeconomic status, and residence as well as religion, family, and peer groups." This hypothesis "is also supported by more direct evidence of drugs and delinquency flowing from a common process" (pp. 69–70).

THE CRACK AND CRIME POLICY ISSUES THAT FACE SOCIETY

The data cited throughout this book clearly describe the extent and consequences of crack use in our society today. Although some observers have noted that societal response was slow in coming (Salholz, 1989), there can be little doubt that once society reacted, it did so with some vigor. By the mid-1980s government policymakers and legislators had concluded that the best means of affecting the crack-crime connection was to enforce existing laws and pass new severe laws against the use and distribution of crack (Fessler, 1990; Kreiter, 1987; Lawrence, 1988; Wilson & DiIulio, 1989). During the 1980s, considerable legislative activity at national and local levels was directed at the increase in cocaine use. For example, Michigan passed a law that provided for life imprisonment for the possession of more than 650 grams of cocaine for individuals with no prior felony convictions (*Harmelin v. Michigan,* 1991). Many other states passed sentencing laws that mandated extensive minimal prison terms for the possession or sale of crack. Some states even considered reintroducing corporal punishment such as flogging to fight crack dealers (see Chambers, 1989). In addition to extensive minimum prison terms, laws were passed that deprived crack dealers of property that might have been bought with dollars obtained from crack sales. The individual had to prove the property was not purchased with drug dollars in order to get the property returned after confiscation. These laws were enforced and have generally been found to be constitutional (for example, see Greenhouse, 1991).

The expectation, or hope, was that vigorous enforcement of a zero tolerance policy would result in raising the cost of crack use, in prison time, and in confiscation of property to such an extent that use would significantly drop. However, as recent DUF (Drug Use Forecasting Program, 1994a) data show, a large majority of felony arrestees in large urban areas continue to be cocaine users and there has been no reduction in use in the last 4 years. Other researchers also have documented that the courts are virtually saturated with crack users. A large proportion of felony cases in today's urban courtrooms are directly (the primary charge involves crack) or indirectly (crack use contributed to the criminal charge) crack cocaine related. The sheer numbers of crack and other drug users arrested and processed through the criminal justice system (see Blenko, 1990; Goerdt, Lomvardias, Fallas, & Mohoney, 1987) caused the establishment of special drug courts to handle the number of cases. These drug courts were established in the nation's largest urban areas such as Chicago and Miami as well as in the country's smaller urban areas such as Berrien County, Michigan (for an overview of drug courts, see Inciardi, McBride, & Rivers, 1996). The development of drug courts has not statistically decreased the extent of cocaine use among arrestees. In addition, evaluations of drug courts by researchers and in the popular press have been mixed (Blenko, Fagan, & Dumanovsky, 1994; Goldcamp & Weilan, 1993). By expediting processing, drug courts have expanded local capacity to process a large number of individuals. They have not so much reduced the number of arrestees as improved the system's capability for handling increased numbers (Davis, Smith, & Lurigio, 1994). However, the ability to handle increased numbers can contribute to prison overcrowding if diversion is not a major part of the system or can diminish the quality of justice if clearing court calendars is the major goal (for a discussion of prison overcrowding resulting from drug law enforcement, see Reske, 1993).

This inundation of the criminal justice system at all levels with crack cocaine users has caused considerable debate about a more appropriate means to impact the crack-crime connection. Our society seems to have reached a conclusion that the crack-crime relationship has not been significantly affected by the zero tolerance era and the massive resources that have been given to law enforcement. From local community groups to federal policymakers and legislators, there has been considerable debate about future policy toward illegal drug use in general and crack cocaine and the crack-crime relationship in particular (e.g., see Cooper, Nadelmann, & Wilson, 1990). This debate has focused on three elements:

1. The legalization of crack cocaine
2. Shifting the emphasis from the supply side (drug law enforcement) to demand reduction (treatment)
3. Prevention of crack use

Crack Legalization

Most Americans probably do not realize that governmental regulation of drug distribution and use, including the distribution and use of cocaine, is a relatively new phenomenon in American history. Until the early part of this century, most of the drugs currently defined as illegal, including cocaine, were part of the free market. Those who distributed these drugs were even organized as a trade group (for a discussion of the history of drug policy in the United States, see Inciardi, 1992; Musto, 1987). During the early 20th century many reforms were directed at addressing what were considered to be major social problems in American health and welfare. These reforms included higher medical ethics advocated by the American Medical Association early in this century, as well as the Pure Food and Drug Act in 1906 and alcohol prohibition in the 1920s. In addition to these reforms, the Harrison Act was passed in 1914. Although this act was ostensibly a tax act, its practical result was to make the manufacture, distribution, and possession of such previously legal drugs as narcotics and cocaine illegal.

Critics claimed that the Harrison Act at the federal level and associated laws at state levels essentially created the drugs-crime association (King, 1974; Lindesmith, 1965). They argue that by making drugs illegal, those who used drugs became, by statutory definition, criminals. In addition, these critics feel that making drugs illegal probably significantly increased the price of drugs and thus drove those who were addicted to the substances to crime in order to finance their drug use. The argument concludes that as a result of the continued demand for drugs, criminal enterprises were organized to meet those demands and were capitalized by users willing to pay high prices to continue their drug use.

Those who advocate the legalization of crack cocaine note that most of the statistical association between crack use and crime is an artifact of existing drug laws. This is clearly illustrated in a recent publication by Inciardi and his colleagues (1994). These researchers found that over 90% of self-reported crimes committed by cocaine users involved violations of drug laws. Those who advocate the legalization of crack believe the war on drugs has resulted in the passing of draconian laws that have eroded our civil rights, corrupted and overwhelmed the criminal justice system, caused the deaths of innocent bystanders, capitalized international criminal organizations, and simply have not worked (for discussions advocating drug legalization, see Nadelmann, 1989; Trebach & Inciardi, 1993).

Although agreeing with many elements of the critique of current drug policy, others have strongly argued against the legalization of drugs. These arguments have largely focused on the lack of a clear legalization program, the probable increase in crack use that would result if crack were made a free, even though regulated, market product and the reality of the personal, physical, psychological, and societal (including criminal) harm that would result from the increase in crack use. These policymakers, treatment providers, and researchers note that those who advocate crack legalization have not dealt with many essential questions. These questions include how the drug would be made available and/or regulated, at what age it would be legal (and how those underage would be kept from crack especially because regulations are totally ineffective at preventing the underage from accessing tobacco or alcohol), and generally how legal crack would be integrated into contemporary society. Perhaps the most basic criticism of calls for legalization involves naivete about the ability of a free, even regulated, market to increase demand. The heavily regulated marketers of tobacco and alcohol have shown remarkable ability to retain and even expand markets in some social groups. There is no reason to believe that crack marketers would not be at least as successful in targeted market expansion (for a discussion in opposition to legalization, see Goldstein & Kalant, 1990; Inciardi & McBride, 1989; Trebach & Inciardi, 1993; Wilson, 1993).

Experiments at legalization have not gone as well as their advocates had hoped. A drug legalization zone experiment in Zurich, Switzerland, in 1991 was stopped about a year later because of increases, not decreases, in crime in areas around the drug zone (*New York Times*, February 11, 1992, p. A10). In addition, Grapendaal and his colleagues (1992), in analyzing the criminal behavior of drug users in a very drug tolerant society in the Netherlands, concluded that the majority of drug users still committed crimes and that crime accounted for about 24% of their income. These researchers further noted that the Netherlands drug legalization policy may have contributed to a permanent underclass whose crimes could be reduced through generous welfare payments but not eliminated.

Overall, in the United States, the public and national policy leaders do not believe the existing arguments or data justify the legalization of crack or other currently illegal drugs. In addition, the current political climate would likely make such discussions very unproductive and hinder the development of an effective broad-based policy directed at alleviating the crack-crime connection. Law enforcement needs to be much better balanced with treatment and prevention and must address issues of the fairness and severity of its application (see Currie, 1993). To many observers, enforcement primarily takes place against inner-city minority groups selling crack on the street and not against the crack or powdered cocaine use of more affluent white suburbanites whose demands and resources fuel the street supply of cocaine (see *New York Times*, May 31, 1994).

Treatment

Key elements of the federal drug policy throughout the 1980s included a strong emphasis on reducing the availability of drugs through destruction of production capability, the interdiction of drug shipments, raising the legal cost of drug use through increased criminal and civil punishment, and vigorous enforcement of all of these laws (Kreiter, 1987). There has been general recognition that this policy was at best unbalanced and ignored the complexity of drug addiction. Particularly, crack has been found to be a highly addictive drug whose use was not significantly affected by increasing the legal and civil consequences of use. This is evidenced by the continuing high rate of cocaine use among those arrested in the United States (Drug Use Forecasting Program, 1994a).

Treatment is an essential part of any national policy to ameliorate the crack-crime relationship (for discussions of a call for national policy change toward treatment, see Cooper et al., 1990; Keigher, 1994; Kleber, 1994; Pierce, 1993). The use of treatment to affect the drugs-crime relationship directly is not new and was clearly a part of national policy in the 1960s and 1970s (see Inciardi & McBride, 1991; Inciardi, McBride, & Rivers, 1996). There is evidence that treatment has some effect on reducing drug use and associated crime. Long-term follow-up studies of drug users, including crack users, indicate a positive relationship between time in treatment and reduced drug use. A study from California clearly shows the strong positive effect of drug treatment (Gerstein, Johnson, Harwood, Fountain, Suter, & Malloy, 1994). In addition, research suggests that drug-using criminal offenders under court-directed treatment are more likely to be retained and more likely to reduce drug use than those drug users not under court control (Hubbard et al., 1988; Simpson, 1981). These findings coupled with other research that shows a strong relationship between less drug use and less crime have resulted in many states diverting drug-using offenders to treatment, providing treatment as a condition of parole, or providing drug treatment to those incarcerated (Inciardi, 1993a; Inciardi & McBride, 1991). An increasing body of research suggests that drug treatment in prison is effective at reducing crack use and impacting the crack-crime connection (Nurco, Thomas, Batemen, Toledano, & Kinlock, 1993).

Many observers have suggested that what our society needs is a much more balanced approach in drug law enforcement to reduce the availability of crack and to provide accessible treatment of sufficient quality and intensity for those addicted to crack cocaine. Treatment availability for indigent crack users is often severely limited in the very cities where crack use is the highest. For example, indigent crack users in many cities often have to wait 6 months or more before admission to a residential facility. Given the nature of crack addiction, its etiology, and associated behaviors, this type of treatment is often the most appropriate. Without the expansion of treatment and without the development of more effective treatment specifically designed for crack use, national policy remains incomplete and much less effective then it could be.

Prevention

The economic costs of crack use are extraordinary. In terms of the crack-crime relationship, they include the costs of goods stolen, health-care costs associated with crime, and the costs of police, courts, and corrections. Although a balanced approach between law enforcement and treatment can considerably ameliorate the crack-crime connection, most observers estimate that it would be much less expensive to prevent the initiation of crack use in the first place.

Today, multifaceted prevention program models have been devised and evaluated. In studies of the etiology of crack use, researchers have reached a number of significant conclusions about the causes of crack use that are directly relevant to prevention policy. These conclusions focus on individual personality development problems, physical and sexual abuse and other family dysfunctions, peer group influence, and broader structural factors such as educational attainment and job opportunities. Prevention programs today tend to base their program on known risk and protective factors for drug abuse particularly emphasizing individual personality, family, peer group, and community influence. The research literature indicates that modern prevention programs have had some success at identifying high-risk groups and reducing the probabilities of drug use initiation based on knowledge of drug abuse etiology (see Hawkins, Catalano, & Miller, 1992; Johnson, Hansen, & Pentz, 1986; Manger, Hawkins, Haggerty, & Catalano, 1992).

Although traditional prevention programs are an important part of a total approach, national policy must also include more macro social issues such as education and economic development. Simple demographic analysis of crack-using populations consistently shows very low levels of education and employment. Generally the majority of crack users have not finished high school and are not regularly employed (see Edlin et al., 1994; Gfroerer & Brodsky, 1993; Inciardi et al., 1994; McBride et al., 1992). When employed, crack users typically hold day laborer or service-type jobs that pay near the minimum wage. The economic opportunities afforded by street crack dealing in the inner city are simply enormously greater than any other economic opportunity available to inner-city youth. A study by the Rand Corporation illustrated this point. They found that in a population of crack street dealers in Washington, D.C., many worked in service jobs and integrated those jobs with street crack dealing as an income supplement (Reuter, MacCoun, & Murphy, 1990).

It is important to remember that statistically, the primary crime-crack connection is in the street-level distribution of crack (Inciardi et al., 1994). The perceived benefit of the economic opportunities provided by street crack dealing does not seem to have been affected by raising the cost of street crack distribution through increased mandatory minimum sentencing and property confiscation. It almost appears that, given the current demand for crack and the very limited opportunities for other income sources, society cannot raise the cost high enough (without a dramatic change in our definition of accept-able punishment) to reduce significantly the extent of street crack distribution and use. Broad societal prevention programs directed at reducing the crack-crime connection must include strong economic development and educational programs in the inner-city areas most affected by crack use.

The social and economic changes in the past decade have resulted in the need for a very highly literate, often technically skilled work force. This is illus-trated by the military. Historically, the military was often a place for the mar-ginal delinquent or young criminal. High school dropouts were readily accepted into the military during most of this century. The military often played a viable role in social control, personality development, and job provi-sion for those who, for whatever reason, had problems in school or the job market and had limited job skills. That has dramatically changed. The military of today has very high demands for technically educated, skilled youth. They simply are not looking for the educationally and psychologically marginal for large-scale military actions. There is no alternative to a strong basic education that prepares young people for a very competitive, rapidly changing job mar-ket. Today, data indicate that inner-city schools have dropout rates many times the national average and at graduation, many inner-city school seniors are years behind the educational attainment test scores of their suburban counterparts. At times it seems our society is more willing to build an unlimited number of jails for inner-city residents than invest in education in these same communi-ties. However, there are simply not enough jails or resources to hold those who our society is not able to educate.

SUMMARY

A review of the issues and data on the crack-crime relationship shows the extensive statistical association between the use of crack cocaine and criminal behavior. However, it also shows the complexity of that association. Although criminal activity appears to occur before the initiation of crack use, the use of crack appears to be involved with increasing and continuing criminal activity and may be correlated with violent behavior. Rather than a direct causal relation-ship, both the use of crack and criminal behavior are probably the result of the same or very similar constellations of variables that include limited education, poverty, unemployment, high rates of physical abuse, and the lack of economic opportunities.

Attempts to reduce crack use and the crack-crime relationship during the last decade or more have focused primarily on law enforcement and raising the consequences of crack use so high that users will be dissuaded from con-tinuing their use. But no evidence indicates this approach has had any im-pact on the crack-crime connection. The majority of arrestees in the nation's major cities continue to use cocaine, and crack users still overwhelm the criminal justice system. Because of the failure of the almost exclusively law enforcement approach to drug policy, there are many calls for a radical re-structuring of national drug policy. These calls have included arguments for drug legalization. However, the probable increase in crack use that would re-sult from legalization, the societal recognition of the consequences of in-creased use, and the limited successes of legalization experiments for crack have minimized the support for crack legalization efforts.

Today, there does appear to be a willingness to develop a better balance be-tween law enforcement and treatment. Evidence shows that treatment can be effective, particularly for drug users involved with the criminal justice system. In addition to treatment, it has been suggested that it is crucial and more cost effec-tive to focus on preventing crack use and any resultant crack-crime connection. Prevention at the individual and group level has been shown to be effective. Fur-ther it has been argued that prevention must also include more macro social ef-forts directed at improving educational retention and attainment and at economic development. Often street crack dealing and its associated crime is the best economic opportunity for uneducated inner-city youth. Our society seems very willing to build prisons to house inner-city criminals. It must be at least as willing to provide the more effective educational and employment skills that could reduce the probability of initiating criminal behavior and crack use.

REFERENCES

Adler, J. (1988, November 28). Crack: Hour by hour. *Newsweek*, 64–71.

Akers, R. L. (1992). *Drugs, alcohol, and society: Social structure, process, and policy.* Belmont, CA: Wadsworth.

Blenko, S. (1990). The impact of drug offenders on the criminal justice system. In R. A. Weisheit (Ed.), *Drugs, crime, and the criminal justice system, (pp.* 27–78). Cincinnati: Anderson.

Blenko, S., Fagan, J. A., & Dumanovsky, T. (1994). The effects of legal sanctions on re-cidivism in special drug courts. *The Justice System Journal, 17,* 53–81.

Chambers, M. (1989). Is mutilation and flogging the answer? *The National Law Journal, 11,* 25–13.

Clayton, R. R., & Tuchfeld, B. S. (1982). The drug-crime debate: Obstacles to under-standing the relationship. *Journal of Drug Issues, 12,* 153–166.

Cooper, M. H., Nadelmann, E. A., & Wilson, J. Q. (1990). Does the war on drugs need a new strategy? *Editorial Research Reports, 2,* 110–122.

Currie, E. (1993). Toward a policy on drugs. *Dissent, 40,* 65–71.

Datesman, S. (1981). Women, crime, and drugs. In J. A. Inciardi (Ed.), *The drugs-crime connection* (pp. 85–104). Beverly Hills, CA: Sage.

Davis, R. C., Smith, B. E., & Lurigio, A. J. (1994). Court strategies to cope with rising drug caseloads. *The Justice System Journal, 17,* 1–18.

Dembo, R. M., Washburn, E. D., Wish, H., Yeung, A., Getreu, B. E., & Blount, W. R. (1987). Heavy marijuana use and crime among youths entering a juvenile detention center. *Journal of Psychoactive Drugs, 19,* 47–56.

Drug Use Forecasting Program. (1994a). *Annual report on adult arrestees.* Washington, DC: National Institute of Justice.

Drug Use Forecasting Program. (1994b). *Annual report on juvenile arrestees.* Washington, DC: National institute of Justice.

Edlin, B. R., Irwin, K. L., Faruque, S., McCoy, C. B., Word, C., Serrano, Y., Inciardi, J. A., Bowser, B. P., Schilling, R. F., Holmberg, S. D., & the Multicenter Crack Cocaine and HIV Infection Study Team. (1994). Intersecting epidemics—crack cocaine use and HIV infection among inner-city young adults. *New England Journal of Medicine, 331,* 1422-1427.

Elliott, D. S., & Huizinga, D. (1985, April 17-18). *The relationship between delinquent behavior and ADM problem behaviors.* Paper presented at ADAMHA/OJJDP "State of the Art" Research Conference on Juvenile Offenders with Serious Alcohol, Drug Abuse and Mental Health Problems, Bethesda, MD.

Fagan, J. (1990). Social processes of delinquency and drug use among urban gangs. In C. R. Huff (Ed.), *Gangs in America* (pp. 183-219). Newbury Park: Sage.

Fagan, J. (1994). Women and drugs revisited: Female participation in the cocaine economy. *Journal of Drug Issues, 24,* 179-226.

Fagan, J., Weis, J. G., & Cheng, Y. (1990). Delinquency and substance abuse among inner-city youths. *Criminology, 24,* 439-471.

Faupel, C. E., & Klockars, C. B. (1987). Drugs-crime connections: Elaborations from the life histories of hard-core heroin addicts. *Social Problems, 34,* 54-68.

Fessler, P. (1990). Bush's $10 billion strategy targets enforcement again. *Congressional Quarterly Weekly Report, 48,* 242-244.

Gawin, F. J. (1991). Cocaine addiction: Psychology and neurophysiology. *Science, 251,* 1580-1586.

Gerstein, D. R., Johnson, R. A., Harwood, H., Fountain, D., Suter, N., & Malloy, K. (1994). *Evaluating recovery services: The California Drug and Alcohol Treatment Assessment (CALDATA).* State of California Department of Alcohol and Drug Programs.

Gfroerer, J., & Brodsky, M. D. (1993). Frequent cocaine users and their use of treatment. *American Journal of Public Health, 8,* 1149-1154.

Goerdt, J. A., Lomvardias, C., Fallas, G., & Mahoney, B. (1987). *Examining court delay: The pace of litigation in 26 urban trial courts.* Williamsburg, VA: National Center for State Courts.

Goldcamp, J. S., & Weilan, D. (1993). *Assessing the impact of the Dade County felony drug court: Final report.* Washington, DC: U.S. Department of Justice, Office of Justice Programs, National Institute of Justice.

Goldstein, A., & Kalant, H. (1990). Drug policy: Striking the right balance. *Science, 249,* 1513-1521.

Goldstein, P. J. (1985). The drugs/violence nexus: A tripartite conceptual framework. *Journal of Drug Issues, 15,* 493-506.

Goldstein, P. J., Bellucci, P. A., Spunt, B. J., & Miller, T. (1993). Volume of cocaine use and violence: A comparison between men and women. In R. Dembo (Ed.), *Drugs and crime* (pp. 141-177). New York: University Press of America.

Grapendaal, M., Leuw, E., & Nelen, H. (1992). Drugs and crime in an accommodating social context: The situation in Amsterdam. *Contemporary Drug Problems, 19,* 303-326.

Greenhouse, L. (1991, June 28). Mandatory life term is upheld in drug cases. *New York Times,* p. A12 (N), p. A15 (L), col. 5.

Harmelin v. Michigan. (1991). 49 CrL 2289.

Harrison, L., & Gfroerer, J. (1992). The intersection of drug use and criminal behavior: Results from the national household survey on drug abuse. *Crime & Delinquency, 38,* 422–443.

Hawkins, J. D., Catalano, R. F., & Miller, J. (1992). Risk and protective factors for alcohol and other drug problems in adolescence and early adulthood: Implications for substance abuse prevention. *Psychological Bulletin, 112,* 64–105.

Hubbard, R. L., Collins, J. J., Rachal, J. V., & Cananaugh, E. R. (1988). The criminal justice client in drug abuse treatment. National Institute on Drug Abuse, Monograph Series, No. 86. In C. Leukefeld and F. Tims (Eds.), *Compulsory treatment of drug abuse: Research and clinical practice* (pp. 57–80). Washington, DC: U.S. Government Printing Office.

Inciardi, J. A. (1992). *The war on drugs II.* Palo Alto, CA: Mayfield.

Inciardi, J. A. (1993a). *Drug treatment and criminal justice.* Newbury Park, CA: Sage.

Inciardi, J. A. (1993b). Kingrats, chicken heads, slow necks, freaks, and blood suckers: A glimpse at the Miami sex for crack market. In M. Ratner (Ed.), *Crack pipe as pimp: An ethnographic investigation of sex-for-crack exchanges* (pp. 37–67). New York: Lexington Books.

Inciardi, J., Horowitz, R., & Pottieger, A. E. (1993). *Street kids, street drugs, street crime: An examination of drug use and serious delinquency in Miami.* Belmont, CA: Wadsworth.

Inciardi, J., Lockwood, D., & Pottieger, A. E. (1993). *Women and crack-cocaine.* New York: Macmillan.

Inciardi, J. A., & McBride, D. C. (1989). Legalization: A high risk alternative in the war on drugs. *American Behavioral Scientist, 32,* 259–289.

Inciardi, J. A., & McBride, D. C. (1991). *Treatment alternatives to street crime (TASC): History, experiences, and issues.* Rockville, MD: National Institute on Drug Abuse.

Inciardi, J. A., McBride, D. C., McCoy, H. V., & Chitwood, D. (1994). Recent research on the crack-cocaine/crime connection. *Studies on Crime and Crime Prevention, 3,* 63–82.

Inciardi, J. A., McBride, D. C., & Rivers, J. E. (1996). *Drug control and the courts.* Newbury Park, CA: Sage.

Inciardi, J. A., & Pottieger, A. E. (1994). Crack-cocaine use and street crime. *Journal of Drug Issues, 24,* 273–292.

Johnson, C. A., Hansen, W. B., & Pentz, M. A. (1986). Comprehensive community programs for drug abuse prevention. In S. Griswold-Ezekoye, L. Kumpfer, & W. J. Bukoski (Eds.), *Childhood and chemical abuse: intervention* (pp. 181–199). New York: Hawthorne Press.

Kandel, D. B., Simcha-Fagan, O., & Davies, M. (1986). Risk factors for delinquency and illicit drug use from adolescence to young adulthood. *Journal of Drug Issues, 16,* 67–90.

Keigher, S. M. (1994). Changing national priorities regarding substance abuse: Detente comes to the war on drugs. *Health and Social Work, 19,* 71–74.

King, R. (1974). The American system: Legal sanctions to repress drug abuse. In J. A. Inciardi & C. D. Chambers (Eds.), *Drugs and the criminal justice system* (pp. 17–37). Beverly Hills, CA: Sage.

Kleber, H. D. (1994). Our current approach to drug abuse—progress, problems, proposals. *New England Journal of Medicine, 330,* 361–365.

Klein, M., Maxson, C. L., & Cunningham, L. (1991). Crack, street gangs, and violence. *Criminology, 29,* 623-650.

Kreiter, M.S. (1987). Fighting drugs: A new look at the new laws and changed attitudes. *Current Health, 2*(13), 12-16.

Lawrence, C. C. (1988). In its last act, Congress clears anti-drug bill. *Congressional Quarterly Weekly Report, 46*(44), 3147-3152.

Lindesmith, A. R. (1965). *The addict and the law.* Bloomington: Indiana University Press.

Manger, T. H., Hawkins, J. D., Haggerty, K. P., & Catalano, R. F. (1992). Mobility communities to reduce risks for drug abuse: Lessons on using research to guide prevention practice. *Journal of Primary Prevention, 13,* 3-22.

McBride, D. C., Burgman-Habermehl, C., Alpert, J., & Chitwood, D. (1986). Drugs and homicide. *Bulletin of the New York Academy of Medicine, 62,* 497-508.

McBride, D. C., Inciardi, J. A., Chitwood, D. D., McCoy, C. B., & The National AIDS Research Consortium. (1992). Crack use and correlates of use in a national population of street heroin users. *Journal of Psychoactive Drugs, 24,* 411-416.

McBride, D. C., & McCoy, C. B. (1981). Crime and drug using behavior: An area analysis. *Criminology, 19,* 281-302.

McBride, D. C., & McCoy, C. B. (1993). The drugs-crime relationship: An analytical framework. *The Prison Journal, 73,* 257-278.

McBride, D. C., & Swartz, J. (1990). Drugs and violence in the age of crack cocaine. In R. A. Weisheit (Ed.), *Drugs, crime and the criminal justice system* (pp. 141-169). American Academy of Criminal Justice Series. Cincinnati: Anderson.

Miami Herald, Oct. 30, 1994, pp. 1A, 18A.

Moore, W. J. (1993). Where'd the drug crisis go? *National Journal, 25,* 485.

Musto, D. (1987). *The American Disease: Origins of Narcotic Control.* New York: Oxford University Press.

Nadelmann, E. (1989). Drug prohibition in the United States: Costs, consequences and alternatives. *Science, 243,* pp. 939-947.

New York Times, Feb. 11, 1992, p. A10.

New York Times, [Editorial] May 31, 1994, p. A14(N), p. A16(L)

Nurco, D. N., Ball, J. C., Shaffer, J. W., & Hanlon, T. (1985). The criminality of narcotic addicts. *Journal of Nervous and Mental Disease, 173,* 94-102.

Nurco, D. N., Thomas, E. H., Bateman, R. W., Toledano, E., & Kinlock, T. W. (1993). Policy implications derived from an experimental intervention involving drug-abusing offenders. *Prison Journal, 73*(3-4), 332-342.

Pierce, N. R. (1993). Needed: A new strategy for drug war. *National Journal, 25,* 1717.

Preble, E., & Casey, J. J., Jr. (1969). Taking care of business: The heroin user's life on the street. *International Journal of the Addictions, 4,* 1-24.

Reske, H.J. (1993). Priorities wrong? Report: Drug war filling prisons. *ABA Journal, 79,* 33.

Reuter, P., MacCoun, R., & Murphy, P. (1990). *Money from crime: A study of the economics of drug dealing in Washington, D.C.* Santa Monica, CA: RAND Corporation.

Rivers, J. E. (1989, July). Drug use and criminal activity among Miami youth involved in the crack-cocaine business. In *Proceedings of the Florida Epidemiology Work Group* (pp. 47-58). Miami: University of Miami Comprehensive Drug Research Center.

Salholz, E. (1989, September 11). Counting trees as the forest burns; why the experts have been slow to respond to the crack epidemic. *Newsweek, 26–29.*

Sheldon, R. G., & Brown, W. B. (1991). Correlates of jail overcrowding: A case study of a county detention center. *Crime and Delinquency, 37,* 347–362.

Simonds, J. F., & Kashani, J. (1980). Specific drug use and violence in delinquent boys. *American Journal of Drug and Alcohol Abuse, 7,* 305–322.

Simpson, D. D. (1981). Treatment for drug abuse: Follow-up outcomes and length of time spent. *Archives of General Psychiatry, 38,* 1449–1453.

Skolnick, J. H., Correl, T., Navarro, E., & Rabb, R. (1988). *The social structure of street drug dealing.* Sacramento: Office of the Attorney General.

Spunt, B. J., Goldstein, P. J., Bellucci, P. A., & Miller, T. (1990). Race/ethnic and gender differences in the drugs-violence relationship. *Journal of Psychoactive Drugs, 22,* 293–303.

Sutter, A. G. (1969). Worlds of drug use on the street scene. In D. R. Cressey & D. A. Ward (Eds.), *Delinquency, crime, and social process* (pp. 802–829). New York: Harper & Row.

Trebach, A. S., & Inciardi, J. A. (1993). *Legalize it? Debating American drug policy.* Washington, DC: American University Press.

Waldorf, D., Reinarman, C., & Murphy, S. (1992). *Cocaine changes: The experience of using and quitting.* Philadelphia: Temple University Press.

Wilson, J. Q. (1993). Against the legalization of drugs. In R. Goldberg (Ed.), *Taking sides* (p. 25). Guilford, CT: Dushkin.

Wilson, J. Q., & DiIulio, J. J., Jr. (1989, July 10). Crackdown: Treating the symptoms of the drug problem. *The New Republic,* 21–25.

Chapter 4

AFRICAN AMERICANS AND THE CRACK-CRIME CONNECTION*

James A. Inciardi
Anne E. Pottieger
Hilary L. Surratt

This one provision, the crack statute, has been directly responsible for incarcerating nearly an entire generation of young black American men for very long periods. It has created a situation that reeks with inhumanity and injustice. The scales of justice have been turned topsy-turvy so that those masterminds, the kingpins of drug trafficking, escape detection while those whose role is minimal, even trivial, are hoisted on the spears of an enraged electorate and at the pinnacle of their youth are imprisoned for years while those responsible for the evil of the day remain free.

—U.S. District Court–Judge Clyde S. Cahill, 1994

Although Judge Cahill's remarks are both melodramatic and somewhat over-stated, his point is well taken. Under the current federal sentencing scheme for cocaine offenses, crimes involving crack cocaine are punished far more severely than those involving powder cocaine (U.S. Sentencing Commission, 1993). In fact, the Federal Sentencing Guidelines treat a given amount of crack as equivalent to 100 times the amount of powder cocaine. Thus this 100 to 1 ratio results in sentences for crack defendants that are considerably more severe than those for defendants whose offenses involve other forms of cocaine (see Figure 4.1).

This oddity in the federal sentencing scheme is best illustrated with the story of Derrick Curry, a 20-year-old African American college student who also was a small-time crack dealer (see Leiby, 1994). In 1990 Curry was one

*This research was supported by HHS Grant No. RO1-DAO4862, "Crack Abuse Patterns and Crime Linkages," from The National Institute on Drug Abuse.

FIGURE 4.1   **Minimum Sentences (in years) for First Offenders under Federal Sentencing Guidelines**

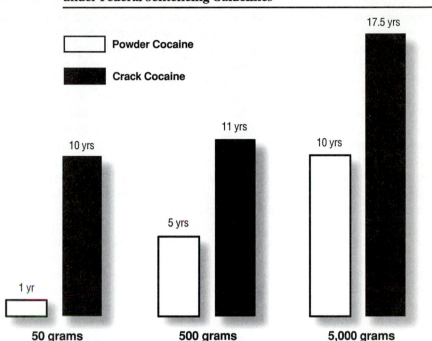

of several Washington, D.C.–area men involved in the distribution of crack who were under surveillance in a joint FBI/DEA sting operation. At one point in the investigation, undercover agents had supplied Curry—who was no more than a low-level drug courier—with a cellular phone in exchange for crack. All of his telephone conversations about his crack deliveries were recorded, and eventually were used as evidence against him. On the day of Curry's arrest, agents found just over a pound of crack in his car, along with a criminal justice textbook and a spiral notebook with his name on it. He was eventually convicted by a federal jury of conspiracy and distribution of crack, and sentenced to prison for 19 years and 7 months, with no possibility of parole.

Derrick Curry's sentence, by almost any available standard, is incomprehensively severe. It is nearly three times the prison sentence served by most murderers in the United States; it is four times the prison sentence served by most kidnappers; it is five times the prison sentence served by most rapists; and it is ten times the prison sentence served by those who illegally possess guns.

Many African American defendants have argued in the federal courts, unsuccessfully for the most part, that this sentencing scheme discriminates against them on the basis of race. They point to the fact that crack is primarily associated with African American sellers and users, whereas powder cocaine is primarily associated with white users and sellers (Cauchon, 1993).

To a large extent, this perception of crack as an African American drug can be traced to the mass media. In their many analyses of the crack epidemic, journalists have portrayed crack use and crack-related crime as essentially problems of African Americans in inner-city neighborhoods. Magazine photographs show young African American men and women smoking crack in abandoned buildings, minority youths with guns in their jeans holding handfuls of crack, and even the former (and once again current) Washington, D.C., mayor Marion Barry, smoking crack. Headlines proclaim "A Tide of Drug Killings: The Crack Plague Spurs More Inner City Murders" and "Prisoners of Crack: Eight Years of Reagan Politics Corrupted a Generation of Urban Black Americans and Devastated Their Communities." Feature articles highlight "Drugs and the Black Community" and "The New Criminal Recruits of the Inner City, the Children Who Deal Crack." Collectively, journalists have presented a crack/crime/African American interconnection that would appear to be a simple well-established fact of American life.[1]

The problem with these media representations is that only part of the story has been clearly and accurately documented—that crack has had a destructive impact on African American inner-city communities. Evidence of more specific crack/crime/African American connections is far more tenuous, and leaves a series of unanswered questions. Is the crack-crime association mere sensationalism, or are crack users commonly involved in criminal behavior (Chapter 3)? Is the crack-crime relationship really a more general cocaine/crime association, or are crack users more crime involved than other cocaine users? Is it really true that most crack users are African American, as typically portrayed in media reports? Are users of any and all forms of cocaine predominantly African American, or are African American cocaine users more likely than white or Hispanic users to use cocaine in the specific form of crack? Has crack spread well beyond inner-city neighborhoods into working-class suburbs, and if so, is there a white crack-crime problem?

These questions, even without answers, suggest a considerably more complex relationship between crack use, crime by crack users, and race/ethnicity than that implied by media reports. These factors cannot be disentangled with urban war zone reporting techniques, but instead require scientific methods of sample selection and data analysis.

---

[1] See Daniel Lazare, "Crack and AIDS: The Next Wave?" *Voice,* May 8, 1990, pp. 29–32; "The Men Who Created Crack," *U.S. News and World Report,* August 19, 1990, p. 3; "Busting the Mayor: Caught in a Web of Drugs, Lies and Videotape Marion Barry Is Arrested on Cocaine Charges," *Newsweek,* January 29, 1990, p. 24; "A Tide of Drug Killings: The Crack Plague Spurs More Inner City Murders," *Newsweek,* January 16, 1989, p. 44; "Prisoners of Crack: Eight Years of Reagan Politics Corrupted a Generation of Urban Black Americans and Devastated Their Communities," *Rolling Stone,* February 9, 1989, p. 61; "Drugs and the Black Community: The Other Side of the Picture," *USA Today,* July 19, 1990, p. 35; "Kids Who Deal Crack," *Time,* May 9, 1988, p. 20.

THE CRACK-CRIME CONNECTION

The relationship between crack use and crime has received considerable attention since the late 1980s, but the available studies rarely have examined race/ethnic differences. Nevertheless, at least the crack-crime linkages seem to be rather clear, particularly with regard to crack selling and violence (Goldstein, Belluci, Spunt, & Miller, 1991; Hamid, 1990; Inciardi, Lockwood, & Pottieger 1993; Inciardi & Pottieger, 1991; Klein & Maxson, 1985; McBride & Swartz, 1990). The media reports appear to be correct in implying that many crack users often are involved in criminal behavior.

Prior research is inconsistent in its answer to the question of whether African Americans are more likely than other ethnic groups to use crack. National studies of households suggest African Americans are more likely than other groups to have done so, but studies of students consistently suggest that the prevalence of crack use is lower among African Americans. For example, the prevalence of crack use is slightly higher among African Americans than among other ethnic groups who participated in the National Household Survey. In 1992, 2.5% of African Americans surveyed had used crack, compared to only 1.3% of Hispanics and 1.2% of whites who are non-Hispanic. Race/ethnic differences in lifetime crack use were greatest among persons aged 26 to 34 years old: The proportion of African Americans who report use (5.6%) is approximately two times that of Hispanic (2.5%) and white (3.1%) Americans (Substance Abuse and Mental Health Services Administration, 1995). However, because whites are the majority of the U.S. population, these proportions yield estimates that, in terms of absolute numbers, most crack users are *not* African American, but white.

Studies of adolescents describe a different image of the relationship between race/ethnicity and crack use. These investigations indicate that most drug use rates, including those concerning crack, are lower for African American adolescents than white adolescents (Bachman et al., 1991; Kandel, Single, & Kessler, 1976; Rebach, 1992; Segal, 1989; Substance Abuse and Mental Health Services Administration, 1995; Wallace & Bachman, 1991).

One primary reason these differences in prevalence occur is the difficulty involved in making precise estimates of the population parameters of illicit drug use. Although the National Household Survey provides national estimates of race/ethnic distributions of crack users, these estimates are imprecise because they seek to measure statistically rare phenomena. Further, the National Household Survey does not include all populations critical to the estimate of race/ethnic differences in crack use. These omitted populations include runaways and other homeless people, addicts in residential treatment, incarcerated populations, and subcultures that are generally inaccessible through standard survey methods. Similarly, surveys of adolescents occur in schools and omit dropouts (Rebach, 1992). Other official surveys—notably the National Institute of Justice's Drug Use Forecasting (DUF) program and NIDA's

Drug Abuse Warning Network (DAWN)—include some of these populations, but they do not separate crack use from other cocaine use and cannot extrapolate the data to population estimates.

Beyond these two points—a strong crack-crime relationship and no more than a tenuous crack–African American association—very little has been published about ethnic differences among crack users, or about differences in criminal behavior between ethnic groups of crack users. In fact, there is surprisingly little research on ethnic differences concerning any type of illegal drug use or its correlates. Moreover, knowledge about the race/ethnicity–drug use relationship is further clouded because most investigations have been based on samples of either students or drug treatment patients, and ethnic minorities have both higher rates of school dropout and lower rates of treatment seeking than whites (Collins, 1992; Rebach, 1992).

The most research attention in this regard has focused on adolescents, primarily students. The findings generally show that ethnic differences in drug use are explained by background variables, particularly income and availability (Adlaf, Smart, & Tan, 1989; Kandel, Single, & Kessler, 1976; Maddehian, Newcomb, & Bentler, 1986; Wallace & Bachman, 1991). More importantly, studies indicate that most drug use rates—including those of alcohol, cocaine, pills of all types, cigarettes, hallucinogens, and inhalants—are *lowest* among black adolescents (Bachman et al., 1991; Kandel, Single, & Kessler, 1976; National Institute on Drug Abuse, 1991; Rebach, 1992; Segal, 1989). Hispanic males, however, are generally found more likely to have used cocaine than either whites or African Americans (Bachman et al., 1991; Marin, 1990; National Institute on Drug Abuse, 1991; Wallace & Bachman, 1991).

Among adult drug users, most research on ethnic differences comes from studies of heroin addicts in treatment in which only two ethnic categories usually are compared: African American and white or Hispanic and white Anglo. These studies suggest that minorities, including African Americans, Puerto Ricans, and Mexican Americans, are overrepresented among heroin users (Anglin, Booth, Ryan, & Hser, 1988; Ball & Chambers, 1970; Kleinman & Lukoff, 1978). Studies of cocaine and crack users also indicate disproportionate use among minorities (Carroll & Rounsaville, 1992; Johnson, Elmoghazy, & Dunlap, 1990). As in the studies of students, however, ethnicity generally is found to interact with other variables. In particular, an interaction effect between gender and ethnicity has been documented in several studies (Austin & Gilbert, 1989; Prendergast, Austin, Maton, & Baker, 1989), and other researchers have presented their results separately for males and females to clarify the ethnic differences within gender categories and to avoid the complexity of this interaction (Anglin et al., 1988; Wallace & Bachman, 1991).

Treatment status also has been recognized as an important confounding factor in the study of ethnic differences in drug use. One recent study, for example, found that 55% of 298 cocaine users in treatment were white, whereas among 101 cocaine users *not* in treatment, only 14% were white (Carroll & Rounsaville, 1992). Treatment status of cocaine users also appears to be confounded by gender and other differences (Boyd & Mieczkowski, 1990; Brunswick, Messeri, & Aidala, 1990; Chitwood & Morningstar, 1985; Griffin, Weiss, Mirin, & Lange, 1989; Rounsaville & Kleber, 1985).

The body of social science research pertinent to the question of a crack-crime/African American linkage can be summarized as follows. First, research is sparse on the specific topic of crack. Second, it has documented a *crack-crime* association. Third, it suggests that any *African American–crack* association is tenuous and inconsistent. Fourth and most importantly, it documents the complexity of drug use–race/ethnicity relationships and the consequent requirement for large demographically diverse samples to study these issues adequately. Drug users who differ in ethnicity invariably also differ in ways that have nothing to do with ethnicity, such as gender, and in ways that are correlated with ethnicity, such as income levels and residence patterns, and in still other ways such as treatment status for which relationships to ethnicity are still not well understood. These other variables offer plausible explanations for the drug-ethnicity differences, but the sample sizes often are too small to permit multivariate analyses.

The purpose of this study is to describe the race/ethnicity question as it relates to a tri-ethnic sample of cocaine users.

STUDYING CRACK-CRIME CONNECTIONS

Drug use patterns and criminal behavior were the focus of a study conducted between September 1987 and August 1991 in Miami, Florida. A total of 699 cocaine users were interviewed, 349 of them in residential treatment and 350 on the street. Eligible participants were those who reported any cocaine use during the "last 90 days on the street." For the street sample, this was the 90 days prior to interview. For the treatment sample, it was the most recent continuous 90 days on the street prior to treatment entry. This 90-day period was required to be within the 2 years before interview. The total time period referenced by all respondents' "last 90 days on the street" was November 1986 through December 1989.

Questions about drug use and criminal behavior were asked during a 30 to 60 minute interview for which respondents were paid $10. Legal protection for subjects was assured by anonymity and a Certificate of Confidentiality from NIDA. This guaranteed that project employees could not be compelled by any court or law enforcement agency to reveal information sources or questionnaire data. Treatment program clients were assured that neither participation nor nonparticipation would affect their program status and that their answers would not be seen by counselors or other program personnel.

Selection of both street and treatment respondents was guided by subsample quotas for gender, age, and ethnicity to ensure a demographically diverse sample. In the treatment programs, this generally meant returning repeatedly to interview every new client in the hard-to-fill subsamples (younger and white or

Hispanic). On the street, subsample targets meant conducting the interview process in several selected neighborhoods to get the required race-ethnic diversity. Street respondents were located through standard multiple-starting-point "snowball sampling" techniques in neighborhoods with high rates of cocaine use by street interviewers familiar with and well known in the target areas. The details of how this kind of street data collection is done are described elsewhere (Inciardi, Horowitz, & Pottieger, 1993; Inciardi, Lockwood, & Pottieger, 1993).

The final sample was 66% male and 34% female. The 285 African American respondents comprised 34% of the males and 54% of the females; the 273 white respondents were 36% of the males and 46% of the females; and the 141 Hispanic respondents made up the remaining 30% of the male respondents. Forty-six percent of all respondents were ages 20 to 29, 28% were ages 13 to 19, and 26% were 30 to 49 years old.

Questions about cocaine use in the last 90 days on the street were asked for six types of cocaine use: snorting, intravenous (IV) use, crack smoking, other (pure, ether-based) freebasing, coca paste smoking, and any other (new) form of cocaine. For each type of cocaine used, respondents were asked how many days it was used and the usual number of doses per day. These two figures were then multiplied together to arrive at an estimated total quantity for each cocaine type used in the respondent's last 90 days on the street. These estimates permitted calculation of each cocaine user's "primary cocaine type"—the one cocaine form, if any, that accounted for 75% or more of all cocaine used by each respondent. For analysis, the estimated dosages for each cocaine type were recoded into seven categories ranging from 0 (none) to 6 (1350+ doses).

Measures for illegal activities were constructed in a similar fashion. For each of 23 crime types, respondents were asked on how many days the offense was committed and the usual number of offenses per day. Total crimes for the 90 days were then estimated for each specific offense type. These numbers were combined into totals for six general crime types—robbery, major property crime (burglary and motor vehicle theft), petty property crime, prostitution and procuring, drug business offenses, and weapon use. For the analysis, the estimated totals for each crime type were recoded into eight categories: 0, 1–11, 12–39, 40–89, 90–299, 300–1,899, 1,900–4,999, and 5,000+ offenses.

THE NATURE OF THE CONNECTION

The first question is whether African American cocaine users were more likely than their white and Hispanic counterparts to use crack as their "primary cocaine type." A breakdown by ethnicity alone suggests no African American/crack association: 74.5% of African Americans, 74.5% of whites, and 58.2% of Hispanics used crack as their primary form of cocaine.

TABLE 4.1   **Primary Cocaine Type: Percentage of Group**

Group			(N)	Crack	Snort	IV	None
Total Sample			(699)	71.4	16.6	4.4	7.6
St	M	13–19	Black	(25)	100.0	0.0	0.0	0.0
			White	(23)	100.0	0.0	0.0	0.0
			Hispanic	(27)	92.6	7.4	0.0	0.0
St	M	20–29	Black	(28)	92.9	0.0	7.1	0.0
			White	(33)	90.9	3.0	6.1	0.0
			Hispanic	(25)	64.0	36.0	0.0	0.0
St	M	30–49	Black	(17)	47.1	5.9	47.1	0.0
			White	(16)	75.0	12.5	12.5	0.0
			Hispanic	(18)	50.0	50.0	0.0	0.0
St	F	13–19	Black	(26)	100.0	0.0	0.0	0.0
			White	(26)	100.0	0.0	0.0	0.0
St	F	20–29	Black	(29)	93.1	0.0	6.9	0.0
			White	(34)	97.1	2.9	0.0	0.0
St	F	30–49	Black	(14)	21.4	14.3	64.3	0.0
			White	(9)	100.0	0.0	0.0	0.0
Tr	M	13–19	Black	(25)	12.0	84.0	0.0	4.0
			White	(21)	33.3	52.4	0.0	14.3
			Hispanic	(22)	36.4	40.9	0.0	22.7
Tr	M	20–29	Black	(36)	69.4	8.3	0.0	22.2
			White	(50)	58.0	16.0	2.0	24.0
			Hispanic	(28)	39.3	28.6	7.1	25.0
Tr	M	30–49	Black	(25)	84.0	8.0	4.0	4.0
			White	(22)	50.0	22.7	0.0	27.3
			Hispanic	(21)	61.9	38.1	0.0	0.0
Tr	F	18–19	Black	(2)	50.0	50.0	0.0	0.0
Tr	F	20–29	Black	(36)	83.3	8.3	0.0	8.3
			White	(20)	75.0	20.0	0.0	5.0
Tr	F	30–49	Black	(22)	81.8	9.1	9.1	0.0
			White	(19)	47.4	21.1	0.0	31.6

Because prior research suggests that gender, age, and treatment status might be related to race/ethnic differences in cocaine type preference, these three factors were held constant so that a specified picture of the relationship between race/ethnicity and primary cocaine type could be examined. The results, as shown in Table 4.1, indicate that among users interviewed on the street, there were very few differences in primary type of cocaine used. In nearly every instance most users preferred crack.

The treatment-recruited users present a different picture because sizeable proportions were not primary users of any specific type of cocaine. Crack use was clearly less common among the cocaine users in treatment than among their counterparts interviewed on the street. Nevertheless, African Americans in treatment were no more likely than other groups to use crack as their primary form of cocaine.

For still another way of looking at the crack/ethnicity connection, correlates were computed for amount of crack used in the last 90 days by only the 499 respondents who were primary crack users. The prior analysis suggests that among cocaine users, being African American is not associated with being a crack user. This analysis asked whether among crack users, African Americans use more crack than whites and Hispanics. The results showed no relationship between amount of crack used and ethnicity or gender. Amount of crack used by primary crack users was significantly, although weakly, correlated with being in treatment, and was clearly related to being older. (Data not shown.)

Given a crack-crime connection, the next question for analysis logically is whether there are differences in the crack-crime relationship for crack users of different ethnicities. This analysis of the crack-crime relationship uses data from the subsample of 257 street recruited primary crack users ages 13 to 29 years old because they were more consistent than any other subgroup of cocaine users in preferring crack as their primary cocaine type.

The criminal involvement of this subsample is extensive, as shown in Table 4.2. Over 96% of each gender/ethnic category reported drug business offenses, most respondents committed petty property crimes, and some also did major property crimes (burglary or motor vehicle theft) or used a weapon of some kind while committing illegal offenses. However, significant gender and ethnic differences also appear: Women, particularly African American women, were more likely to engage in prostitution and procuring; men were more likely than women to commit major property crimes; women were more likely than men to commit petty property crimes; and weapon use was most common among African American women.

The extent to which the crimes of these crack users are related to their crack use varies by crime type. As indicated in Table 4.3, there is a strong correlation between amount of crack used and number of drug business offenses in all gender/ethnic subgroups. Amount of prostitution is also correlated with amount of crack used for both African American and white women. Major property crimes, in contrast, are related to crack use only among Hispanic males, and minor property crimes are correlated only for African American females. Because very few committed robberies (as shown in Table 4.2), robbery is not significantly related to amount of crack used for any of the subgroups. Number of weapons used is related to amount of crack used for Hispanics and whites, but not for African Americans.

TABLE 4.1	Crime Types Done in the Last 90 Days by 257 Primary Crack Users Ages 13–29 Interviewed on the Street: Percentage of Respondents Committing Any, by Sex and Ethnicity

	Male			Female	
CRIME TYPE	BLACK (N = 51)	WHITE (N = 53)	HISPANIC (N = 41)	BLACK (N = 53)	WHITE (N = 59)
Robbery	5.9	0.0	0.0	5.7	0.0
Major property	13.7	15.1	26.8	3.8	0.0
Petty property	64.7	62.3	78.0	88.7	79.7
Prostitution/ procuring	2.0	0.0	0.0	67.9	37.3
Drug business	100.0	100.0	100.0	96.2	96.6
Weapon use	21.6	18.9	19.5	32.1	16.9

Two-tailed chi-square tests significant at $p < .05$:
Gender (controlling race/ethnicity): major property, $p < .01$
   petty property, $p < .01$
   prostitution/procuring, $p < .001$
Race (controlling gender): prostitution/procuring, $p < .01$
Gender/ethnicity combination only:
   weapon uses, black women versus all others, $p < .001$

These results display no clear pattern of differences by ethnicity in the re-lationships between degree of crime involvement and amount of crack use. This is partially due to the overall level and diversity of criminal behavior in this subsample. All respondents were criminally active and most committed a variety of crimes during the 90 days before interview. In addition, in spite of the lack of criminal specialization in this subsample, respondents in every eth-nic and gender group were most likely to be involved in street-level drug sales—and for all subgroups, this was the offense most likely to be highly cor-related with total crack used.

To explore the crack-crime relationship further, analyses were performed on an additional set of questions about methods of obtaining the crack used in the last 90 days. (Data not presented in tabular form.) Whites and Hispanics were more likely than African Americans to obtain crack by paying for it in cash or getting it for free (for example, by sharing with friends or having it pro-vided by a dealer friend or spouse). African Americans, in contrast, were more likely than whites and Hispanics to obtain crack by earning it as pay (most often for drug sales), stealing it, or trading stolen goods for it.

This similarity between whites and Hispanics in contrast to the pattern for African Americans is what would be expected in a Miami sample if the differ-ence was primarily one of socioeconomic status. In Miami, as in many other U.S. cities, general socioeconomic indicators such as income, education, and

TABLE 4.3	Amount of Crack Used in Relation to Amount of Crime Committed in the Last 90 Days by 257 Primary Crack Users Ages 13–29 Interviewed on the Street: Spearman Correlation Coefficients, Controlling Sex and Ethnicity

	Male			Female	
CRIME TYPE	BLACK (N = 51)	WHITE (N = 53)	HISPANIC (N = 41)	BLACK (N = 53)	WHITE (N = 59)
Robbery	.03	—	—	.11	—
Major property	-.09	.27	.44*	.16	—
Petty property	.13	.26	-.05	.33*	.13
Prostitution/ procuring	.18	—	—	.32*	.51**
Drug business	.50**	.63**	.67**	.53**	.59**
Weapon use	.22	.49**	.58**	.15	.41**

* Significant at $p < .05$.
** Significant at p {less than or equal} .001.
— No offenses committed

residential patterns show markedly higher rates of poverty among African Americans than among whites. And indicators for Miami Hispanics, especially Cubans, are generally similar to those for Miami whites.

One aspect of ethnic socioeconomic differences is the availability of economic resources. Income from a job was unusual for respondents in the young street crack user subsample. None of the teenagers and only 4 (3.0%) of the respondents ages 20 to 29 had jobs. Welfare, disability, or other assistance was also rare; such income was reported by 5.0% of the 60 women ages 20 to 29 and none of other subsample members. Unexpectedly, some kind of investment income was actually more common—18 of these respondents had bank account interest or income from stocks or rental property. Further, reports of investment income varied by ethnicity: 1.0% of African Americans, 2.4% of Hispanics, and 14.3% of whites. Income from employment, assistance, and investment income indicate that whites were more likely to have such conventional economic resources than were African Americans and Hispanics.

Most respondents, however, did have some legal source of support, most commonly parents, spouse, or other people. Thus only 1 in 6 of the young street crack user subsample reported obtaining all or nearly all their living expenses from crime. However, living arrangements may have a very different kind of crack-crime relevance—some persons who help pay for a crack user's living expenses may also help support a crack-crime lifestyle. Respondents were asked three questions about living circumstances: (1) Persons lived with last week, including (a) parents (with or without siblings), (b) spouse/opposite-sex partner, and (c) other people; (2) Do any of these people use crack or other cocaine?; and (3) Do any deal it? All co-residents reported as dealers were also reported as users. Results for primary crack users ages 13 to 29 indicated that over 90% of respondents living with a spouse or friends reported living with another cocaine user, compared to less than half of those still living at home. Women were especially likely to live with a cocaine user or dealer: More than half of both African American and white women ages 20 to 29 lived with dealers, as did a third of younger African American women.

The "live with user or dealer" answers were used to construct a four-category indicator for the relative cocaine involvement of co-residents. The four categories were as follows: lives with (1) nonusers only, (2) nobody, (3) at least one user who does not deal, or (4) at least one dealer. This measure of cocaine involvement of co-residents was significantly correlated with being female (correlation of .34), and being African American (.35). The importance of greater cocaine involvement of co-residents is demonstrated by its correlation with other crack-crime indicators: more crack used (correlation of .46), a greater percentage of living expenses paid for by crime (.48), and more overall crime (.60).

Although no causal inferences can be made from this analysis, the results indicate that ethnic differences—particularly African American/white differences—exist both in elements of their lifestyle and influences on it. White respondents had the least apparent need to commit crimes in order to pay for living expenses, and whites and Hispanics were less likely than African Americans to reside with other cocaine involved persons. African American respondents reported that more living expenses were paid for by crime and more cocaine involvement occurred among co-residents. These results suggest that some differences that appear to be ethnic are socioeconomic in nature. It is socioeconomic factors such as (1) the degree of access to income sources other than crime, and (2) the likelihood of living in a high drug/crime rate environment that are important for understanding the crack-crime connection.

DISCUSSION

In the 1991 case of *State v. Russell* (477 N.W.2d 886 [Minn. 1991]), the Minnesota Supreme Court invalidated a state law that punished the possession of crack cocaine more harshly than that of powder cocaine. The court ruled against the differential punishment largely on the grounds that it constituted an "illicit racial discrimination" because most persons convicted of possessing powder cocaine were white whereas most of those convicted of possessing crack were African American.

More specifically, under Minnesota Statute 152.023(2), a person is guilty of a "third degree" offense if he or she possesses 3 or more grams of cocaine base ("crack cocaine"). Under the same statute, a person must possess 10 or more grams of cocaine powder to be guilty of the same offense. A person who possesses less than 10 grams of powder is guilty of a fifth degree offense (Section 152.025). Pursuant to these statutes, possession of 3 grams of crack carries a penalty of up to 20 years in prison; possession of an equal amount of powder cocaine carries a penalty of up to 5 years in prison.

In *State v. Russell,* five African American men who were charged with violating Section 152.023(2) jointly moved the trial court to dismiss the charges on the ground that the statute had a discriminatory effect on African American persons and violated the equal protection guarantees of both the Minnesota and U.S. constitutions. The trial court noted that crack was indeed used primarily by African Americans and powder cocaine primarily by whites. Among the many statistics provided to the trial court were those showing that of all persons charged with possession of cocaine base in 1988, 97% were African American; of those charged with possession of powder cocaine, 80% were white. The trial court agreed with the defendants and invalidated the sentencing scheme.

On an appeal brought by the state, it was contended that the state legislature had a permissible and legitimate interest in regulating the possession and sale of both crack and powder cocaine, and that it was reasonable for lawmakers to believe the 3 grams of crack/10 grams of powder classification would regulate the possession of those drugs by the street-level dealers at whom the statute was primarily aimed. The Minnesota Supreme Court was not persuaded, however, and affirmed that the sentencing scheme was in violation of the state constitution on equal protection grounds.

Is it possible that the Minnesota Supreme Court's holding in *Russell* was wrongly decided?

The analysis in this chapter suggests that crack may not be an African American drug and powder cocaine a white American drug. Among young crime-involved cocaine users, whites and blacks are equally likely—and highly likely—to use crack rather than powder cocaine. However, the data presented here are from one study of one community, collected in a manner that may not be representative of the crack- and cocaine-using populations. Drug users in Miami are not necessarily representative of the nation as a whole. However, other data are accumulating that tend to corroborate the Miami findings. Most recently, a reanalysis of data from the 1988 National Household Survey compared race-ethnic group differences in crack smoking (Lillie-Blanton, Anthony, & Schuster, 1993). The findings provided evidence that given similar social and environmental conditions (neighborhood, education, income, age, and gender), crack use does not depend on race-specific factors. This suggests that race-specific explanations of crack use likely obscure the role that social and environmental factors play in the overall epidemiology of crack use.

REFERENCES

Adlaf, E. M., Smart, R. G., & Tan, S. H. (1989). Ethnicity and drug use: A critical look. *International Journal of the Addictions, 24,* 1-18.

Anglin, M. D., Booth, M. W., Ryan, T. M., & Hser, Y. (1988). Ethnic differences in narcotics addiction: II. Chicano and Anglo addiction career patterns. *International Journal of the Addictions, 23,* 1011-1127.

Austin, G. A., & Gilbert, M. J. (1989). Substance abuse among Latino youth. *Prevention Update, 3,* 1-26.

Bachman, J. G., Wallace, J. M., O'Malley, P. M., Johnston, L. D., Kurth, C. L., & Neighbors, H. W. (1991). Racial/ethnic differences in smoking, drinking, and illicit drug use among American high school seniors, 1976-89. *American Journal of Public Health, 81,* 372-377.

Ball, J. C., & Chambers, C. D. (1970). Overview of the problem. In J. C. Ball & C. D. Chambers (Eds.), *The epidemiology of opiate addiction in the United States* (pp. 5-21). Springfield, IL: Charles C Thomas.

Boyd, C. J., & Mieczkowski, T. (1990). Drug use, health, family and social support in "crack" cocaine users. *Addictive Behaviors, 15,* 481-485.

Brunswick, A., Messeri, P. A., & Aidala, A. A. (1990). Changing drug use patterns and treatment behavior: A longitudinal study of urban black youth. In R. R. Watson (Ed.), *Drug and alcohol abuse prevention* (pp. 263-311). Clifton, NJ: Humana Press.

Carroll, K., & Rounsaville, B. J. (1992). Contrast of treatment-seeking and untreated cocaine abusers. *Archives of General Psychiatry, 49,* 646-671.

Cauchon, D. (1993, November 10). Crack sentencing disparities weighed. *USA Today,* p. 10A.

Chitwood, D. D., & Morningstar, P. C. (1985). Factors which differentiate cocaine users in treatment from nontreatment users. *International Journal of the Addictions, 20,* 449-459.

Collins, R. L. (1992). Methodological issues in conducting substance abuse research in ethnic minority populations. *Drugs & Society, 6,* 59-77.

Goldstein, P. J., Belluci, P. A., Spunt, B. J., & Miller, T. (1991). Volume of cocaine use and violence: A comparison between men and women. *Journal of Drug Issues, 21,* 345-367.

Griffin, M. L., Weiss, R. D., Mirin, S. M., & Lange, U. (1989). A comparison of male and female cocaine abusers. *Archives of General Psychiatry, 46,* 122-126.

Hamid, A. (1990). The political economy of crack related violence. *Contemporary Drug Problems, 17,* 31-78.

Inciardi, J. A., Horowitz, R., & Pottieger, A. E. (1993). *Street kids, street drugs, street crime.* Belmont, CA: Wadsworth.

Inciardi, J. A., Lockwood, D., & Pottieger, A. E. (1993). *Women and Crack-Cocaine.* New York: Macmillan.

Inciardi, J. A., & Pottieger, A. E. (1991). Kids, crack and crime. *Journal of Drug Issues, 21,* 257-270.

Johnson, B. D., Elmoghazy, E., & Dunlap, E. (1990, November 8). *Crack abusers and noncrack drug abusers: A comparison of drug use, drug sales, and nondrug criminality.* Paper presented at the annual meeting of the American Society of Criminology, Baltimore, MD.

Kandel, D. B., Single, E., & Kessler, R. (1976). The epidemiology of drug use among New York state high school students: Distribution, trends and changes in use. *American Journal of Public Health, 66,* 43–53.

Kennedy, R. (1994). The state, criminal law, and racial discrimination: A comment. *Harvard Law Review, 107,* 1255–1278.

Klein, M. W., & Maxson, C. (1985). "Rock" sales in South Los Angeles. *Sociology and Social Research, 69,* 561–565.

Kleinman, P. H., & Lukoff, I. F. (1978). Ethnic differences in factors related to drug use. *Journal of Health and Social Behavior, 19,* 190–199.

Leiby, R. (1994, February 20). A crack in the system. *Washington Post,* pp. F1, F4–F5.

Lillie-Blanton, M., Anthony, J. C., & Schuster, C. R. (1993). Probing the meaning of racial/ethnic group comparisons in crack cocaine smoking. *Journal of the American Medical Association, 269,* 993–997.

Maddehian, E., Newcomb, M. D., & Bentler, P. M. (1986). Adolescents' substance use: Impact of ethnicity, income and availability. *Advances in Alcohol and Substance Abuse, 5,* 63–78.

Marin, B. V. (1990). Hispanic drug abuse: Culturally appropriate prevention and treatment. In R. R. Watson (Ed.), *Drug and alcohol abuse prevention* (pp. 151–165). Clifton, NJ: Humana Press.

McBride, D. C., & Swartz, J. A. (1990). Drugs and violence in the age of crack cocaine. In Ralph Weisheit (Ed.), *Drugs, crime and the criminal justice system* (pp. 141–169). Cincinnati: Anderson.

National Institute on Drug Abuse. (1991). *National household survey on drug abuse: Population estimates.* Rockville, MD: Author.

Prendergast, M. L., Austin, G. A., Maton, K. I., & Baker, R. (1989). Substance abuse among black youth. *Prevention Research Update, 4,* 1–27.

Rebach, H. (1992). Alcohol and drug use among American minorities. *Drugs & Society, 6,* 23–57.

Rounsaville, B. J., & Kleber, H. D. (1985). Untreated opiate addicts: How do they differ from those seeking treatment?" *Archives of General Psychiatry, 42,* 1072–1077.

Segal, B. (1989). Drug-taking behavior among school aged youth: The Alaska experience and comparisons with lower 48 states. *Drugs and Society, 4,* 1–17.

Substance Abuse and Mental Health Services Administration.(1995). *National household survey on drug abuse: Main findings 1992.* Rockville, MD: Author,

United States Sentencing Commission. (1993, November 9). *Hearing on crack cocaine.* Washington, DC.

Wallace, J. M., & Bachman, J. G. (1991). Explaining racial/ethnic differences in adolescent drug use: The impact of background and lifestyle. *Social Problems, 38,* 333–357.

Chapter 5

WOMEN AND CRACK

Lisa R. Metsch
H. Virginia McCoy
Norman L. Weatherby

Chemically dependent women are among the most wounded and needy members of our society, yet their special problems have long gone underrecognized and under-treated. (Mondanaro, 1989)

This chapter discusses the unique impact of the subculture of crack distribution and its use on the lives of women who use crack. The discussion begins with a historical perspective of women and drug use.

HISTORICAL OVERVIEW OF DRUG USE AND GENDER

Social definitions and socially imposed consequences of the use of psychoactive drugs by men and women have differed throughout history. The 4,000-year-old Code of Hammurabi actually contained different rules for men and women about the consumption of alcohol and other drugs (Blume, 1994). Since that time, societal expectations for the use of intoxicating substances typically have been more willing to permit drug use by men while stigmatizing or proscribing use by women. The socially enduring perspective that drug use is a deviant behavior incompatible with the normative role of women has isolated drug addicted women more than addicted men from the attention of conventional society (Inciardi, Lockwood, & Pottieger, 1993). Crack-dependent women, moreover, are ostracized because of risks to in utero crack-exposed unborn children, crack-attributed sexual promiscuity, and related factors that carry greater perils of social exclusion and legal sanction than they do for men (Fagan, 1994). Women who use drugs consequently have been ignored for the most part as have their unique needs for drug treatment and related health and social services. Little gender-specific information about drug use among women exists (Bourgois, 1989), and most of the existing research concentrates on the consequences of drug use for the health of the fetus rather than the mother. The amount of information required to adequately understand, treat, and prevent the misuse of drugs by women simply has not been published (Inciardi et al., 1993), although an increase in knowledge has occurred during the last 10 years (Fullilove, Lown, & Fullilove, 1992).

PREVALENCE OF CRACK USE AMONG WOMEN

In 1992 more than 400,000 women above the age of 11 were estimated to have used some form of cocaine within the last 30 days (Center for Substance Abuse Treatment, 1994). The extent of crack use among pregnant women is of particular concern because the National Pregnancy and Health Survey data indicate that more than 40,000 infants born annually are exposed in utero to crack (Ostrea, 1992; Wallace, 1991).

Crack directly impacts the dynamics of addiction and treatment for women and their families. The rate of dependence has increased and the rates of treatment entry and treatment retention have declined among women who smoke crack (Inciardi et al., 1993; Reed, 1987).

POWDER COCAINE, CRACK COCAINE, AND SEX ROLES

Anyone who has had extensive experience with crack knows that the use of this stimulant alters relationships. Perhaps no relationship is more profoundly transformed than the relationship between men and women.

The impact of crack on women is an extension of the impact that the illicit drug use setting in general, and the cocaine subculture in particular, have on women and men. The rights of women, which increasingly have been claimed but not fully realized in American society through legislation and adjudication, are unprotected within the illicit world of drug use. The economic discrimination that women experience in the general society is several times greater in the settings of illicit drug distribution and use that largely exist outside of the protection of the courts. Men generally control the wealth and the distribution of drugs and thus exercise considerable control over women's access to drugs. Deprived of that access, women, more often than men who seek to use drugs, are forced to find alternative means of obtaining drugs.

Stereotypes of Sex Roles

A study of patterns of the acquisition and use of cocaine that was conducted between 1979 and 1981 observed a gender-based hierarchy in cocaine distribution.

Men were more likely than women to obtain cocaine for personal use through dealing, and access to cocaine for both women and men usually was controlled by men. Although a plurality of men and women purchased the cocaine they used, women were twice as likely as men to be given the cocaine they ingested (Morningstar & Chitwood, 1995). In most instances the source of that gift was men, not other women.

This relationship between male users, who tended to control the supply of the drug, and female cocaine users, who often depended on men for access to the drug, became dramatized in the stereotypical roles of the cocaine cowboy and the cocaine whore that were popularized by the media in the 1980s. The cocaine cowboy was depicted as the dangerously macho egomaniac who deals cocaine, and the cocaine whore was viewed as the degraded slave of cocaine who will trade sex for the drug. Although these are not accurate images of the majority of behavior patterns among men and women, they do depict dimensions of real contrast because more men were involved in dealing activity and more women received cocaine in the form of gifts (for a discussion of sex role stereotypes of cocaine users, see Morningstar & Chitwood, 1995).

The kernel of truth depicted in those stereotypes of women and men who use powder cocaine is intensified in the world of crack, particularly in the inner city or other areas that are severely depressed economically. As with other forms of cocaine, the distribution and economic control of crack typically are male dominated and access to crack for women often is controlled by men.

Women and Social Problems of Crack Use

Specific characteristics of crack seem to increase the detrimental impact that crack can have on women who smoke this drug. The low price ($10 for "dime rocks," $5 for "metal rocks," as little as $2 for "kibbles and bits") and ready availability of crack fuels its proliferation in low-income neighborhoods. Crack has become the chosen form of cocaine for many who fear or dislike drug injection or who seek a cheap alternative to snorting cocaine. The low price and availability has introduced crack to relatively naive users who are much younger and far less experienced in the use of major drugs of abuse than had been the case with powder cocaine.

Crack has a high abuse potential because it is a powerful reinforcer. The stimulant produces an immediate but temporary, intensely gratifying high that quickly is followed by a depression, or crash, characterized by acute malaise and intense craving. Crack crosses the blood-brain barrier a few seconds after it is inhaled and creates an instantaneous high and intense gratification often described as a sexual euphoria or orgasm. Crack users often integrate the perception that crack heightens sex with their perception of the intense high that crack produces:

> You know, I mean it's like, it's like the greatest sex, like your whole body is gonna come. It starts in your head and your tail, and then moves up and down and around and out, and to the tips of your fingers. All of a sudden you are

electrified all over, and, for a few minutes, you're on top of the whole world.
(McCoy, Miles, & Inciardi, 1995, p. 172)

This cycle of euphoria and craving typically promotes patterns of compulsive use (Inciardi, 1992; Wallace, 1991). Many users smoke crack for as long as they have supplies of the drug or the resources to obtain more. Although a single hit of crack is inexpensive, hundreds of dollars can be spent on each episode of use. A crack binge may last 3 to 4 days during which crack is smoked almost constantly.

Research suggests that women who experiment with crack may be more likely to become addicted and addicted more rapidly than their male counterparts (Stephens, 1991). This may be due in part to the combination of psychological and physical effects of crack that have been perceived to make it a particularly powerful reinforcing drug of abuse for women (McCoy et al., 1995). Women may be vulnerable to crack because of its ability to help women cope with depression, low self-esteem, and learned helplessness, problems that typically affect women more often then men. Crack and other forms of cocaine may provide users with a temporary sense of accomplishment, self-worth, and power. Some women have reported they felt worthwhile for the first time in their lives while they were high on crack (Mondanaro, 1989). The appetite suppression and energizing abilities of crack also are effects that are attractive to women.

These characteristics create a high-risk setting for all users, and for women of the inner city in particular. Many persons who are inexperienced in the use of stimulants are introduced to crack early in their drug use careers because of the low price per unit of use. Few if any new users are experienced enough to know how to cope with the reinforcing properties of the euphoric high and the intense craving that follows that temporary high. Even experienced snorters of powder cocaine are challenged by crack. When the compulsive use of any drug, including crack, occurs, the cost of the drug quickly becomes a major expense item (James, Gosho, & Wohl, 1979). Many women soon exhaust their funds but not their craving. In the inner city these women often are unemployed and have few if any employment opportunities (Anglin & Hser, 1987; Burt, Glynn, & Sowder, 1979; Cuskey, Moffett, & Clifford, 1971).

Women who use crack may turn to a variety of illicit sources for funds to obtain drugs if they do not have alternative financial resources (Department of Justice, 1994; see Chapters 3 and 4 for a discussion of crack and crime). Crack-using women often become involved in a street addict lifestyle in which crime is an expected, common part of the addict's self-concept (Inciardi et al., 1993). One user describes the variety of her activities this way:

> Hustling is how I get by. What that means is that I get up at noon, boost [shoplift] something at the OMNI [shopping mall] on my way to cop some drugs. I'll sell half the drugs for a profit and sell the watch or perfume that I boost to someone on the street. Then some car date will wave me down an' I'll give him a quick blow and if he's careless I'll empty his pockets [rob him].

> Later in the day I might help in a break-in, deliver some coke to a Montana [a Cuban drug dealer]. . . . At night I'll be back on the stroll. (Inciardi et al., 1993, p. 107)

This woman relies on several types of crime to support her chronic crack habit. Notice that with the exception of the resale of half of the crack she purchased from a dealer for her personal use, she did not sell drugs to support her habit. The sex roles of women and men in the illicit settings of drug use often impact the acquisition behaviors of women, and gender differences in criminal activity frequently place women in a disadvantaged status in that regard. This crack user, like many other women, may have encountered barriers to significant participation in drug dealing that provides a major source of drugs for many male users. Often obstructed from dealing, women are more likely than men to partially or wholly finance their compulsive crack use by exchanging sexual activity for crack or money to buy crack. This is not to say that most women engage in sex for crack exchanges. Although women are more likely than men to do so, women engage in several types of crime to support a chronic crack habit.

Studies of women and crack generally have focused on prostitution and sex-for-crack exchanges (Chaisson et al., 1991; Inciardi et al., 1993; Ratner, 1993), but studies of users of other drugs indicate that prostitution is not the most common crime among drug-using women (Anglin & Hser, 1987; DeLeon, 1986; Inciardi & Chambers, 1972; Inciardi, Pottieger, & Faupel, 1982). Fagan (1994) further maintains that women's roles in some contemporary crack markets are becoming more diversified as they earn more money in higher level drug-selling positions. Nevertheless, many impoverished women have no other means of support, encounter considerable barriers to significant participation in drug dealing, and have little choice but to resort to a "survival instinct" that utilizes sexual activity to obtain most of their material needs and wants (McCoy et al., 1995). The manager of an AIDS prevention center in a south Florida community explained the survival instinct that was responsible for much of the sexual activity of women who used her center:

> A women who needs Pampers and food for her baby gets a boyfriend. When she needs money for rent, she gets another boyfriend. She might have three or four boyfriends, but what she's doing isn't considered to be prostitution. It's survival. (McCoy et al., 1995, p. 172)

Pressure to support chronic crack use can distort this survival instinct into behaviors that endanger health.

SEXUAL TRADING BEHAVIORS

A crack habit rapidly can exhaust revenues obtained from legal employment sources and the more socially accepted activities related to survival instinct. It can propel even the very young into high risk anonymous sexual behavior. A 17-year-old crack user expressed this fact very clearly:

> When you needs the cracks, and you needs money for other things 'cause your rent money went on the boards [was used to buy crack], you got to survive, and you know, to do that, the pussy [sex] works! (McCoy et al., 1995, p. 172)

Crack, even more than other forms of cocaine, is viewed as an aphrodisiac that promotes and intensifies extensive sexual behavior. Several ethnographic studies suggest that crack engenders "hypersexual" behavior among many users (McCoy et al., 1995). One recent study found sex-for-drugs exchanges to be far more common among contemporary female crack addicts than they ever were among female heroin users at the height of the heroin epidemics in the late 1960s and early 1970s (Inciardi, Lockwood, & Pottieger, 1991).

The combination of survival sex and the apparent increase in hypersexual behavior associated with crack appears to have generated a subculture that endorses and promotes sexual activity while it exploits many of the women who participate in that subculture. Women in the San Francisco area who exchange sex for crack, for example, are referred to as "tossups," literally something to be used and then tossed or thrown away (Fullilove, Fullilove, Bowser, & Gross, 1990). They are called "skeezers," "freaks," and other extremely pejorative appellations such as "base whores," "gut buckets," and "rock monsters" in other locales (Inciardi, 1991). Perhaps the exploitation of women reaches its nadir in the crack house (Chapter 2) where some women become "house girls" who are kept to provide any sexual behavior requested by patrons. These women receive crack, alcohol, junk food, and a place to sleep in exchange.

The disinhibiting effects of crack seem to make these exchanges and conditions psychologically more tolerable. Crack reportedly also enables both women and men to engage in sexual acts that they might not consider if they were not using this drug (Inciardi, 1991; Wallace, 1991). Crack users themselves use the term *freaking* to refer to sexual behavior that usually is well beyond the norm of sexual activity in which they would otherwise engage. Examples of freaking include having sex simultaneously with multiple partners or sex with other women for the viewing pleasure of men (Ratner, 1993).

Health Risks Associated with the Use of Crack

The prevalence of sexually transmitted diseases (STDs), including HIV, has been associated with the drug-related high-risk sexual practices of many crack users (Booth, Watters, & Chitwood, 1993; Chaisson et al., 1991; Edlin et al., 1994; Ellenbrock, Lieb, & Harrington, 1992; Fullilove et al., 1990; Marx, Aral, Rolfs, Sterk, & Kahn, 1991; Weatherby et al., 1992). Some studies suggest that women may be at greater risk than men. For example, a recent study of three inner-city communities with a high prevalence of illicit drug use observed that the associations among crack use, high-risk sexual practices, and STDs were stronger among women than among men who used crack (Edlin et al., 1994).

TABLE 5.1	Self-Reported Health History				
Disease/Condition	**Male**			**Female**	
	N	**%**		**N**	**%**
Pneumonia	126	19.9		73	25.3
Hepatitis	100	15.8		34	11.8
Tuberculosis	43	6.8		12	4.2
Endocarditis	13	2.0		16	5.5
STDs					
Genital herpes	19	3.0		11	3.8
Gonorrhea	319	50.2		116	40.1
Syphilis	139	21.9		88	30.4
Chlamydia	6	.9			
Genital sores	104	16.4		51	17.6

SOURCE: McCoy, H. V., & Miles, C. (1992). A gender comparison of health status among users of crack cocaine. *Journal of Psychoactive Drugs, 24* (4), 389-397.

In other instances, the risk between men and women is similar. This was the case in a study of crack users in Miami who were interviewed in the early 1990s. Table 5.1 contains information about their self-reported histories of STDs and other health problems.

The STD most commonly reported by this group was gonorrhea, with a prevalence rate of 50.2% for men and 40.1% for women. The second most common STD was syphilis, reported by 21.9% of the men and by 30.4% of the women. Genital sores were reported by approximately 16% of the men and 17% of the women. Genital herpes was relatively rare, with prevalence for both men and women of approximately 3% to 4%. Chlamydia was only reported by six (0.9%) men and was not reported by any women.

Crack also has been linked to the increased incidence of several sexually transmitted diseases, especially syphilis (Chirgwin, DeHovitz, Dillon, & McCormack, 1991; Forney, Inciardi, & Lockwood, 1992; Inciardi et al., 1991; Marx et al., 1991; Weissman, Sowder, & Young, 1990). Rolfs, Goldberg, and Sharrar (1990) found that an increasing proportion of female syphilis patients were users of illegal drugs, especially crack. This study indicated that trading sex for drugs rather than for money was an important pattern for syphilis patients. Crack use has been associated with multiple simultaneous STDs as well (Fullilove et al., 1990; Rolfs et al., 1990). Chirgwin and colleagues (1991) report that both genital ulceration and HIV infection are common among habitués of crack houses.

The transmission of HIV has been associated with the use of crack cocaine because of high-risk sexual practices among crack users (Booth et al., 1993; Chiasson et al., 1991; Edlin et al., 1992; Ellenbrock et al., 1992; Fullilove et al., 1990; Marx et al., 1991; Weatherby et al., 1992). In at least three inner-city communities the prevalence of HIV among women who use crack has been observed to be higher than for men who smoke crack (Edlin et al., 1994). Heterosexual contact is the only AIDS risk category in which women outnumber men. Crack-using women are at risk for HIV because they often have multiple sex partners (McCoy, 1992), have sex with injection drug users, sometimes inject drugs while smoking crack, and have high rates of sexually transmitted diseases that may increase their risk for HIV (Marx et al., 1991; Piot & Laga, 1989). The relationship among crack use, risk behavior, and HIV is the subject of Chapter 6.

Other Health Problems

Table 5.1 also documents the prevalence of four additional major health problems. One out of 4 women had experienced pneumonia and more than 1 in 10 had hepatitis. The levels of tuberculosis and bacterial endocarditis also exceed that of the general population. Taken together these data indicate that women as well as men who are chronic users of crack are more likely than the general population to experience major health problems. These problems may be the result of an unhealthy lifestyle that is exacerbated by their use of crack.

ACUTE HEALTH RISKS ASSOCIATED WITH THE USE OF CRACK

Crack use can produce a myriad of health-associated problems that are related to the ingestion of this form of cocaine. Adverse reactions to crack are similar to those associated with other forms of cocaine, including an increased risk of acute toxic reactions such as cardiac irregularities, respiratory paralysis, paranoid psychosis, brain seizure, pulmonary dysfunction, and gastroduodenal complications (McCoy & Miles, 1992).

USE OF CRACK AND OTHER FORMS OF COCAINE DURING PREGNANCY

False Fears and Real Problems

When knowledge of crack first came to the attention of the public in the 1980s, the media quickly exaggerated the prevalence of the use of crack (Chapter 1). During this time obstetricians and midwives in hospitals of major cities began to deliver "crack babies," the premature, tiny, and very sick babies born to women who are addicted to crack. These providers feared that hospital neonatal intensive care units were about to be overrun with crack babies who, if they survived, would require extensive care because they would be developmentally impaired. In keeping with the public panic reaction to the crack problem, the prevalence of crack and other illicit drug use among pregnant women was estimated to exceed 500,000 per year. This was a 10-fold overestimation. Data from the National Pregnancy and Health Survey now estimate that the actual number of women who used crack or other drugs at least once during pregnancy and gave birth in 1992 was approximately 45,100, about 1.1% of all pregnant women. Clearly the size and the severity of the epidemic of in utero-exposed crack babies has been overstated. Nevertheless, crack use during pregnancy is a real health and social problem for many women and their offspring.

About 40,000 infants who are born annually to women who abuse drugs have either symptoms of drug withdrawal or a medical diagnosis that indicates health problems that may be related to drug use (Dicker & Leighton, 1994). Many of these infants are the children of women who smoke crack.

Most pregnant women who use cocaine also use one or more of the following drugs: cigarettes, alcohol, and marijuana. In addition, pregnant women who use cocaine may live in older, often substandard housing units where they may be exposed to environmental health hazards such as lead. Many pregnant women who use crack also tend to have poor health, inadequate nutrition, and little or no prenatal care. This polydrug use, poor health and nutrition, inadequate prenatal care, and possible substandard living conditions all increase the likelihood of problems in pregnancy that may result in low birth weight babies and infants with birth defects. Consequently, it is difficult to determine the extent to which birth problems and subsequent developmental problems are the result of crack use and which problems are the product of other drug use and the environment (Bandstra, 1992; Neuspicl, Markowitz, & Drucker, 1994). Nevertheless it is possible to summarize what currently is known about effects of cocaine abuse during pregnancy on the mother and her baby. The following discussion is about cocaine use, including crack use, because the in utero exposure effects are the same for crack and all other forms of cocaine.

EFFECTS OF COCAINE USE ON THE PREGNANT WOMAN AND HER FETUS

Use of cocaine and tobacco leads to high blood pressure in the pregnant woman because the blood vessels in her body become constricted. Acute hypertension may cause her to have a stroke or heart attack. The blood vessels in the placenta, which is attached to the lining of her uterus and through which the fetus gets nutrition and oxygen, also become constricted and may be damaged, even if the woman stops using cocaine. If the placenta becomes so damaged it becomes detached from the uterus, the fetus may not survive. If the baby is born alive, it may die from asphyxiation, suffer brain damage, and serious related problems. If the placenta remains attached, but the fetus does not get adequate nutrition and oxygen, the baby may be born alive but suffer from intrauterine growth retardation. This condition is diagnosed when the infant is significantly smaller than expected given the length of time the woman was pregnant (Chasnoff, Griffith, MacGregor, Kirkes, & Burns, 1989; Sexson, 1993).

Cocaine use also may cause strong contractions of the uterus. If these contractions do not stop, the pregnant woman may go into labor and deliver her baby prematurely. If the contractions are excessively strong, the delivery may occur suddenly, too quickly for it to be controlled even in a hospital setting (Bandstra, 1992).

EFFECTS OF MATERNAL COCAINE USE ON THE INFANT

Prematurity and low birth weight are among the more common consequences of crack during pregnancy. Pregnancies should last more than 37 weeks, and infants should weigh more than 5.5 pounds (2,500 grams) at birth. Newborns who weigh less than about 3 pounds, 5 ounces (1,500 grams) have the most difficulties. A common problem among premature infants is respiratory distress syndrome. This condition requires ventilation to assist with respiration and may involve hospital care that can last for several weeks (Sexson, 1993).

Infants born to women who use cocaine and/or alcohol during pregnancy are more likely to have birth defects than are infants of women who do not use these drugs. Cocaine causes many of the same birth defects that have been observed in infants whose mothers use alcohol during pregnancy. Fetal alcohol syndrome (FAS), the most common problem associated with drug use, was diagnosed in about 40 newborns in every 100,000 live births during 1990. Infants with FAS have distinctive facial features, tend to be low birth weight babies, and may have internal organs that are not correctly developed. They also have cognitive and behavioral problems that may persist through childhood (Department of Health and Human Services, 1990). Less common birth defects include genitourinary tract malformations and cardiac problems (Bandstra, 1992; Wheeler, 1993). These birth defects may be observed among babies of women who only occasionally use cocaine, but whose cocaine use occurred at the particular point in pregnancy during which the cardiovascular and genitourinary systems were developing (Dicker & Leighton, 1994).

Various health problems of pregnant women may be transmitted to their babies. Sexually transmitted diseases (STDs) such as syphilis and HIV can be transmitted to the infant before or during childbirth. About one fourth of infants born to HIV-positive women who are not taking the antiviral drug AZT develop HIV infection (Minkoff et al., 1990).

Researchers are investigating whether cocaine use during pregnancy and continued cocaine use by mothers after the children are born have long-term effects on the development of children as they mature and enter school. Developmental disabilities, including impairment of memory, intelligence, and motor coordination, have been reported in infants who were exposed in utero to drugs. Early findings indicate that cocaine-exposed infants who were not born prematurely may develop normally if they are raised in a supportive home. Infants born prematurely, especially those with very low birth weight, may have developmental problems that persist throughout childhood. It is not yet known whether such disabilities are a direct result of cocaine abuse during pregnancy. They may result from in utero polydrug exposure or prematurity itself. Certainly the home environment of a child has a major impact on his or her development. Children who are not adequately nurtured are at a definite disadvantage in their development (Wheeler, 1993).

PRENATAL CARE AND DRUG TREATMENT FOR PREGNANT CRACK USERS

Public concern about crack babies was fueled by published photographs of very small, very sick babies in neonatal intensive care units, some of whom had been abandoned by their crack-using mothers. The General Accounting Office estimated in 1990 that the median cost for caring for a drug-exposed infant was $4,100 higher than the cost of care for infants who were not exposed to drugs during pregnancy. The estimated cost increases to as much as $135,000 for the very low birth weight premature infants who need intensive care for several months. If the infant is a "boarder baby," abandoned at the hospital at birth, the continuing cost for foster care is approximately an additional $6,000 per year (Hawk, 1994).

Many of these costs, along with the human and societal costs of children born with disabilities due to drug abuse during pregnancy, could be averted if prenatal care along with drug treatment for pregnant women was available.

Pregnant women who use drugs and who want both prenatal care and drug treatment face a number of obstacles. Few drug treatment programs readily admit pregnant women because of worries about lawsuits if the infant is born with problems and because most drug treatment personnel are not trained to provide prenatal care. Waiting lists are long, comprehensive treatment is expensive, and the system of private and public programs is fragmented and uncoordinated. Programs that rely on techniques of confronting drug users may not be effective with pregnant women who are anxious and depressed. Women who come for care worry about going to jail and losing the custody of their children when they admit they use drugs. In addition to all of these obstacles, a major problem for pregnant women who want to enroll and stay in intensive residential or day treatment is that few programs have on-site child care.

Despite the public perception that drug-using women often abandon their children because the maternal instinct is damaged by cocaine dependence, most mothers will not stay in treatment for long if it means separation from their children. Paradoxically, society seems willing to provide high-cost neonatal intensive care for preterm low birth weight babies born to pregnant women who use drugs, but is not willing to avoid problem pregnancies by providing lower cost effective prenatal care and drug treatment services (Aday, 1993; Institute of Medicine, 1990).

TREATMENT AND POLICY ISSUES

Most drug use policy issues related to health-care delivery and drug prevention and treatment in the United States impact all drug users, including women who use crack. Nevertheless, women historically have been ignored when treatment programs are developed and evaluated.

The obvious way in which women differ from men—in their ability to bear children—has in large part been the mirror by which public health issues of women and crack use have been reflected. Issues concerning women and crack largely have been limited to the consequences of in utero exposure of the fetus during pregnancy and subsequent consequences for those children. Although considerable work remains to be done on drug use and pregnancy, it is imperative that research concerns be expanded to consider the wide spectrum of questions about women who use crack.

The exclusion of women from much of the research on drug abuse has compromised the generalizability of many potentially important studies. This oversight becomes alarming when results from studies with entirely male samples are used to design programs for female participants (Hughes, 1990). Many commonly used treatment components may be less appropriate for women than men. For example, a confrontational approach in therapy probably is less effective for women than men. Women may revert to old patterns of learned helplessness when faced with such adversity in treatment (Reed, 1987). Evaluations of treatment program effectiveness for women and men will provide information on which gender-appropriate treatment components can be constructed.

Inappropriate generic treatment models tend to be self-perpetuating because the absence of female-specific programming and clinical expertise makes it difficult for treatment programs to attract and retain female clients (Beschner & Thompson, 1981; Cuskey & Wathey, 1982; Lex, 1991; Mondanaro, 1989, pp. 1–16; Reed, 1981, 1985; Rosenbaum & Murphy, 1981). Fortunately, the omission of females as participants—which historically was too often true—today requires full justification in most types of federally funded health-related research studies.

Other positive changes are occurring. Recent federal health financing and health-care delivery programs have increased access to drug abuse treatment programs for indigent women while providing intervention and prevention services for their children and families (Department of Health and Human Services, 1992). Demonstration research and service programs are evaluating whether comprehensive long-term residential treatment services for women will decrease alcohol and other drug use, reduce reliance on social and health welfare systems, and improve functioning in specific life skill and vocational areas (Metsch et al., 1995). A unique aspect of these programs is the addition of arranged child care, either on or off site, which allows for the provision of intervention and prevention services for the clients' children in a safe and supportive environment. Although these programs are still primarily client centered, the curricula also include family-focused components such as parenting classes and family outreach programs. Specific treatment needs and programs are discussed in Chapters 8 and 9.

POSTSCRIPT

The use of crack by women has had several consequences—consequences felt by the women themselves, their children, and the larger community in which they live. One crack-dependent woman in residential drug treatment relates her crack use and the problems that followed:

> I started smoking crack when I was 26 years old. I was prostituting at the time but I was working at a local fast-food restaurant and I said I got to find me another way to get high cuz I can't snort cocaine cuz see something happened on the job while I was snorting cocaine, so after the nose bleed I was on the biscuit table fixing up biscuits and I was having the cocaine right out there beside me and the boss came around the corner so I poured the cocaine in the biscuit mix and mixed it up and served it. It wasn't really enough to do any real damage to anybody you know. But it was just the idea that I did something like that you know.

Soon after this experience, the woman was introduced to crack cocaine by another prostitute who said to her:

> "Wilma, I got this new kind of high for you." And she pulled out this little white hard rock that looked like a pebble. And I said, "Girl, what this?" And I'm looking at it cuz it's all shiny and all. And she said do you have this and that so I got her everything she asked for like aluminum foil, rubber band, a glass with water in it and then she started fixing it up. I said, "What the hell are you doing?" And she said, "Girl this high will make you feel so good, it will make you feel better than cocaine, better than drinking even." I said, "No-way, uh-uh, nothing is better than drinking." And she said it was better so she took a hit and the smoke started coming to the bottom of the glass where the water was and then she held it [the smoke] like that when she blew it out slow. And she said, "Girl, you wanna try this?" And I said, "No way." She kept bugging me so she put a piece up there and I did exactly what she did and I fell to my knees. And then I said I don't want any more of that. And when I came back to my senses, I ended up doing what she was doing.

Continued use of crack cocaine resulted in the woman losing her job, her home, and becoming pregnant with her second child:

And from there I lost my apartment, my clothes, my furniture and I ended up quitting my job. I mean I lost everything that I owned. My dad had custody of my son at the time and I was out there prostituting and I moved back in with my mother. I was out there tricking and I got pregnant with my second child. I don't know who the father was, see I was tricking for drugs and everything.

During the interview, she also described how her crack-using behavior had consequences for her pregnancy and her children:

So I continued to get high and I didn't have no prenatal care with my child, none whatsoever. I was prostituting again. Five to ten dollars—whatever to get my next hit. The result of that after my baby was born was that she had to stay in the hospital for two weeks cuz she was a preemie—only 4 pounds, 8 ounces at birth.

This same woman reported later in the interview that she was HIV positive as a consequence of her drug-involved risky behaviors and that while she used crack she continued to engage in unsafe sex without concern for whom she infected.

This woman subsequently entered a residential drug abuse treatment program. She recognizes the need for changing her drug-using and other risky behaviors. In addition, she realizes her responsibilities as a parent. She states,

I don't know what life has for me out there. All I know is that today I don't wanna drink or get high. I don't wanna smoke cigarettes. All I want to do is be a responsible parent.

For this woman and the many like her, crack cocaine has had a devastating impact. Her life, the lives of her children, family members, friends, and community have changed. Stopping the use of crack cocaine in general, and among women in particular, must become a priority. Failure to do so will reproduce in countless lives the harsh realities this woman has experienced.

REFERENCES

Aday, L. A. (1993). *At risk in America: The health and health care needs of vulnerable populations in the United States.* San Francisco, CA: Jossey-Bass.

Anglin, M. D., & Hser, Y. (1987). Addicted women and crime. *Criminology, 25,* 359–397.

Bandstra, E. S. (1992). Assessing acute and long-term physical effects of in utero drug exposure on the perinate, infant and child. In M. M. Kilbey & K. Asghar (Eds.), *Methodological issues in epidemiological, prevention and treatment research on drug-exposed women and their children.* NIDA Research Monograph 117. Rockville, MD: National Institute on Drug Abuse.

Beschner, G. M., & Thompson, P. (1981). *Women and drug abuse treatment: Needs and services.* Rockville, MD: National Institute on Drug Abuse.

Blume, S. B. (1994). Women and addictive disorders. In B. Wilford (Ed.), *Principles of addiction medicine.* New York: American Society of Addiction Medicine.

Booth, R. E., Watters, J. K., & Chitwood, D. D. (1993). HIV risk related sex behaviors among injection drug users, crack smokers, and injection drug users who smoke crack. *American Journal of Public Health, 83*(8), 1144-1148.

Bourgois, P. (1989). In search of Horatio Alger: Culture and ideology in the crack economy. *Contemporary Drug Problems, 16,* 619-649.

Burt, M. R., Glynn, T. J., & Sowder, B. J. (1979). *Psychosocial characteristics of drug-abusing women.* NIDA Services Research Monograph Series. Bethesda, MD: Burt Associates.

Center for Substance Abuse Treatment. (1994). *Practical approaches in the treatment of women who abuse alcohol and other drugs.* DHHS Pub. No. (SMA) 94-3006. Rockville, MD: Department of Health and Human Services.

Chaisson, J. A., Stoneburner, R. L., Hildebrandt, D. S., Ewing, W. E., Telzak, E. E., & Jaffe, H. W. (1991). Heterosexual transmission of HIV-1 associated with the use of smokable freebase cocaine (crack). *AIDS, 5*(9), 1121-1126.

Chasnoff, I. J., Griffith, D. R., MacGregor, S., Kirkes, K., & Burns, K. A. (1989). Temporal patterns of cocaine use in pregnancy. *Journal of the American Medical Association, 261*(12); 1741-1744.

Chirgwin, K., DeHovitz, J. A., Dillon, S. & McCormack, M. (1991). HIV infection, genital ulcer disease, and crack cocaine use among patients attending a clinic for sexually transmitted diseases. *American Journal of Public Health, 81,* 1576-1579.

Cuskey, W. R., Moffett, A. D., & Clifford, H. B. (1971). Comparison of female opiate addicts admitted to Lexington Hospital in 1961 and 1967. *HSMHA Health Reports, 86,* 332-340.

Cuskey, W. R., & Wathey, R. B. (1982). *Female addiction: A longitudinal study.* Lexington, MA: Lexington Books.

DeLeon, G. (1986). Male and female drug abusers: Social background, drug and criminal histories. In *Phoenix House: Social and psychological profiles in a therapeutic community.* Unpublished report to NIDA.

Department of Health and Human Services. (1990). *Seventh special report to the U.S. Congress on alcohol and health.* DHHS Pub. No. (ADM) 90-1656. Rockville, MD: Author.

Department of Health and Human Services. (1992). *Maternal drug abuse and drug exposed children: Understanding the problem.* DHHS Pub. No. (ADM) 92-1949. Rockville, MD: Author.

Department of Justice, Bureau of Justice Statistics. (1994). *Women in prison.* Washington, DC: U.S. Government Printing Office.

Dicker, M., & Leighton, E. A. (1994). Trends in the U.S. prevalence of drug-using parturient women and drug-affected newborns, 1979 through 1990. *American Journal of Public Health, 84*(9), 1433-1438.

Edlin, B., Irwin, K. L., Faruque, S., McCoy, C. B., Word, C., Serrano, Y., Inciardi, J. A., Bowser, B. P., Schilling, R. F., Holmberg, S. D., & the Multicenter Crack Cocaine and HIV Infection Study Team. (1994). Intersecting epidemics—crack cocaine use and HIV infection among inner-city young adults. *New England Journal of Medicine, 331,* 1422-1427.

Edlin, B. R., Irwin, K. L., Ludwing, D. D., McCoy, H. V., Serano, Y., Word, C., Bowser, B. P., Faruque, S., McCoy, C. B., Schilling, R. F., & Holmberg, S. D. (1992). Risky sex behavior among young street-recruited crack cocaine smokers in three U.S. cities: An interim report. *Journal of Psychoactive Drugs, 24*(3), 364–371.

Ellenbrock, T. V., Lieb, S., & Harrington, P. E. (1992). Heterosexually transmitted human immunodeficiency virus infection among pregnant women in a rural Florida community. *New England Journal of Medicine, 327,* 1704–1709.

Fagan, J. (1994). Women and drugs revisited: Female participation in the cocaine economy. *Journal of Drug Issues. 24,* 179–225.

Forney, M. A., Inciardi, J. A., & Lockwood, D. (1992). Exchanging sex for crack-cocaine: A comparison of women from rural and urban communities. *Journal of Community Health, 17,* 73–85.

Fullilove, M. T., Lown, A., & Fullilove, R. E. (1992). Crack hos and skeezers: Traumatic experiences of women crack users. *The Journal of Sex Research, 29*(2), 275–287.

Fullilove, R. E., Fullilove, M. T., Bowser, B. P., & Gross, S. A. (1990). Risk of sexually transmitted disease among black adolescent crack users in Oakland and San Francisco, California. *Journal of the American Medical Association, 263,* 851–855.

Hawk, M. A. (1994). How social policies make matters worse: The case of maternal substance abuse. *The Journal of Drug Issues, 24*(3), 517–526.

Hughes, T. L. (1990). Evaluating research on chemical dependency among women: A woman's health perspective. *Family Community Health, 13*(3), 35–46.

Inciardi, J. A. (1991). *Kingrats, chicken heads, slow necks, freaks, and blood suckers: A glimpse at the Miami sex for crack market.* Paper presented at the annual meeting of the Society for Applied Anthropology, Charleston, SC.

Inciardi, J. A. (1992). *The war on drugs II: The continuing epic of heroin, cocaine, crack, crime, AIDS, and public policy.* Mountain View, CA: Mayfield.

Inciardi, J. A., & Chambers, C. D. (1972). Unreported criminal involvement of narcotic addicts. *Journal of Drug Issues, 2:* 56–64.

Inciardi, J. A., Lockwood, D., & Pottieger, A. E. (1991). Crack-dependent women and sexuality: Implications for STD acquisition and transmission. *Addiction and Recovery, 11,* 25–28.

Inciardi, J. A., Lockwood, D., & Pottieger, A. E. (1993). *Women and crack cocaine.* New York: Macmillan.

Inciardi, J. A., Pottieger, A. E., & Faupel, C. E. (1982). Black women, heroin and crime: Some empirical notes. *Journal of Drug Issues, 12,* 241–250.

Institute of Medicine. (1990). Treating drug problems. In D. R. Gernstein and H. J. Harwood (Eds.), *A study of the evolution, effectiveness, and financing of public and private drug treatment systems* (Vol. 1). Committee for the Substance Abuse Coverage Study, Division of Health Care Services, Institute of Medicine. Washington, DC: National Academy Press.

James, J., Gosho, C., & Wohl, R. W. (1979). The relationship between female criminality and drug use. *International Journal of the Addictions, 14,* 215–229.

Lex, B. W. (1991). Some gender differences in alcohol and poly-substance users. *Health Psychology, 10,* 121–132.

Marx, R., Aral, S. O., Rolfs, R. T., Sterk, C. E., & Kahn, J. G. (1991). Crack, sex, and STD. *Sexually Transmitted Diseases, 18*(2), 92–101.

McCoy, H. V. (1992). *Women, crack and crime in the context of the AIDS epidemic.* Paper presented at the American Society of Criminology, New Orleans, LA.

McCoy, H. V., & Miles, C. (1992). A gender comparison of health status among users of crack cocaine. *Journal of Psychoactive Drugs, 24*(4), 389–397.

McCoy, H. V., Miles, C., & Inciardi, J. A. (1995). Survival sex: Inner-city women and crack-cocaine. In J. A. Inciardi & K. McElrath (Eds.), *The American drug scene: An anthology.* (pp. 172–177). Los Angeles: Roxbury

Metsch, L. R., Rivers, J. E., Miller, M., Bohs, R., McCoy, C. B., Morrow, C., Bandstra, E. S., Jackson, V., & Gissen, M. (1995). Implementation of a family-centered treatment program for substance-abusing women and their children: Barriers and resolutions. *Journal of Psychoactive Drugs, 27*(1), 73–78.

Minkoff, H. L., McCalla, S., Delke, I., Stevens, R., Salwen, M., & Feldman, J. (1990). The relationship of cocaine use to syphilis and human immunodeficiency virus infection among inner city parturient women. *American Journal of Obstetrics and Gynecology, 163*(2), 521–526.

Mondanaro, J. (1989). *Chemically dependent women: Assessment and treatment.* Lexington, MA: Lexington Books.

Morningstar, P. J., & Chitwood, D. D. (1995). How men and women get cocaine: Sex-role stereotypes and acquisition patterns. In J. A. Inciardi & K. McElrath (Eds.), *The American drug scene: An anthology* (pp. 178–185). Los Angeles: Roxbury.

Neuspiel, D. R., Markowitz, M., & Drucker, E. (1994). Intrauterine cocaine, lead, and nicotine exposure and fetal growth. *American Journal of Public Health, 84*(9), 1492–1497.

Ostrea, E. M. (1992). Detection of prenatal drug exposure in the pregnant woman and her newborn infant. In M. M. Kilbey & K. Asghar (Eds.), *Methodological issues in epidemiological prevention and treatment research on drug exposed women and their children.* NIDA Research Monograph 117, DHHS. Washington, DC: U.S. Government Printing Office.

Piot, P., & Laga, M. (1989). Genital ulcers, other sexually transmitted diseases, and the sexual transmission of HIV. *British Medical Journal, 298*(6774), 623–624.

Ratner, M. S. (Ed.). (1993). *Crack pipe as pimp.* Lexington, MA: Lexington Books.

Reed, B. G. (1981). Intervention strategies for drug dependent women. In G. Beschner, B. G. Reed, & J. Mondanaro (Eds.), *Treatment Services for Drug Dependent Women* (Vol. 1). Rockville, MD: National Institute on Drug Abuse.

Reed, B. G. (1985). Drug misuse and dependency in women: The meaning and implications of being considered a special population or minority group. *International Journal of the Addictions, 20,* 13–62.

Reed, B. G. (1987). Developing women-sensitive drug dependence treatment services: Why so difficult? *Journal of Psychoactive Drugs, 19*(2), 151–164.

Rolfs, R. T., Goldberg, M., & Sharrar, R. G. (1990). Risk factors for syphilis: Cocaine use and prostitution. *American Journal of Public Health, 80,* 853–857.

Rosenbaum, M., & Murphy, S. (1981). Getting the treatment: Recycling women addicts. *Journal of Psychoactive Drugs, 19,* 217–226.

Sexson, W. R. (1993). Cocaine: A neonatal perspective. *The International Journal of the Addictions, 29*(7), 585–598.

Stephens, R. C. (1991). *The street addict role: A theory of heroin addiction.* Albany: State University of New York Press.

Wallace, B. C. (1991). *Crack cocaine: A practical treatment approach for the chemically dependent.* New York: Brunner/Mazel.

Weatherby, N. L., Shultz, J. M., Chitwood, D. D., McCoy, H. V., McCoy, C. B., Ludwig, D. D., & Edlin, B. R. (1992). Crack cocaine use and sexual activity in Miami, Florida. *Journal of Psychoactive Drugs, 24*(4), 373–380.

Weissman, G., Sowder, B., & Young, P. (1990, June 20–24). *The relationship between crack cocaine use and other risk factors among women in a national AIDS prevention program.* Poster session presented at the VI International Conference on AIDS, San Francisco, CA.

Wheeler, S. F. (1993). Substance abuse during pregnancy. *Primary Care, 20*(1), 191–207.

Chapter 6

DUAL EPIDEMICS: CRACK COCAINE AND HIV/AIDS

Clyde B. McCoy
Lisa R. Metsch
Robert S. Anwyl

A drastic rise in the number of regular crack cocaine users nationwide has led to a disturbing concomitant phenomenon: the exchange of sexual services for crack or for money to buy the drug. Major American cities have seen increasing numbers of these men and women, commonly referred to within the drug subculture and in rap lyrics as "skeezers" or "crack whores," who dramatize the intersection of the major social issues of the 1990s: drugs, AIDS, gender roles, and the crisis of the inner city. (Ratner, 1993, overleaf)

INTRODUCTION

Because crack is inhaled, rather than injected, crack use was not linked with HIV during the early stages of the AIDS epidemic. Instead, media reports began describing crack use as a separate "epidemic" or "plague" that was devastating entire communities (Inciardi, 1987). These journalistic accounts emphasized the high addiction liability of the drug, the crimes committed by users to support their habits, the involvement of youth in the sale of crack, the violence associated with attempts to control crack distribution networks, and the "hypersexuality" among users.

Meanwhile, drug abuse research was focused on the growing problem of HIV transmission through shared injection equipment among injection drug users (IDUs). These studies also discovered that sex partners of IDUs were at high risk for HIV infection, but crack users were not yet understood to be at high risk. In fact, there was speculation that crack use might become a safe alternative to cocaine injection because no needles were used that could transmit the virus (Des Jarlais & Friedman, 1988).

Less noted by the media, but of growing concern among public health authorities, were rising rates of syphilis and other sexually transmitted diseases (STDs) among crack users (Guinan, 1989; Schultz, Zweig, Sing, & Htoo, 1990). An official from the Centers for Disease Control (CDC) commented in 1988 that "the crack house of today has become what the gay bathhouse was yesterday with regard to all sexually transmitted diseases" (Goldsmith, 1988, p. 2009). Actually, the popular media had reported extensive sexual activity by crack users, especially in the more sensational accounts, but the emphases typically were on hypersexuality related to the frequent exchange of sex acts of all types with anonymous partners for crack or for money to buy crack (Gross, 1985).

The possibility that crack use was associated with HIV surfaced with the recognition by researchers that crack users engaged in high-risk sex and had high rates of other STDs. Research confirmed the media reports that many crack users engaged in frequent risky sexual activities with large numbers of sex partners when they exchanged sex for crack and money for crack (Chiasson et al., 1991; Chirgwin, DeHovitz, Dillon, & McCormack, 1991; Inciardi, 1989; Fullilove & Fullilove, 1989; Fullilove, Fullilove, Bowser, & Gross, 1990; Marx, Aral, Rolfs, Sterk, & Kahn, 1991). Shortly thereafter, sex-for-crack exchanges and consequent risk of HIV infection were targeted for systematic study.

Research reports now began to document the nature and extent of the risk of HIV infection among crack users (Booth, Watters, & Chitwood, 1993; Chiasson et al., 1991; Chirgwin et al., 1991; Edlin et al., 1992, 1994; Fullilove et al., 1990; Marx, 1991; Rolfs, Goldberg, & Sharrar, 1990). By the mid-1990s the linkage between crack and HIV had become clearer. In the February 29, 1995, *New York Times,* Dr. Scott Holmberg of the CDC stated, "Maybe as much as half of the new infections among heterosexuals are occurring in relation to crack cocaine" (Kolata, 1995, p. B6). However, specifying the level of HIV risk associated with crack use has been difficult because many crack users engage in multiple risk activities.

THE EPIDEMIOLOGY OF CRACK COCAINE AND HIV/AIDS

The AIDS epidemic began with an almost exclusive focus on male-to-male sexual transmission. The first recognized drug-related HIV risk group was injection drug users (IDUs) and the second group was the sex partners of IDUs. Epidemiological data have been collected by the CDC on these groups through its surveillance reporting system for several years. Incidence and prevalence data on AIDS cases for crack users resulting from sexual transmission remain hidden, however, within the CDC reporting category of "heterosexual transmission."

The June 1995 CDC HIV/AIDS Surveillance Report identified the cumulative number of AIDS cases from heterosexual transmission as 35,683 which was approximately 8% of the diagnosed adult AIDS cases reported to that date. The number of reported cases in this category has increased persistently and at an increasing rate during the past decade; nearly one fourth (8,178) of the adult cases attributable to heterosexual contact were reported during the 12 months just prior to the report date. In that 1-year period, the number of reported AIDS cases attributable to heterosexual transmission increased by one third (Centers for Disease Control, 1995). Transmission has evolved beyond the IDU–sex partner vector to include new groups that were not part of the original gay and IDU risk communities. Thus male-to-female and female-to-male transmission of HIV, where neither partner is known to be a member of a group at high risk for AIDS, appears to be increasing rapidly (Haverkos, 1994).

HIV has a long incubation period, and diagnosis of AIDS and/or profound symptoms of its onset can occur several years after the initial HIV infection. Those who have been exposed to HIV usually will have antibodies to HIV in their system that can be detected via laboratory tests of blood samples. Sera that contain antibodies to HIV are said to test "positive" and the person is said to be "seropositive." By examining rates of seropositive samples in defined populations of tested individuals, it is possible to construct scientific estimates of HIV incidence (the appearance of new cases) and HIV prevalence (the number of living individuals who are infected at a given time). Thus some of the knowledge gap regarding the risk factors and extent of HIV among crack addicts and their sex partners can be filled with seroprevalence data from specific research studies.

A study of risk factors for HIV infection was conducted at an STD clinic in an area in New York City where the cumulative incidence of reported AIDS in adults through mid-1990 was 9.1 per 1,000 population and where the use of illicit drugs, including crack, was common (Chiasson et al., 1991). The overall seroprevalence among the 3,084 volunteer subjects was 12%, with 80% of those seropositive reporting risk behaviors associated with HIV infection, including male-to-male sexual contact, intravenous drug use, and heterosexual contact with an IDU. The seroprevalence in individuals who did not report these risks was 3.6% in men (50 of 1,389) and 4.2% in women (22 of 522). The risk factors associated with infection among these men were a history of syphilis, crack use, and sexual contact with a crack-using prostitute; among the women, prostitution and the use of crack were the associated risk factors.

Another New York City study examined the risk factors of 87 women admitted to a municipal hospital for pelvic inflammatory disease, 49 (56%) of whom were self-reported crack users. Of these women, 10 (20%) tested HIV positive. As noted earlier, the crack use/HIV association is not a simple one; these women reported not only crack-related unsafe sex behaviors (sex for crack or crack money and casual sex partners when high), but also injection drug use and sexual relations with IDUs (Des Jarlais et al., 1991).

Given the potential of sex-for-crack exchanges for spreading HIV to new populations, the National Institute on Drug Abuse (NIDA) supported ethnographic studies of the phenomenon in eight cities: Chicago, Denver, Los Angeles, Miami, Newark, New York, Philadelphia, and San Francisco (Ratner, 1993). A total of 340 crack users were interviewed in depth (69% of whom were women). Of the 233 women, 108 had participated in sex-for-crack exchanges, as had 69 of the men. HIV testing was done with 168 of the subjects, and 14% were positive for HIV antibodies. Of the 24 males who were noninjectors and who had engaged in heterosexual sex-for-crack exchanges, 12% were HIV positive.

Recently published data from one of the many National AIDS Demonstration Research projects funded by NIDA during the latter half of the 1980s illustrates the significance of crack use in increasing behavioral risks for HIV infection. The Miami project initially was designed to develop and evaluate the efficacy of HIV interventions among male IDUs. The investigators and NIDA agreed to add primary female sex partners of the IDUs to the study sample when preliminary data from these and other research projects identified the importance of the issue. Of primary pertinence here are the data from the sample of 235 female sex partners of IDUs who had not injected drugs themselves. A sizable portion (40.9%) of these women reported crack use; the remainder reported either no drug use or use of noninjecting drugs other than crack. HIV seropositivity was 19.8% among crack-using women compared to a still high 10.8% among the women who were sex partners of IDUs but who were not crack users.

Major differences in HIV risk behaviors were reported by women who used crack and those who had not. Some of the more notable of these differences include the following: 64.5% of the crack-using women had exchanged sex for money compared to 18.4% of the women who were not crack users; 24.2% of the crack-using women acknowledged having had sex for drug exchanges, but only 2.7% of the noncrack users had done so; crack-using women reported multiple sex partners (mean of 13.6) in the month prior to interview in contrast to virtually monogamous (mean of 1.6) sexual partnerships for women who did not use crack. This latter difference narrowed when the sex partners question was repeated but specified IDU sex partners. Crack-using women reported a mean of 2.1 IDU sex partners in the previous month compared to 1.2 IDU sex partners for noncrack-using women (remember that these women were sex partners of a known IDU).

Neither group of women in this sample reported consistent use of condoms, but the crack-using women had notably higher rates of STDs than their noncrack-using counterparts. Gonorrhea (42.7% of crack-using women, 23.7% of women who were not crack users) was the STD most commonly reported, followed by syphilis (30.2% vs. 13.8%), and genital sores (17.7% vs. 6%). It would appear that crack use increases the risk for HIV infection among women, specifically from crack use–inspired sexual behavior (McCoy, Miles, & Inciardi, 1995).

| TABLE 6.1 | HIV Seroprevalence in Three Cities |

	Women		Men		Total
	CRACK SMOKERS (N = 560)	NON SMOKERS (N = 406)	CRACK SMOKERS (N = 577)	NON SMOKERS (N = 424)	
CITY	PERCENTAGE HIV POSITIVE (NO. TESTED)				
New York	29.6 (203)	9.3 (54)	15.4 (253)	12.7 (110)	19.0 (620)
Miami	23.0 (161)	6.6 (151)	17.8 (163)	7.4 (149)	13.9 (624)
San Francisco	2.0 (196)	1.0 (201)	5.6 (161)	0.6 (165)	2.2 (723)

SOURCE: Edlin, B. R., Irwin, K. L., Faruque, S., McCoy, C., Word, C., Serrano, Y., Inciardi, J. A., Bowser, B. P., Schilling, R. F., Holmberg, S. D., & The Multicenter Crack Cocaine and HIV Infection Study Team. (1994). Intersecting epidemics: Crack cocaine use and HIV infection in inner-city young adults. New England Journal of Medicine, 21, 1422–1427.

Comparable HIV seroprevalance data were found in a slightly more recent study of young adults recruited from the inner-city streets of Miami, New York, and San Francisco (Edlin et al., 1994). In this epidemiological study, 23.0% of 161 women crack users in Miami were HIV seropositive versus 6.6% of 151 noncrack smokers. Similar patterns were found for crack users and noncrack users among samples of women in New York (where the rates for both subgroups were slightly higher) and San Francisco (where the rates for both subgroups were considerably lower). HIV seroprevalence data also were reported for crack-using and noncrack-using men; the pattern of higher rates of HIV seropositivity among crack users than among noncrack users was observed but, except in San Francisco, the differences between the two groups was not as pronounced (see Table 6.1).

To provide further context for these data, sex-for-crack exchanges seem to be far more common than sex for heroin ever was among female narcotic users, even at the height of the heroin epidemic from 1967 through 1974 (Ball & Chambers, 1970; Rosenbaum, 1981). The higher rates of HIV seroprevalence among crack smokers than noncrack smokers in the studies just reviewed support the conclusion that sex behavior that accompanies the use of crack is an important vector for the transmission of HIV/AIDS.

SEXUAL ACTIVITY AND THE RISK FOR HIV

Cocaine has a historical reputation as an aphrodisiac, although sexuality is notoriously a subject for rumor, exaggeration, and legend. This aphrodisiac effect certainly was one of the major allures in the earlier popularity of snorting (nasal ingestion) of powdered cocaine hydrochloride, and there is no pharmacological reason to expect any different effects regarding crack use. In fact, from the beginning of extensive crack use in the United States, many commentators have emphasized the reported hypersexuality among crack addicts. Such behavior has been observed in several ethnographic studies (Inciardi, Lockwood, & Pottieger, 1993).

Cocaine's reputation in this regard probably stems from the mental exhilaration and disinhibition felt by users that are translated as heightened sexual pleasure, particularly by new users. Casual cocaine users consistently report that the drug tends to delay sexual climax and to result in explosive orgasms. Clinical researchers confirm that enhanced sexual enjoyment, derived from disinhibition, maintenance of erection, delay of ejaculation, and intensified orgasm, is initially experienced by cocaine users (Grinspoon & Bakalar, 1985; Weiss & Mirin, 1987).

Pharmacologists and psychiatrists tend to focus on the chemically induced disinhibition effect of cocaine ingestion. Regardless of the form of the drug or the means of ingestion (snorting, freebasing, injecting, or crack smoking), one effect of cocaine use is relaxation of normal restraints on various aspects of the user's behavior, including sexual behavior. Heroin also has this reputation, as do alcohol and various misused prescription medications such as benzodiazepines (including Valium). It is important to note, however, that the disinhibiting effects of the stimulant cocaine are different from those resulting from use of central nervous system (CNS) depressants. The CNS depressants tend to give the user feelings of relief from everyday tensions, from exceptionally stressful life events, or from mood disorders. They typically impart a sense of well-being. In contrast, cocaine's stimulant effects typically are manifested in feelings of elation and overestimates of one's physical and mental capabilities. The euphoria and disinhibitions occur quickly and virtually simultaneously following the use of crack.

Crack also differs from alcohol, heroin, and most other CNS depressants in that it is not inherently physiologically self-limiting, either in threshold amounts needed for a high or ceiling amounts tolerated before unconsciousness, although life-threatening adverse reaction is a continual possibility. These characteristics of crack plus its rapid effect, the brief duration of the high, and its high addiction liability frequently result in compulsive use and compulsive behavior to obtain the drug using any means believed necessary. In these ways, crack psychopharmacology does figure prominently in the sex for crack or money equation.

A common crack-using pattern is not a single hit with brief transient effects, but repeated hits, strung together in a binge that continues until the crack supply or the resources to obtain it are gone, be that minutes, hours, or days. During such binges, crack users neglect to eat, to sleep, and to maintain basic personal hygiene. They typically spend most of their time between binges seeking and obtaining the resources to binge again. Although crack users often suffer from mouth ulcers and burned lips and tongues from hot vapors and crack pipe stems (McCoy & Miles, 1992), they tend to give low priority to obtaining medical care for themselves even during their relatively sober periods. The result often is a severely compromised health status. The financial and emotional burden from this compulsive crack use pattern can be staggering for users and their families, depriving them not only of basic life necessities such as food and shelter, but also of the psychosocial benefits of a trustworthy, caring, productive, and responsible spouse, parent, child, and sibling.

Sociocultural factors combine with pharmacological effects to present gender-specific problems for women who use crack (as elaborated in Chapter 5). The crack-sex association for females revolves around their need to pay for crack. Crack-using women tend not to be in the work force, to be undereducated, and to have few job skills. In ways not dissimilar to the legitimate job market, access to various means of gaining illegal income in the street subculture is even further limited for such crack-using women compared to men. Consequently, prostitution has long been an accessible, lucrative, and reliable means for women to finance their drug use (Goldstein, 1979).

Female crack users tend to characterize their prostitution as economic necessities. As detailed in Chapter 5, crack's disinhibiting effects are instrumental in facilitating some of the behaviors involved in sex for crack, allowing women crack users to perform sex acts demanded by customers that these women might otherwise find unacceptable. In summary, considerations of the nature of addiction, of the economic limitations, perceived necessity and psychological rationalization involved in sex for crack exchanges, and of disinhibition produced by pharmacology are important contextual factors in any discussion that focuses on sexual behavior of women that sometimes is too easily summarized as hypersexuality.

Another important point in the sex-for-crack scenario is a commonly heard theme among male crack users: Having sex, and particularly receiving oral sex, while smoking both enhances the drug's effects and conveys a sense of power and control that users usually do not experience in other aspects of their lives. This phenomenon is graphically illustrated in the street language of a 40-year-old male crack user/dealer:

> I've been shit on all my life, first by my parents and teachers and now by everybody. . . . Everybody seems to be always kickin' me in the ass. . . . The cracks puts me in charge of things. With the cracks I can get people to do things. For crack I can get women to do anything. (McCoy & Inciardi, 1995, p. 103)

Some women crack users also report a preference for receiving oral sex while they smoke. In the words of a 36-year-old woman who initiated crack use in the early 1980s:

> I know it is weird and hard to explain, but it's true: crack and oral sex go together. Men like it and women like it, and maybe for the same reasons. I like it because if my partner does it slow and gentle, it's soothing, it sort of smooths off the rough edges. It just makes me feel good, and makes the drug better, and because I'm so high most of the time I don't much care if anyone is watching. It's a good thing. (McCoy & Inciardi, 1995, p. 103)

Both fellatio and cunnilingus are common forms of sexual activity in crack houses. However, investigations of orogenital sex as a potential mechanism of heterosexual HIV transmission have been rare to date (Fischl, 1988; Puro et al., 1991). More often, this issue has been explored using study populations of homosexual men (Keet, van Lent, Sandfort, Coutinho, & van Griensven, 1992; Lifson et al., 1990; Rozenbaum, Gharakhanian, Cardon, Duval, & Coulaud, 1988). Only one fully documented published case of female-to-male orogenital HIV transmission is known to date (Spitzer & Weiner, 1989). Thus orogenital sexual activity as a potential HIV transmission vector is an area of needed research. This need is underscored by the commonality of HIV risk factors and co-factors of STDs, genital ulcers, lip and tongue lesions, and penile and vaginal abrasions among those who exchange sex for crack.

Field reports and media accounts alike have described crack users as readily engaging in any variety of sexual activity, at any time, under any circumstances and with numerous partners. This seems particularly accurate in urban crack houses across the United States where crack users in poor states of health, likely to have untreated STDs and compromised immune systems, have marathon drug binges and sex orgies without the protection of condoms. These unsanitary and health-threatening conditions resemble those that have contributed to the heterosexual transmission of HIV in Africa and other developing countries.

It has long been known that the initial enhancement of sexual pleasure and endurance changes to sexual dysfunction with chronic cocaine use; males report impotence and the inability to ejaculate, females complain about the inability to climax, and both genders report eventual decreased desire for sex (Grinspoon & Bakalar, 1985; Weiss & Mirin, 1987). These earlier accounts pertained to those who had used cocaine in other forms. Based on observations and interviews in crack houses, the desire for sex may not diminish appreciably among chronic crack users, but they do seem to experience some frustration and consequent loss of enjoyment. In one study of crack house sexual activities, some men reported they could ejaculate only after extremely vigorous masturbation or prolonged vaginal intercourse. Many of the female partners in these exchanges reported that the lengthy intercourse resulted in both vaginal and penile bleeding (Inciardi et al., 1993).

The friction between penis and vagina during vaginal intercourse stimulates the generation of significant amounts of vaginal secretions. In laboratory tests, virologists have been able to isolate live HIV from secretion samples provided by infected women and from semen provided by infected men. A crack house customer interviewed in one study reported that the skin on his penis had ruptured during intercourse with a menstruating crack house prostitute. He indicated that this was not a new experience for him (McCoy & Inciardi, 1995). The risk of female-to-male HIV transmission is particularly high under these conditions (Inciardi, Chitwood, & McCoy, 1992). These potentially infected genital secretions, potentially infected semen from prior customers, and potentially infected menstrual blood all come into contact with the often chafed skin of a client's penis during crack house sex. With this information in mind, note the description of crack house sexual activities from an ethnographer's notebook:

> In the bloop house/freak house/wild thang, all the sex and voyeurism and highs are happening at once. All orifices are involved. There is no sequentiality, no reasoning. The one door to the room is bolted, everyone is naked and there is no bathroom. You cannot just run down the hallway and clean up. (McCoy et al., 1995)

In the scenes described here or during more workaday sex-for-crack exchanges, some women who work in crack houses repeatedly perform acts of oral, vaginal, and anal sex with virtually no elapsed time between customers. Women who perform vaginal sex in crack houses do so with many different men in succession; thus infected semen from previous customers can still be present in vaginal fluids to expose later customers to infection risk. (A related practice was reported by Magana [1991] in which numerous migrant workers would become "milk brothers" by having vaginal intercourse in rapid succession with the same heroin-addicted prostitute.)

Prophylactics rarely are used in crack houses (although there are indications that crack-using street prostitutes are beginning to require their customers to use condoms). Because condom use is rare, not only are the women exposed to the semen of all of their male partners, but successive male partners are exposed to the semen of the women's previous partners (Inciardi et al., 1992). Consequently, crack house sex-for-crack exchanges represent a heterosexual situation where male-to-female, female-to-male, and male-to-male transmission of HIV can occur.

CRACK, CONDOMS, AND HIV PREVENTION

Presently there is neither an effective vaccine against HIV infection nor a cure for AIDS. For the foreseeable future, public health responses must concentrate on slowing the spread of HIV/AIDS through primary prevention programs and efforts to reduce the danger of those at high risk through behavioral change. This chapter has elaborated the high-risk status of the lifestyle of many crack users, particularly those who exchange sex for crack or money for crack. One obvious method to reduce the risk of HIV infection by sexual transmission is the use of condoms that serve as barrier prophylactics.

Male condoms have been used since the time of the early Egyptians who covered the penis with animal membranes. In more modern times, universal and consistent use of condoms has been checked by religious and moral groups that oppose birth control or believe condoms promote promiscuity. Significant numbers of males and some females say they do not use condoms because of inconvenience (reduction of spontaneity or difficulty in applying), desensitization, or discomfort. Historically, low profile promotion of condoms to prevent STDs and pregnancy has not proven very effective.

Since the advent of the AIDS epidemic, promotion of condom use has increased, marketing approaches have become more sophisticated, and condoms have been moved from beneath the counter to prominent displays in pharmacies and other retail stores. Numerous studies have found male condoms to effectively prevent the sexual transmission of HIV. Nevertheless, significant proportions of populations at risk of HIV infection still do not use condoms, some not consistently and others not at all.

Difficult prevention/intervention problems remain with regard to the promotion and acceptance of condom use among crack users. For example, a 1991–1992 study of 641 crack users found that only 33% of those who exchanged sex-for-crack or money for crack said they always used condoms; 38% of the men and 4% of the women who participated in sex-for-crack exchanges reported never using condoms. Among study participants who did not engage in sex-for-crack transactions, condom use was even less frequent; only 22% of these crack users said they always use condoms and 55% reported never using them. These investigators conclude that such infrequent/inconsistent use of condoms by such a high-risk group would do little to substantially reduce the spread of STDs or HIV infection (Weatherby et al., 1992).

The female condom is an innovation that may eventually equal or even surpass the male condom as an effective prophylactic against both pregnancies and STDs. It differs from the male condom in that it is controlled by the woman; provides protection from pre-ejaculation fluids; provides barrier protection for virtually the entire vaginal area, thus providing better protection against STD transmission; and is less likely to rupture. The female condom was approved for sale by the U.S. Food and Drug Administration in 1993, and large-scale studies are needed to test its acceptability and efficacy among crack-using populations in the United States.

It is now clear that effective HIV behavioral risk intervention programs must target both drug use and sexual behaviors and must include persuasive motivating information. A variety of programs exist that are intended to reduce HIV risk behavior. These programs employ various techniques: written and verbal presentations of HIV behavior risk reduction information; skills training and assertiveness education for females (Kelly & St. Lawrence, 1990); HIV testing and counseling (Landis, Earp, & Koch, 1992); audiovisual presentations and individual counseling (Martin et al., 1990); and couples counseling in conjunction with social supports (Padian, O'Brien, Chang, Glass, & Francis, 1993).

These and other interventions, although imperfect, have more potential to be effective than simple passive distribution of written AIDS prevention information. Interventions should be culturally appropriate for specific target populations, attend to their attitudes, values, and concerns, and be sensitive to social and economic barriers that can inhibit behavioral change. Some interventionists stress that persons at risk for HIV infection must use specific technical and interpersonal skills to change their high-risk sex and drug use behaviors. Such risk reduction programs employ a variety of techniques that supplement information with group interaction and training exercises.

A recent Miami-based study that was part of a multiple city federally funded research program evaluated the effectiveness of HIV interventions in reducing risk behaviors in a sample of 185 male and female crack users who were divided into two groups using a random assignment experimental design. A standard intervention group followed a protocol designed by staff members of NIDA and a multisite group of investigators. The second group received an innovative intervention that was locally designed. Six month follow-up measures indicated significant reduction in high-risk behavior from baseline for *each* of the two groups. Significant differences in drug use and sexual behavior changes also were noted between the standard and innovative intervention groups (McCoy et al., in press).

DUAL EPIDEMICS BEYOND THE METROPOLITAN INNER CITY

The HIV, STD, and crack use epidemics affect large segments of the population in many of our nation's inner cities (Edlin et al., 1992, 1994; McCoy, McKay, Hermanns, & Lai, 1990; Steel & Haverkos, 1992; Weatherby et al., 1992). These epidemics now extend far beyond inner cities to impact suburbs, smaller cities, and small rural towns and villages across the United States and throughout most of the countries of the world. The following example illustrates the association among crack cocaine, sexual activity, and HIV in a small rural U.S. community.

Belle Glade is a small farming town on the southeastern tip of Lake Okeechobee, in the heart of Florida's vegetable and sugar cane region. Its permanent population is increased each winter by migrant workers who come to harvest vegetables and to pick the citrus fruit. A separate group of migrant agricultural workers, predominantly from the Caribbean islands, live in the area from November through March each year, cutting and processing sugar cane. In 1985 more than one quarter of the area's population had personal incomes below the poverty level; the per capita income for Belle Glade that year was $7,704 (University of Florida, 1989). The incidence of disease, in general, and STD rates, in particular, were extremely high (Trapido, Lewis, & Comerford, 1990).

That same year Belle Glade achieved instant national notoriety when it was announced its incidence rate of reported AIDS cases was the highest in the nation. The absolute number of reported cases was not large; only 31 cases of AIDS had been reported for this area through 1985, but each subsequent year produced increasingly high rates for a small town of approximately 29,000 permanent residents.

A 1986 field study in the Belle Glade area by the CDC, using case interviews and neighborhood-based seroprevalence tests, concluded that the

HIV/AIDS cases in Belle Glade have resulted from the same transmission mechanisms as elsewhere, principally through sexual contact and injection drug use (Castro et al., 1988).

However, the unpublished results of continuing field studies by University of Miami ethnographers reveal that currently there actually are few drug injectors in the Belle Glade area, probably because many IDUs have already died of AIDS. These investigators have concluded that the crucial dynamic in Belle Glade is an integral association between the local drug trade and sex industries, specifically in sex for crack exchanges (McCoy et al., 1995). Two quotes echo the experiences of crack users in inner cities:

> I smoke so much rock, I don't care about how I look. I don't change my clothes or bathe. I have sex with anyone, I don't even look at them. I just want the rock.

> Everyone knows how you get AIDS, but the crack takes away your reason.

These statements reveal feelings of despair and defeat, but still fail to approach the desperation reflected in the statement of a crack-using woman recently interviewed by one of the authors. She said,

> So in April 1994, I found out that I was HIV positive. And that news just really, well, I couldn't believe it. This situation just makes me want to get high, more and more and more. Cuz I don't have nothing to live for, you know, so I continued to have unprotected sex knowing that I'm HIV positive. And I just did not care who I hurt.

The woman subsequently recovered from her initial reaction of anger and futility. She was enrolled in a residential drug treatment program when interviewed.

Whenever drug treatment is accessible, the preferred intervention is to reduce HIV behavioral risks for crack users. Current drug treatment services cannot meet the demonstrated need or demand, however, and policymakers are encouraged to employ additional approaches similar to those developed in the NIDA multisite study. AIDS intervention efforts must be dynamic. They must address specific community circumstances, cultural differences, perceptions of vulnerability, and the social roles of crack users.

REFERENCES

Ball, J. C., & Chambers, C. D. (1970). *The epidemiology of opiate addiction in the United States.* Springfield, IL: Charles Thomas.

Booth, R. E., Watters, J. K., & Chitwood, D. D. (1993). HIV risk related sex behaviors among injection drug users, crack smokers, and injection drug users who smoke crack. *American Journal of Public Health, 83,* 1144–1148.

Castro, K. G., Lieb, S., Jaffe, H. W., Narkunas, J. P., Calisher, C. H., Bush, T. J., Witte, J. J., & the Belle Glade Field Study Group. (1988). Transmission of HIV in Belle

Glade, Florida: Lessons of other communities in the United States. *Science, 239,* 193–197.

Centers for Disease Control. (1994). *HIV/AIDS surveillance report, 6,* 1–27.

Chiasson, M. A., Stoneburner, R. L., Hildebrandt, D. S., Ewing, W. E., Telzak, E. E., & Jaffe, H. W. (1991). Heterosexual transmission of HIV-1 associated with the use of smokeable freebase cocaine (crack). *AIDS, 5,* 1121–1126.

Chirgwin, K., DeHovitz, J. A., Dillon, S., & McCormack, M. (1991). HIV infection, genital ulcer disease, and crack cocaine use among patients attending a clinic for sexually transmitted diseases. *American Journal of Public Health, 81,* 1576–1579.

Des Jarlais, D. C., Abdul-Quader, A., Minkoff, H., Hoegsberg, B., Landesman, S., & Tross, S. (1991). Crack use and multiple AIDS risk behaviors. *Journal of Acquired Immune Deficiency Syndromes, 4,* 446–447.

Des Jarlais, D. C., & Friedman, S. R. (1988). Intravenous cocaine, crack, and HIV infection [Letter] *Journal of the American Medical Association, 259,* 1945–1946.

Edlin, B., Irwin, K. L., Faruque, S., McCoy, C. B., Word, C., Serrano, Y., Inciardi, J. A., Bowser, B. P., Schilling, R. F., Holmberg, S. D., & the Multicenter Crack Cocaine and HIV Infection Study Team. (1994). Intersecting epidemics: Crack cocaine use and HIV infection among inner-city young adults. *New England Journal of Medicine,* 331; 1422-1427.

Edlin, B. R., Irwin, K. L., Ludwig, D. D., McCoy, H. V., Serano, Y., Word, C., Bowser, B. P., Faruque, S., McCoy, C. B., Schilling, R. F., & Holmberg, S. D. (1992). Risky sex behavior among young street-recruited crack cocaine smokers in three U.S. cities: An interim report. *Journal of Psychoactive Drugs, 24,* 222–237.

Fischl, M. A. (1988). Prevention of transmission of AIDS during sexual intercourse. In V. T. DeVita, S. Hellman, & S. A. Rosenberg (Eds.), *AIDS: Etiology, diagnosis, treatment, and prevention.* Philadelphia: J. B. Lippincott.

Fullilove, M. T., & Fullilove, R. E. (1989). Intersecting epidemics: Black teen crack use and sexually transmitted diseases. *Journal of the American Women's Medical Association, 44,* 146–153.

Fullilove, R. E., Fullilove, M. T., Bowser, B. P., & Gross, S. A. (1990). Risk of sexually transmitted disease among black adolescent crack users in Oakland and San Francisco, California. *Journal of the American Medical Association, 263,* 851–855.

Goldsmith, M. F. (1988). Sex tied to drugs STD spread. *Journal of the American Medical Association, 260,* 2009.

Goldstein, P. (1979). *Prostitution and drugs.* New York: Dorset.

Grinspoon, L., & Bakalar, J. B. (1985). *Cocaine: A drug and its social evolution.* New York: Basic.

Gross, J. (1985, November 29). A new purified form of cocaine causes alarm as abuse increases. *New York Times,* pp. 1A, B6.

Guinan, M. E. (1989). Women and crack addiction. *Journal of the American Women's Medical Association, 44,* 129.

Haverkos, H. W. (1994). *The third wave: Heterosexual transmission in developed countries.* Paper presented at the National Institute on Drug Abuse and Northern Arizona University Second Science Symposium on Drug Abuse, Sexual Risk, and AIDS: Prevention Research 1995–2000, Flagstaff, AZ.

Inciardi, J. A. (1987). Beyond cocaine: Basuco, crack, and other coca products. *Contemporary Drug Problems, 14,* 461–492.

Inciardi, J. A. (1989). Trading sex for crack among juvenile drug users: A research note. *Contemporary Drug Problems, 16,* 689–700.

Inciardi, J. A., Chitwood, D. D., & McCoy, C. B. (1992). Special risks for the acquisition and transmission of HIV infection during sex in crack houses. *Journal of Acquired Immune Deficiency Syndromes, 5,* 951-952.

Inciardi, J. A., Lockwood, D., & Pottieger, A. E. (1993). *Women and crack cocaine.* New York: Macmillan.

Keet, I. M. P., van Lent, N. A., Sandfort, T. G. M., Coutinho, R. A., & van Griensven, G. J. P. (1992). Orogenital sex and the transmission of HIV among homosexual men. *AIDS, 6,* 223-226.

Kelly, J. A., & St. Lawrence, J. (1990). The impact of community based groups to help persons reduce HIV infection risk behaviors. *AIDS Care, 2,* 25-35.

Kolata, G. (1995, February 28). New picture of who will get AIDS is crammed with addicts. *New York Times,* pp. B6.

Landis, S. E., Earp, J. L., & Koch, G. G. (1992). Impact of HIV testing and counseling on subsequent sexual behavior. *AIDS Education and Prevention, 4,* 61-70.

Lifson, A. R., O'Malley, P. M., Hessol, N. A., Buchbinder, S. P., Cannon, L., & Rutherford, G. W. (1990). HIV seroconversion in two homosexual men after receptive oral intercourse with ejaculation: Implications for counseling safe sexual practices. *American Journal of Public Health, 80,* 1509-1511.

Magana, J. R. (1991). Sex, drugs, and HIV: An ethnographic investigation. *Social Science and Medicine, 33,* 5-9.

Martin, G. S., Serpelloni, G., Galvan, U., Rizzetto, A., Gomma, M., Morgante, S., & Rezza, G. (1990). Behavioral change in injecting drug users: Evaluation in an HIV/AIDS education programme. *AIDS Care, 2,* 275-279.

Marx, R., Aral, S. O., Rolfs, R. T., Sterk, C. E., & Kahn, J. G. (1991). Crack, sex, and STD. *Sexually Transmitted Diseases, 18,* 92-101.

McCoy, C. B., Anwyl, R. S., Metsch, L. R., Inciardi, J. A., Wingred, J., Miles, C., & Bletzer, K. (1995). The drugs/AIDS connection in Belle Glade, Florida. Unpublished manuscript.

McCoy C. B., & Inciardi, J. A. (1995). *Sex, drugs, and the continuing spread of AIDS.* Los Angeles: Roxbury.

McCoy, C. B., Weatherby, N. L., Metsch, L. R., McCoy, H. V., Rivers, J. E., & Correa, R. (In press). Effectiveness of HIV interventions among crack users. *Drugs and Society.*

McCoy, H. V., McKay, C. Y., Hermanns, L., & Lai, S. (1990). Sexual behavior and the risk of HIV infection. *American Behavioral Scientist, 33,* 432-450.

McCoy, H. V., & Miles, C. (1992). A gender comparison of health status among users of crack cocaine. *Journal of Psychoactive Drugs, 24,* 389-397.

McCoy, H. V., Miles, C., & Inciardi, J. A. (1995). Survival sex: Inner city women and crack cocaine. In J. A. Inciardi & K. McElrath (Eds.), *The American drug scene.* Los Angeles: Roxbury.

Padian, N. S., O'Brien, T. R., Chang, Y., Glass, S., & Francis, D. P. (1993). Prevention of heterosexual transmission of human immunodeficiency virus through group counseling. *Journal of Acquired Immune Deficiency Syndromes, 3,* 307-318.

Puro, V., Narciso, N., Girardi, E., Antonelli, L., Zaccarelli, M., & Visco, G. (1991). Male-to-female transmission of human immunodeficiency virus infection by oro-genital sex. *European Journal of Clinical Microbiology and Infectious Diseases, 10,* 47.

Ratner, M. S. (Ed.). (1993). *Crack pipe as pimp.* Lexington, MA: Lexington Books.

Rolfs, R. T., Goldberg, M., & Sharrar, R. G. (1990). Risk factors for syphilis: Cocaine use and prostitution. *American Journal of Public Health, 80,* 853-857.

Rosenbaum, M. (1981). *Women on heroin.* New Brunswick, NJ: Rutgers University Press.

Rozenbaum, W., Gharakhanian, S., Cardon, B., Duval, E., & Coulaud, J. P. (1988). HIV transmission by oral sex. *Lancet, 1,* 1395.

Schultz, S., Zweig, M., Sing, T., & Htoo, M. (1990). Congenital syphilis: New York City, 1986–1988. *American Journal of Diseases of Children, 144,* 279.

Spitzer, P. G., & Weiner, N. J. (1989). Transmission of HIV infection from a woman to a man by oral sex. *New England Journal of Medicine, 320,* 251.

Steel, E., & Haverkos, H. W. (1992). Epidemiologic studies of HIV/AIDS and drug abuse. *American Journal of Drug and Alcohol Abuse, 18,* 167–175.

Trapido, E. J., Lewis, N., & Comerford, M. (1990). HIV-1 and AIDS in Belle Glade, Florida: A re-examination of the issues. *American Behavioral Scientist, 33,* 451–464.

University of Florida. (1989). *Florida statistical abstracts.* Gainesville: Author.

Weatherby, N. L., Shultz, J. M., Chitwood, D. D., McCoy, H. V., McCoy, C. B., Ludwig, D. D., & Edlin, B. R. (1992). Crack cocaine use and sexual activity in Miami, Florida. *Journal of Psychoactive Drugs, 24,* 373–380.

Weiss, R. D., & Mirin, S. M. (1987). *Cocaine.* Washington, DC: American Psychiatric Press.

Chapter 7

HOMELESS ADULTS AND CRACK

Prince C. Smith
J. Bryan Page

Obviously my parents wanted me out, when their VCR was missing, when their TV was missing and my dad's money was missing out of the bank . . . cause we had a joint account . . . I'd go in there and draw some money and buy crack.
—An 18-year-old homeless man

This chapter describes the place that crack occupies in the lives of homeless adults living in the inner cities of South Florida. This approach places crack use in the larger context of homelessness, based on our studies of several types of homeless people. These data were part of an ethnographic component of a comprehensive study that included components on policy, public attitudes, model programs, census of shelters and congregation zones, and psychiatric epidemiology. This study was coordinated by Barry University.

FIELD TEAM AND METHODS

The ethnographic team conducted field work in the contiguous counties of Dade and Broward between December 1988 and December 1989.

The methods used in this study required direct contact with homeless people in their natural habitats. The field team identified locations where homeless people congregate in groups of five or more, made observations in those settings, and audiotape-recorded life histories that focused on the origins of homelessness. After observational sessions, the field workers dictated notes that were transcribed and coded according to the coding scheme constructed by the field team.

Observation and Mapping Areas of Congregation

The field workers visited the known sites of congregation to record their exact locations and sizes and to note the composition and activities of the population that congregated at these sites. Forty-one sites where homeless people congregated in groups of five or more were identified. Most of the team's observations took place in these noninstitutional locales.

Initial Contact with Homeless People

First contacts with homeless people generally originated from introductions by individuals who knew other people who were homeless. Drug users known to the field team introduced team members to other drug users who were homeless. Administrators and workers in the temporary shelters and soup kitchens introduced field workers to homeless people. Very often, homeless people introduced field workers to other homeless people. In rarer cases, field workers initiated direct contact spontaneously in congregation areas. This kind of contact, however, was labor intensive, requiring hours of presence in the congregation sites before it was possible to establish contact.

Ongoing Observational Sessions

Once field workers had established contact in specific locales, it was possible to make repeated visits to those sites. Observational roles were established at four sites in Dade County and three in Broward. The field team amassed more than 1,000 person hours of observation in these seven sites. They observed approximately 225 people in Dade County, and 276 in Broward County. The team had direct, face-to-face, speaking contact. Of these contacts, 33 allowed themselves to be interviewed in depth and 8 allowed themselves to be followed through their daily (or nightly) routines. The data reported below were collected from these individuals.

VARIETIES OF HOMELESSNESS

One way of viewing homelessness is to examine the factors the homeless person associated with the loss of home. The ethnographic team identified three general conditions that were consistently related to not having a place to live. The most important was having one's life go out of control. The second condition was the desire for some aspects of the homeless lifestyle, especially the freedom afforded by such a lifestyle. The third was having made mistakes that drove the individual into a homeless lifestyle. These three perspectives are not mutually exclusive, and elements of all three may occur in an individual case of homelessness. Nevertheless, most individuals strongly favored one of these three views of their homeless condition.

Life Out of Control

Loss of control appears in several varieties, including addiction, chronic mental illness, an abusive home environment, lack of skills in handling the demands of life, and extreme economic hardship.

Addiction.   The largest subgroup of homeless people interviewed by the field team were the drug abusers. Warheit (1989) also found this to be true in his epidemiologic study of residents of shelters. The homeless people who were drug impaired had managed, in the course of pursuing their addictions, to cut off every social and personal resource that could possibly have afforded them support in times of difficulty. Because their addictions were so strong, they were not in control of what was happening to them. Attributions of addiction as the etiology of homelessness dominate the life history materials collected during this project. A few examples follow:

Interviewer: How did you become homeless?
Respondent: Oh, that is tough. . . . Well, let us say ah . . .
I: Just tell me what happened, why you find yourself on the street.
R: Well, this . . . I was on drugs . . .
I: Were you on drugs at [names neighborhood]?
R: U'hum.
I: Were you on drugs early on? Were you on drugs?
R: Yes, I was, but not right now.
I: When did you stop doing drugs?
R: Ah, I haven't been on drugs for about a year now.
I: For about a year?
R: Yes.
I: So, how did you find yourself on the street?
R: Well, I haven't been able to find a job, I just haven't been able to get back on my feet. No fuss, ah . . . My kids, you know, I have 3 kids, and . . .
I: You have three kids?
R: Yes, they are down here, they's staying with their father's mother and. . . it's just been hard for me to get back on my feet . . . first finding a job.
I: What happened to the place you were living at [neighborhood]? What happened? What happened, why can't you live there now?
R: I lost the place. I had a 3 bedroom home.
I: Got a 3 bedroom home?
R: Yes I did.
I: And you lost the place?
R: Yes.
I: How did you lose it?
R: Drugs.

Similar circumstances were reported by intact but homeless families.

I: How did you come to be evicted?

R: Well, my boyfriend lost his job and we were like three weeks behind in rent.

I: Three weeks?

R: And it's like a motel apartment.

I: U'hum.

R: So, we were rent(ing) by the week and they said that we were $355 behind rent, but he just got a job a week ago, and he put his whole paycheck on it, $156, and they kick us out after they took our money.

I: They took your money and then they kicked you out?

R: U'hum. They told us we couldn't get any of our belongings unless we came up with the rest of the money.

I: What do you do? Do you normally work? Do you work, or have you just been taking care of the baby, which is a big job anyway?

R: Since she was born, I've been home, but before I was.

I: What were you working as?

R: Subway, cashier.

I: A cashier at the metro?

R: Subway, the sub shop.

I: Oh, the sub shop. How old is your baby?

R: 4 months.

I: Four months. What was your boyfriend doing for a living? What was the type of work that he's doing?

R: He's a roofer.

I: A roofer? Do you see any other problem having influenced your becoming homeless, economic . . . you said the economic was one thing, you didn't have enough money to pay the rent. Is there any other problem that might have contributed?

R: Drugs.

I: Drugs? Who has the drug problem?

R: We both.

I: You both do?

R: But he's a little worse than I am. I could do without, it's like he needs.

I: What kind of drugs does he use?

R: Crack.

Obsessive use of crack was often identified by the interviewees as an important factor in how they became homeless. Their accounts often began as hard luck stories involving employment problems and unfair landlords. But when the interviewer asked, "Were there any other problems that might have contributed?", the answer often added crack use as a major contributing factor.

Mental Illness.   Accurate identification and diagnosis of mental illness was not part of the ethnographic study. A companion study of psychiatric epidemiology among homeless people in shelters, however (Warheit, 1989),

found high proportions of homeless respondents to fit criteria for mild to severe mental illness, including depression (30%), drug dependence (40%),
and schizophrenia (15%). Field workers in the ethnographic study believed
that a substantial proportion of the solitary homeless adults they interviewed had difficulties handling relatively simple daily tasks and expressing
coherent thoughts. Few of these homeless people could be termed consistently aberrant in behavior, but many seemed disoriented and out of touch
with reality.

Abusive home environment.   People whose home environments exposed
them to abuse were present in all groups studied by the field team. The varieties of abuse that were related to homelessness included physical, sexual,
and verbal abuse, often in combination.

Lack of skills.   Some people simply lacked the mental ability to meet the
demands of adult life. Others appeared not to have acquired essential skills in
management of money, so that economic emergencies were inevitable.

Economic hardship.   Although cases of this nature were relatively rare,
there were some homeless people who appeared to be in poor economic circumstances that could not be traced to some other more basic problem.
These people were not chronically homeless, but their responsibilities (such
as providing for a family) did not allow them to provide food and clothing
and also secure stable shelter. In the absence of other problems, economic
factors in homelessness often are acute and may be remediable.

Desire for a Homeless Lifestyle

It was relatively easy for field workers to find homeless people who had chosen
to be homeless. They articulated the merits of their lifestyle, pointing out its ad-
vantages over mainstream lifestyles. The fundamental issue in this point of view
was freedom.

Freedoms.   Respondents cited (1) freedom from responsibility, (2) freedom
from demands of family, and (3) freedom to travel.
    Homelessness, from one point of view, offers individuals wide latitude in
their behavior. Homeless people who participated in our study often commented they liked the idea of not owing anyone anything and having no
monthly bills to pay. Knowing that nobody was depending on them for food or
shelter was also said by some to be an advantage of homelessness. These people
tended not to resort to shelters and soup kitchens because they found the rules
and restrictions enforced in those places too limiting. Furthermore, the forced
choices that must be made when one accepts aid from institutions led, according to these individuals, to acceptance of unsatisfactory conditions. Getting
food from a soup kitchen led to eating bad food. Sleeping in a shelter led to

being kept awake by snoring alcoholics. People who were homeless by choice tended to prefer handouts with no strings attached.

Among people who chose to be homeless, families were contacted at one's convenience for information purposes only. Not having family nearby to demand time and attention was a freedom this variety of homeless person prized. Individuals who were homeless by choice stated that not having people depending on you for basic necessities made possible great personal freedom.

The freedom to travel was very important to people who were homeless by choice. They enjoyed telling of the many places they had visited and of the adventures they had had during their travels. Several claimed to have traveled the equivalent of the length of the United States three or four times in the last 12 months. In their perception, their homelessness had made their travels possible.

Ambivalence and Relationship to Loss of Control.   There is probably much truth to what the people who are homeless by choice say about personal freedom as it relates to homelessness. Nevertheless, they are ambivalent about leading such a life. Some were drug users who may have had chronic problems elsewhere, even though they did not evidence any drug dependence during our brief field work. One fairly common theme among crack users was their conflicts with family over liking to use drugs once in a while. According to the homeless persons, their less-than-once-a-day use was not a problem; according to the rest of the family, it was. In the face of this conflict, some occasional users chose to be homeless.

Personal Mistakes

The field team identified another variant in the etiologic condition of homeless people in which the individual blames him or herself for homelessness or attributes the lack of home to being disappointed by a spouse or lover. This is the rarest of the three types of homeless people contacted by the field team.

Ruined My Own Life.   Blaming oneself for one's homelessness may have its origins in thinking (perhaps mistakenly) that it is possible to counteract addiction with greater self-control, or that treating a spouse or lover differently would have changed the course of things. However self-blame is interpreted, some homeless people feel they have actively and perversely destroyed their own lives. This category may represent a stage in the life histories of homeless people, or may represent a different variation on homeless individuals' ways of interpreting their own experiences.

Broken Hearts.   Some homeless men claimed that when they lost their wives, they lost interest in maintaining a household, subsequently becoming homeless. In the absence of any other impairment or problem, the field workers termed these individuals "broken hearts." Again, because of lack of time depth in our perspective, the field team may have missed history of loss of control through drugs or finances that would have led to assigning a different etiologic condition to these cases. Still, the conditions described here are not mutually exclusive, and loss of control and broken heart may have interacted in a history of chronic homelessness.

Drug Impairment

The majority of homeless people cited drug impairment as their main problem. The field team identified five types of homeless who were drug impaired.

Workers.   *Workers* are people who maintain their addictions as best they can by working for a living and spending their wages on their drug of choice. They are left without enough money to rent lodging, so they sleep on the street. Workers can only be found in the shelters and congregation areas during the night. Their only form of illegal activity is drug use.

Losers.   Homeless adults who do not work, but wait around for opportunities to make money by petty thievery, begging, or scavenging are known on the street as *losers.* They disdain the kinds of jobs usually taken by workers, feeling such labor is unnecessary because they can provide for themselves in an almost passive manner. As one homeless man put it, a loser "stays in the jungle and chases you for drugs."

Dumped People.   *Dumped people* historically tended to be alcoholics whose families and friends had abandoned them, but today some dumped people are crack addicts. Some are men who were thrown out into the streets because crack destroyed their traditional relationships with women. They live exclusively on handouts, and show even less initiative than losers.

Hustlers.   Living by their wits in the streets is the hallmark of the *hustlers.* They are no more inclined to work for money than the losers, but their areas of endeavor require energy and creativity not demanded by the losers' activities. Hustlers act as messengers and couriers for illegal activities. They sell stolen merchandise on the street or pose as unlucky motorists in need of gas money. They wash car windows at intersections. Their preference is to swindle or dupe their clientele with a scam rather than appeal to pity.

Chicken Heads.   Some women who live out on the streets are called *chicken heads* because of the type of sexual behavior they practice to support their drug habit. This name comes from the motion of their heads when performing fellatio, which is similar to that of a chicken when it is walking or pecking the ground. These women sell sex as long as there is a market, primarily oral sex. A homeless male defined a chicken head as a woman who has sex for "the rock." The drug of choice of chicken heads usually is crack. Their sexual behavior places them at the high risk of HIV infection.

The following life story of a chicken head illustrates the living conditions in which crack use occurs among homeless adults.

Daphne is a 38-year-old African American[1] female. She is originally from a town in Arkansas. She spent last night as a homeless person in Miami at a bayfront public park. Daphne's boyfriend, Steve, also is a homeless person. At night they set up their bedroom camps in this park. Daphne is an attractive woman, although her hygiene is poor. On our first contact she apologized for not looking better and not being able to take a bath and to dress up before coming to the northern end of the park for the interview session.

Daphne grew up in the state of Arkansas where she completed high school at the age of 17. She went on to a state university in Arkansas where she obtained her bachelor's degree in nursing by age 23. At age 27, she worked as a registered nurse at an army hospital in Texas where she met her husband, Sid, an auto mechanic. Sid was originally from South Florida, and after raising a family for about 7 years in Texas, Daphne and Sid moved to South Florida. Daphne relates that Sid was having problems with heroin and she eventually became hooked on heroin and cocaine. As a result of playing the good and faithful wife to Sid, he got her hooked on cocaine.

She worked for about four years in a state facility in South Florida. Her supervisor eventually realized she had a problem with drugs. As a result of being identified as a drug abuser, Daphne's supervisor gave her an ultimatum. She would be fired, or she could take time off on a part-time basis to go into a rehabilitation program. With the assistance of her supervisor, she went into a community drug rehabilitation program in Miami. After being in the program for 7 months on a part-time basis, she was unexpectedly required to give a urine specimen. She tested positive for the use of heroin and cocaine, and was asked to leave the outpatient program or to be transfer into the residential program where she would be under 24-hour supervision. Because of her job, her home, and her family (she had four children ranging in age from 12 to 17), she refused to go into the residential program. She also was experiencing a number of problems with her husband and had recently separated from him. Sid had been to prison for drug related crimes.

About three weeks after leaving the program, she was asked to resign from her job when the report came that she had left without completing the program and had tested positive for heroin and cocaine. Three weeks later she began working at a private nursing agency where she made as much as $17 an hour working at night, caring for elderly people. Her drug problem

---

[1]Ethnicity: There are intercultural variations in the kinds of problems leading to homelessness found among people of different cultural backgrounds. Possibly the most crucial point in discussion of intercultural variation is the importance of family. Among Hispanics and Haitians (apparently both underrepresented among homeless people), the only way one can become completely homeless is by losing one's family. Among Hispanics, whole families may become situationally homeless, but only individuals who are already isolated from their families can become solitary homeless. Because the migration process among Haitians in South Florida is relatively new, solitary homeless people reflect the vicissitudes of solitary migration. This appears to be true of other black Caribbean groups. African American homeless people can point to the existence of their families, but they also are aware of why they have become estranged from them.

increased as a way of coping with the marital problems. Adding to her concerns, her 16-year-old daughter became pregnant and her teenage son ran away from home and began to sell drugs.

Daphne said her demands for money for drugs increased during that period and she became friends with an individual named Steve. Steve had a good life, two cars, was working as a manager of a local fast-food restaurant, and he helped her meet her needs. Neither initially realized that the other had a drug problem. Seven months later she was convicted of forging a check of a patient and was sentenced to 7 months in prison. During that period of time, Steve, who was living in her house with her children, became intimate with her 16-year-old daughter. While Daphne was in prison, the girl became pregnant, ran away from home, and went to stay at her grandmother's house in Arkansas.

Steve lost Daphne's house because he failed to make payments on the mortgage. Authorities for the state took her kids. One son ran away to his grandparents and became a dope dealer for his uncle. After her release from prison, Daphne stayed for about 4 months with a girlfriend who accused her of stealing jewelry and kicked her out. Daphne regained custody of her children with the assistance of her former mother-in-law. She lived in a shelter where she was accused of theft and evicted.

After spending four weeks on the road with Steve in his car, Daphne placed her children in protective custody with a state agency because she could not take care of them. Two weeks later Steve had no car. He claimed the car was repossessed but she knew that he had owed a drug dealer some money, and in order to save his skin, he had to give him the car.

She has perceived herself as homeless for the past 6 months, because she has been living in the park, sleeping on bus benches, and sleeping behind empty containers on the docks when Steve worked for the labor pool.[2] She states that her life on the street is one of constant fear; she has to look constantly over her shoulder, she explains. Daphne has been raped twice on the street. She states that one night when she was sleeping in an empty container at the port of Miami she was raped by two longshoremen, but she did not report the rape because nobody would believe her and because she should not have been sleeping there.

When Steve works at night, Daphne spends most of her time downtown hanging out with other prostitutes. This provides her with some safety. When she hangs out with a group of other girls who are hustling, men won't molest her because they know some girls carry pistols. She claims that she has been involved in five-and-dime prostitution. At times, just to get by she has sold her body. She is presently on crack and injects heroin. On an average day, she will leave the park early in the morning with Steve, go over to the labor pool, and hang out with the guys. If Steve obtains a job for that day, she walks up to a homeless shelter to have breakfast. She spends the rest of the day washing

---

[2]*Labor pools* are businesses that hire people for brief ad hoc jobs. The jobs may vary from construction and removal of temporary bleachers in preparation for the Orange Bowl parade to installation of light fixtures on expressways. They usually pay minimum wage and take full deductions for income tax and social security. Men working the labor pool are paid by the day, leaving work at the end of the day with $21 to $26 in their pockets.

clothes and getting some sleep. Sometimes she hangs out with a number of guys they know pretty well because she feels safe with them.

Daphne has tried three times to get off the streets. She has gone to the Salvation Army Women's program and stayed in the shelter for about 5 nights. After they learned about her drug problem, she was referred to a drug rehabilitation program but they could not take her due to the lack of space. She also went to a community health center, which she left because she thought they were putting her down.

Daphne does not keep in touch with her children. She did write to her daughter and her mother in Arkansas asking for help. Just before Christmas she called them collect and they hung up on her three times. She wanted a bus ticket to go back to Arkansas to see if she could start over.

Daphne has recently learned from a contact in a shooting gallery that her son was sentenced to 5 years in a state prison for selling marijuana and cocaine. Within the last 6 months Daphne has been arrested four times for disorderly conduct, sleeping in public, and having sex in public. She states that all those were trumped up charges. Daphne has learned from her homelessness that when you are on the street you have no friends.

Daphne also functions among the street people as a "chicken head." She says that women make it much better on the street because they can do a lot of things for the guys to get money without having to put themselves down or at any risk.

Not all homelessness among crack users is as attributable to drug use as it is in Daphne's case. Abuse of drugs may be a result of being homeless rather than a precipitating cause of homelessness. Some homeless adults said they were not involved in drug abuse beyond the recreational level before becoming homeless, but that life in the streets is so demeaning and hard for them that drugs offer the only kind of escape they can afford.

The rising availability and popularity of crack clearly has had a devastating effect on homeless people. A 33-year-old homeless man described how crack affects the formation of social structures in the homeless culture: ". . . there's people in which you . . . you generally like to smoke with or whatever that can tell you where . . . what's open, what's not . . . what's got beds, and what's on the floor, what's got mattresses, where is (there) glass . . . broken windows, things under this nature." Sharing the drug at times leads to sex and securing a place to stay in an apartment for this individual as well, ". . . if I can sleep in somebody's house instead of an abandoned building, I will . . . especially with this chick . . . (she's) just an associate that I know. I don't even know her last name to be honest . . . I been knowing her and screwing around and smoking with her about two months now . . . all she's interested in is another hit too." On why he had not sought a female companion, ". . . I don't want one, you know, cause I wouldn't do her right . . . I would neglect her, if I could get all the dope I need, maybe, yeah (I would want one) . . . This is confidential, right? . . . I ain't going to lie to you . . . I don't care about nothing but another rock."

Drug impairment was probably the most significant correlate of chronic homelessness. Crack use was common among homeless people, especially the solitary men. Generally, the homeless men took no pride in smoking "the rock" or spending their labor pool dollars on it. They described crack as the "ultimate high" and a "powerful craving." As a 39-year-old homeless man reported about crack, "it takes control of you."

Another homeless man reported that it was very difficult to keep money in his pocket from one labor pool job to the next, with crack dealers so present. Crack dealers work the lines at the soup kitchens, know what check cashing stores cash labor pool checks without identification and hang out there, and are present at the parks with a supply of marijuana and crack.

SUMMARY

The lifestyles of some types of homeless adults revolve around crack cocaine, working all day to be able to buy some by late afternoon, or begging, hustling, or prostituting to get a piece of rock.

Where crack use stands relative to the origins of homelessness is still debatable. In some instances, crack use is the reason for being expelled from the family home. In other cases crack use appears to follow homelessness as an adaptation to a hostile and grim environment.

Whether or not crack use preceded homelessness, it could not always qualify as a root cause. Homelessness also has origins in other problems, including dysfunctional relationships with spouses or other family members, which provide motives for initiating crack use. For others, it is sensible to view crack use as a unifying feature of the users' lives. Whether they work for it, beg for it, or give oral sex for it, the few blissful moments on the pipe are the users' primary goals in life.

REFERENCES

Warheit, G. (1989). *Psychiatric epidemiology of homelessness in South Florida.* South Florida Homelessness Studies, Vol. 2. Miami: Barry University.

Chapter 8

BARRIERS TO TREATMENT AMONG CRACK-DEPENDENT AND OTHER DRUG-ABUSING INNER-CITY WOMEN

Duane C. McBride
Patricia B. Mutch
Carole Kilcher
James A. Inciardi
H. Virginia McCoy
Anne E. Pottieger

Earlier chapters have discussed many health and social problems of women who use crack. However, very few clinical or community-based studies of substance abuse treatment needs and/or barriers to treatment for women who use crack or other drugs have been published. The first part of this chapter discusses the principal reasons for this deficiency and recent social developments associated with the women's movement that are generating new studies concerning women who use drugs. The remainder of the chapter presents findings from a study of the needs for health and human services and the barriers to services for women at risk for drug abuse problems.

For generations, drug abuse treatment programs have targeted their services almost exclusively toward men. Three factors have influenced this bias. First, rates of illegal drug use have always been higher among men. Second, many treatment referrals have come from courts and correctional agencies, where more than 80% of all defendants and inmates are men. Third, most drug abuse treatment systems in the United States are funded through male-dominated legislatures, managed by male administrators, and operated by male clinicians (Inciardi, Lockwood, & Pottieger 1993; Mondanaro, 1989; Rosenbaum, 1981).

At the same time, although research on substance abuse can be traced back at least six decades, the bulk of this work has been concerned with either alcoholism or heroin addiction among men. Furthermore, there is the long tradition in the substance abuse literature of ignoring gender as a drug use variable. When early research efforts on drug and alcohol problems did include women, a surprisingly large percentage of the work focused not on women's lives but on the impact of a pregnant woman's addiction on the health of the fetus (Ashbrook & Solley, 1979; Glynn, Pearson, & Sayers, 1983; Polit, Nuttall, & Hunter, 1976). The recent frenzy surrounding crack-exposed infants suggests this topic remains a strong focus of public attention, and a significant share of research funds continue to be devoted to the drug/pregnancy connection rather than drug treatment and prevention issues among women who are not pregnant (Johnson, 1991).

Through the close of the 1960s, one category of research on women and drug use that did receive some attention was clinical analyses of female heroin addicts and alcoholics as self-destructive, unstable, sexually maladjusted, insecure, socially immature, and other variations on a diagnosis of "inadequate personality" (Ashbrook & Solley, 1979; Burt, Glynn, & Sowder, 1979; Colten, 1979; Polit, Nuttall, & Hunter, 1976). Similar diagnoses were made of male heroin addicts and alcoholics, but such analyses were a markedly smaller percentage of all research on men. The literature of this period was in fairly strong agreement that although chemically dependent males were "sick," their female counterparts were even sicker (Austin, Macari, Sutker, & Lettieri, 1977). As Barbara G. Lex (1991) of Harvard Medical School pointed out in the specific case of alcohol, these allegations of greater psychological disturbance among women were being made at the same time that other researchers were presuming gender distributions were not important enough to report because chemical dependence was similar in men and women. Other researchers argued that substance abuse was essentially a male problem because sociocultural factors protected women from involvement in highly deviant behavior.

THE DRUG CRISIS AND THE WOMEN'S MOVEMENT

By the 1970s, research on women's drug problems began to change because of two social upheavals during the late 1960s: the American drug crisis and the women's movement. The explosion of drug use among high school and college students in the 1960s provoked a major change in how illicit drug use was explained. The emphasis shifted from psychopathology to peer groups and subcultures, making strictly psychiatric explanations of the use of heroin and other illicit drugs suspect. Several now classic ethnographic studies showed male heroin users as being not the passive, socially inadequate escapists of psychoanalytic theory, but alert, resourceful, purposive "hustlers"— "ripping and running," "taking care of business," engaged in that multitude of activities required to secure heroin and avoid arrest (Agar, 1973; Feldman, 1968; Preble & Casey, 1969; Sutter, 1966). These studies of male street culture set the stage for research on how female heroin users and later female crack users viewed their own lives.

The drug crisis also led to the funding of the first large-scale epidemiological studies of illicit drug use. The results confirmed that many adolescents and young adults in the conventional household population were in fact using illegal drugs. Rates for marijuana use among female students, in particular, turned out to be surprisingly high—lower than rates for males, but much higher than had been predicted under the assumption that women are highly unlikely to engage in illegal activities. Further, rates of increase for most illicit drug use by young women were higher than those for young men in the 1967 to 1972 period (Cisin, Miller, & Harrell, 1978). This trend toward convergence of male-female rates apparently did not continue past the mid-1970s, but gender differences for all types of drug use remain much lower for youth than for older Americans (Colten & Marsh, 1984; Ferrence & Whitehead, 1980).

Another aspect of the 1960s drug crisis of particular consequence for research on women was heroin use. It now seems clear that the general increase in illicit drug use during this time was also a time of increase specifically in heroin use, with a major heroin epidemic peaking around 1968–1969 in large cities, and later in smaller cities (Greene, 1974; Hunt & Chambers, 1976). Further, heroin appears to be one of the illicit drugs for which usage rates grew faster for women than for men. This is indicated by national statistics—arrest rates for narcotic offenses, gender distributions of addicts appearing for treatment, epidemiologic studies of specific cities, and incidence of pregnant addicts admitted to hospitals (Colten & Marsh, 1984; Cuskey, Richardson, & Berger, 1979; Nurco, Wegner, Baum, & Makotsky, 1979; Prather & Fidell, 1978; Ramer, Smith, & Gay, 1972). By the mid-1970s women accounted for 25% or more of the heroin addicts appearing for treatment. Because this represented a one-third increase over figures reported only 10 years earlier, it became increasingly apparent to some clinicians that the particular treatment needs of women would have to be given more attention.

The second major influence on the study of drug use among women during the late 1960s was the feminist movement. Almost simultaneously with the drug crisis, a revived women's movement began to apply pressure for change in virtually every American institution from the federal government to the Miss America pageant (Deckard, 1975). In the social sciences, the movement sparked a series of feminist critiques of existing research, theory, and policy, and it stimulated new interest in all aspects of women's behaviors and experiences, including drug use.

An initial focus of feminist attention was the licit medical use of prescribed sedatives and tranquilizers by middle-class women and its relationship to the gender-roles embodied in physician prescribing patterns and pharmaceutical company advertising (Gutierres, Patton, Raymond, & Rhoads, 1984; Hughes & Brewin, 1979). The resulting publicity helped educate both physicians and female patients. However, it should be noted that this problem persists: Physicians still write more prescriptions for psychoactive drugs for women than men, more women than men are seen in emergency rooms with overdoses of prescription drugs, and it has been reported that the formerly middle-class problem of prescription drug misuse is now being seen in low-income women as a result of prescriptions written for women on Medicaid (Galbraith, 1991). Further, cynical manipulation of women's fears and desires still provide advertisers and manufacturers with huge profits from sales directly to women of over-the-counter stimulants and depressants, alcohol, and cigarettes (Kilbourne, 1991).

A second variety of early feminist studies of drug use reflected concern about the needs of women treated for drug use problems, including the growing number of female heroin addicts appearing in treatment centers, as noted earlier. Some of the first studies investigated how these women viewed their lives. These studies produced a series of horror stories about treatment programs: sexual exploitation, humiliation, sexual voyeurism by male staff and male clients, being used as an aid in the treatment of male addicts (e.g., role-playing exploitive situations), and being excluded from aspects of the program deemed unnecessary for women such as employment training (Eldred & Washington, 1975; Levy & Doyle, 1974). Partially as a result of these studies, several major research projects were funded by the National Institute on Drug Abuse (NIDA) and the National Institute on Alcohol Abuse and Alcoholism (NIAAA) to study ways in which drug treatment programs could serve women (Beschner & Thompson, 1981; Reed, 1981).

The 1975 to 1985 period also produced several new types of research on women and substance abuse. One type were studies of female heroin users who were not in treatment or prison. They included intensive interviews with prostitutes by Paul J. Goldstein and by Jennifer James, an ethnography of women heroin users on the street by Marsha Rosenbaum (which notably remains the sole such work, in contrast to the half dozen completed on men), and several large studies entailing street interviews with female heroin users as well as other female criminal offenders in the same communities (Goldstein, 1979; Inciardi & Pottieger, 1986; Inciardi, Pottieger, & Faupel, 1982; James, 1976; James, Gosho, & Watson, 1976; Rosenbaum, 1981). A second type of study repudiated the popular notion that the increased participation of women in the work force produced an increase in problem drinking among women (Ferrence, 1980; Ferrence & Whitehead, 1980; Fillmore, 1984).

These new investigations advance the understanding of the social psychology of drug and alcohol use among women and differences of substance use patterns of men and women. However, to some extent traditional research limitations have continued. Pregnancy and psychopathology appear to remain primary foci for some studies of drug use among women, and reports continue to appear with all male samples or, more commonly now, analyses that ignore gender.

Two major issues concerning drug use by women still have received little attention. They include treatment seeking and barriers to treatment. Recently, empirical research and public hearings have brought these concerns into sharper focus. Annual survey data from the National Household Survey on Drug Abuse document decreasing differences in drug use prevalence by gender (NIDA, 1990; SAMHSA, 1993). Increasingly, men and women are reported to use most types of substances at similar rates and frequencies. Female injection drug users, moreover, are at a high risk for HIV infection, and represent the primary source of HIV infection among infants (CDC, 1993; Corea, 1992; Faden, Geller, & Powers, 1991; McCoy & Inciardi, 1994; Miller, Turner, & Moses, 1990). And finally, congressional hearings and other public testimony have documented systematic biases against women in public health research, clinical trials, and basic service provision (Denenberg, 1993; Jonsen & Stryker, 1993; Novello & Wise, 1991). Because of women's fertility, reproductive, and other unique health issues, researchers typically considered men to be less problematic subjects in clinical trials. In a sense, men were considered the "normal" population to study.

This general societal view has significantly affected attitudes toward gender and drug abuse. Males have been viewed by decision makers as the population most at risk for drug abuse and its concomitant personal and social consequences. As a result, women have often been overlooked in drug treatment needs assessment research, and little is known about women and their treatment needs. Generally, male models of etiology and appropriate intervention are applied in programs for female clients, despite research that indicates considerable differences in female and male drug use etiology, specific service needs, and barriers to meeting those needs (Report Lists Barriers, 1993; Root, 1989; Toray, 1993; Wallen, 1992).

RESEARCH ON INNER-CITY WOMEN

As a consequence of this research and testimony, the federal government has become more sensitive to the specific health and human service needs of women, including drug-abusing women. For example, the NIDA and other agencies in the National Institutes of Health now require all grant and contract applicants to include adequate representation of women in study populations or to have defensible reasons for their exclusion. Furthermore, the federal block grant funding process now requires states to give the highest priority to serving women and their dependent children.

In a local area response to this federal initiative, and in an attempt to address the treatment deficits of women, the Southwestern Human Resources Commission of the State of Michigan Public Health Department commissioned a needs assessment study focusing on the service requirements of inner-city women at risk for drug abuse problems and the barriers they faced in their attempts to access treatment. The needs assessment utilized a mixed methodology involving the collection of regional indicator data, key informant interviews, and surveys of women at high risk for drug abuse (see Kimmel, 1992; Mutch, McBride, Amey, & Gray, 1991; Mutch, McBride, Kilcher, Hartmann, Gray, & Amey, 1993). The analysis in this chapter focuses on the survey of women at risk for drug abuse in a tri-county area of southwestern Michigan—Berrien, Cass, and Van Buren counties. These data document drug abuse problems, treatment needs, and barriers to treatment of women who reside in inner city settings within non-metropolitan communties. Women were defined to be "at risk" if they were unemployed, had limited education, and had significant child-care responsibilities. To access the target population, a list of 22 relevant human service providers was compiled, drawn from public health, social welfare, and other relevant human service agencies.

The survey involved a 20-minute, self-administered questionnaire covering such areas as demographic characteristics, living conditions, traumatic childhood experiences, patterns of past and current drug abuse, frequency of current drug abuse, sources of drugs, treatment experiences, drug/alcohol use during pregnancy, service needs, and perceived barriers to drug treatment services.

Participation in the survey was both voluntary and anonymous. As an incentive to participate, certificates for food (provided by a local grocery store) were raffled among each agency's participants. A total of 145 questionnaires were administered, of which 136 were completed.

STUDY LOCALE

The study area was three counties situated in the southwest corner of Michigan, along Lake Michigan and bordering the Indiana state line. The population of Berrien County, the largest of the three, was 173,678 in 1990. The other two counties, Cass and Van Buren, had populations in 1990 of 56,743 and 37,654, respectively. All three counties contain numerous rural communities, small towns, and villages. The largest city in the tri-county area is Benton Harbor, with a population of just under 15,000.

Sections of Benton Harbor are similar to inner-city areas of larger metropolitan areas. During much of the 20th century, Benton Harbor was the principal manufacturing city in the region, with numerous foundries and factories that produced both small and large home appliances. This industrial activity attracted laborers of many race/ethnic groups from throughout the country. During the past two decades, however, although many industries still maintain corporate offices in the area, almost all of the manufacturing work has moved to other locales where labor costs are lower. The official unemployment rate for the region is about 8%, with neighborhood surveys of Benton Harbor indicating rates as high as 50%. The regional household income was about $27,000 as compared to the state average of just over $31,000. Finally, the region has relatively high rates of sexually transmitted diseases, infant mortality, and teen violent crimes (Schmidt, 1994). In 1991 *Money* magazine ranked Benton Harbor 398th (out of 400) in its list of most livable cities in the United States.

Further, interstate highway 94 connecting Chicago and Detroit goes through two of the counties. Because this area is approximately halfway between Chicago and Detroit with many exits from the interstate into otherwise isolated communities, the area has traditionally been a transfer point for drugs. This is demonstrated with data from the Berrien County Forensic Laboratory, which analyzes all state and local law enforcement drug seizures in the area. The number of illegal drug seizure samples submitted to the lab increased from 2,539 in 1987 to 5,925 in 1993. The proportion of samples that contained cocaine increased from 18.2% in 1987 to 43.9% in 1993 (Annual Report of the Berrien County Forensic Laboratory, 1994). These data suggest that the context within which this study took place involved the increasing availability of drugs, particularly cocaine and typically crack.

FINDINGS

The 136 women surveyed had a median age of 25.3 years, with more than two-thirds under age 30. There were almost equal proportions of African Americans (47.1%) and whites (46.3%), with the remaining distributed among Hispanics, Native Americans, and Asians. Some 54% had at least a high school education or GED. Their primary sources of income included legal employment (30.8%), public assistance (48.9%), and support from spouses and relatives (15%), with such other sources as friends and relatives, social security, and illegal activities totaling just over 5%. Given that the target population was drawn from public agencies offering economic and social services, this distribution of demographic characteristics was not unexpected.

Most (84%) of the women had children, and the majority (54%) had two or more. Most cared for their children themselves or with help from parents or other relatives. Few of the women lived alone (14.9%), with the majority living exclusively with their children (19.4%) or with parents, spouses, friends, and/or relatives (65.7%). Almost half of the women (46.1%) reported having been emotionally abused as children, and 32.6% had histories of physical or sexual abuse. In addition, 37.4% reported their parents drank heavily, and 15.6% indicated their parents had used illegal drugs. One in 10 residents (10.9%) reported their parents had been incarcerated, and approximately one fourth (23.4%) of the respondents said they themselves had been incarcerated.

As indicated in Table 8.1, alcohol was the substance most commonly used by the women surveyed, with three fourths having "ever used" and two-thirds reporting some use in the past year. Marijuana was the most frequently used illegal drug, followed by crack or powder cocaine, and amphetamines. Injection drug use was uncommon in this population, as was the use of barbiturates and hallucinogens.

The data in Table 8.2 indicate that significant proportions of the women used alcohol or other drugs on a daily basis. One in four (25.7%) of the crack

TABLE 8.1	Drug Use: Lifetime (Ever) and Annual (in Last Year) (Prevalence: N = 136)	
	Lifetime	**Annual**
Alcohol	76.6%	65.4%
Marijuana	53.7	39.0
Inhalants	3.0	0.7
Amphetamines	10.3	6.7
Crack cocaine	24.8	23.2
Cocaine (noninjected)	11.7	5.8
Cocaine (injected)	3.6	1.5
Barbiturates	3.6	2.2
PCP	1.5	—
LSD	4.4	0.7
Heroin	2.2	1.4

users smoked the drug every day, and an additional 25.9% used crack one or more times a week.

Half of the women were introduced to drugs by a spouse or male friend, 30.8% were introduced by a family member or other relative, and the remaining 19.2% by female friends. In addition, 48.5% were provided with drugs by a spouse or male friend, 36.4% of the women obtained the drugs on their own, and 15.1% through a family member or female friend. Also, 67.4% of the women had friends who used drugs. These data suggest the use of drugs by these women occurs within a pattern of relationships supportive of drug use. (Data not presented in tabular form.)

Of the women reporting drug and/alcohol use in the past year, only a third said they received any type of treatment services. Of these, the majority were in treatment for 3 months or less, and almost all found treatment to be very (66.7%) or somewhat (31.1%) helpful. In addition, 43.3% of the alcohol users attended Alcoholics Anonymous meetings and another 17.7% attended

TABLE 8.2	Frequency of Drug Use in Last Year			
	Monthly	**1–3 x Mo.**	**1–5 x Wk.**	**Daily**
Alcohol (N = 89)	27.3%	36.4%	18.2%	18.1
Marijuana (N = 53)	22.2	46.3	18.5	13.0
Inhalants (N = 1)	100.0	—	—	—
Amphetamines (N = 9)	58.3	16.7	25.0	—
Crack cocaine (N = 32)	11.1	37.0	25.9	25.7
Powder cocaine (N = 8)	22.2	22.2	33.3	22.2
Inj. cocaine (N = 2)	50.0	—	—	50.0
Barbiturates (N = 3)	50.0	50.0	—	—
LSD (N = 1)	100.0	—	—	—
Heroin (N = 2)	—	100.0	—	—

Al-Anon or Alateen meetings. Moreover, 19.4% of the drug users attended Narcotics Anonymous meetings and 5.8% attended Cocaine Anonymous meetings. All of the women attending these meetings found the self-help groups to be either very (70.5%) or somewhat (29.5%) helpful. (Data not presented in tabular form.)

Almost all of the women (96.2%) had had at least one pregnancy and two thirds had been pregnant at least twice. Half of the women reported they smoked during pregnancy; a fourth drank alcohol and 23% used other drugs during pregnancy. Of those who smoked, two thirds did so during all of their pregnancies; of those who drank, 44.1% did so during all of their pregnancies; and of those who used illicit drugs, 33% did so during all of their pregnancies. Those who used tobacco during pregnancy were likely to use every day (76.8%); 20% of those who drank used on a daily basis; and 22.2% of those who used drugs while pregnant used on a daily basis. The most likely self-reported outcomes of drug and/or alcohol use during pregnancy were miscarriages (17%) or low birth weight (80%), with half of the latter cases also involving other complications. (Data not presented in tabular form.)

TABLE 8.3	Human Service Needs (N = 110)
	%
Basic Services	
Dental care	53.3
Housing	52.1
Medical care	43.5
Clothing	38.4
Transportation	34.7
Food	34.5
Legal assistance	18.5
Family Needs	
Day care for children	42.9
Parenting skills	27.4
Communication skills	20.9
Family therapy	17.4
Day care for senior citizens	8.1
Other short-term counseling	4.6
Education for children	38.3
GED	33.1
Substance Abuse Services	
Drug education/prevention	13.9
Self-help groups	8.9
Outpatient treatment	7.7
Detoxification	6.9
Inpatient treatment	2.7
Substance abuse screening	2.6
Substance abuse referral	2.6
Short-term counseling	1.8

TABLE 8.4	Human Service Needs (N = 110) %
Mentions	
Limited or no transportation	60.7
Services not available in my neighborhood	52.3
Discourteous staff	44.9
Lack of child care	43.9
Hours not convenient	25.2
Dangerous neighborhood	8.4

Each woman was asked about her need for basic health and human services. The data document a need for services that ensure survival (Table 8.3). The majority expressed a strong need for housing and health care. Between 34% and 43% indicated a need for medical care (only a few physicians in the area accept Medicaid), food, clothing, housing, and transportation. Family needs such as education, child care, family therapy, and parenting and communication skill building also were needed. A strikingly low proportion expressed any need for substance abuse treatment services. These data indicate that for most of the women their basic needs of shelter, clothing, child care, and health care would have to be met before they would recognize the need for substance abuse treatment.

An important purpose of this study was to examine the perceived barriers to services reported by those in need of them. Availability and accessibility of services were major problems. The majority of women did not have social and health programs in their neighborhoods. As indicated in Table 8.4, transportation problems were listed by over 60% of the respondents as a barrier to service access. Because the towns and cities in the tri-county region are small, there is no mass transit system. There is a dial-a-ride service that residents may call, but departure and arrival times tend to be problematic, making the service unreliable for scheduled appointments.

Furthermore, existing treatment services frequently were unacceptable. Approximately half (44.9%) of the respondents said agency staff were disrespectful. Demeaning attitudes toward a woman's problems and sexual flirtation or harassment by male clients and staff were primary difficulties. A lack of child care was also a prominent problem for many of the women.

DISCUSSION

In order to address fully the drug treatment service needs of at-risk women, it is important to suspend stereotypical assumptions about standard service needs and listen to the women themselves (Hendrickson, 1992). The primary needs reported by the women in this survey were medical and dental services, food and clothing, as well as housing and child care. The primary barrier to services was a general lack of access because of either inadequate transportation or the absence of services in respondents' neighborhoods. In addition, women indicated the need to be treated with respect. Providers need to listen to these women and provide gender-specific and effective services. Providers must recognize gender differences in the etiology and maintenance of drug use.

Because of the way the sample for this survey was drawn, the data probably underestimate the needs and barriers to treatment. The respondents were women who appeared for services. At least on the day of the survey, they were able to find transportation and overcome other barriers.

Attempts to meet the substance abuse treatment needs of women in similar circumstances should include the following:

1. Substance abuse treatment must include active, continuous assistance—such as case management—to access basic shelter and health-care needs.
2. The provision of transportation for regularly scheduled treatment appointments is neccessary. In many areas the lack of regularly scheduled public transportation to treatment locales is a major barrier, particularly for poor women.
3. Treatment services for women should include child care. Survey and clinical data document that women at the highest risk for substance abuse are in their childbearing years, and many have one or more children (Levy & Rutter, 1992; Sonderegger, 1992).
4. An increase in the number of female staff and specific training in gender and drug use issues would be beneficial. Staff training should focus on male/female differences in substance abuse etiology, barriers to services, and specific treatment needs.
5. Treatment programs must be sensitive to institutional sexism that may pervade male-oriented service programs. Issues of respect, appropriate forms of sexual interaction, and the potential for sexual harassment in treatment programs must be addressed.

REFERENCES

Agar, M. (1973). *Ripping and running: A formal ethnography of urban heroin addicts.* New York: Seminar Press.

Annual report of the Berrien County Forensic Laboratory. (1994). Submitted to the Berrien County Commission by Andrews University Forensic Laboratory, Berrien Springs, MI.

Ashbrook, D. L., & Solley, L. C. (1979). *Women and heroin abuse: A survey of sexism in drug abuse administration.* Palo Alto, CA: R & E Research Associates.

Austin, G. A., Macari, M. A., Sutker, P., & Lettieri, D. J. (Eds.). (1977). *Drugs and psychopathology.* Rockville, MD: National Institute on Drug Abuse.

Beschner, G. M., & Thompson, P. (1981). *Women and drug abuse treatment: Needs and services.* Rockville, MD: National Institute on Drug Abuse.

Burt, M., Glynn, T. J., & Sowder, B. J. (1979). *Psychosocial characteristics of drug-abusing women.* Rockville, MD: National Institute on Drug Abuse.

Centers for Disease Control and Prevention (CDC). (1993, October). *HIV/AIDS Surveillance, 5.*

Cisin, I., Miller, J. D., & Harrell, A. V. (1978). *Highlights from the national survey on drug abuse: 1977.* Rockville, MD: National Institute on Drug Abuse.

Colten, M. E. (1979). A descriptive and comparative analysis of self-perceptions and attitudes of heroin-addicted women. In *Addicted women: Family dynamics, self-perceptions, and support systems* (pp. 7-36). Rockville, MD: National Institute on Drug Abuse.

Colten, M. E., & Marsh, J. C. (1984). A sex-roles perspective on drug and alcohol use by women. In C. S. Widom (Ed.), *Sex roles and psychopathology* (pp. 219-248). New York: Plenum Press.

Corea, G. (1992). *The invisible epidemic.* New York: HarperCollins.

Cuskey, W. R., Richardson, A. H., & Berger, L. H. (1979). *Specialized therapeutic community program for female addicts.* Rockville, MD: National Institute on Drug Abuse.

Deckard, S. B. (1975). *The women's movement: Political, socioeconomic, and psychological issues.* New York: Harper & Row.

Denenberg, R. (1993). The community: Mobilizing and accessing resources and services. In F. L. Cohen & J. D. Durham (Eds.), *Women, children, and HIV/AIDS* (pp. 251-262). New York: Springer.

Eldred, C. A., & Washington, M. N. (1975). Female heroin addicts in a city treatment program: The forgotten minority. *Psychiatry, 38,* 75-85.

Faden, R., Geller, G., & Powers, M. (1991). *AIDS, women and the next generation.* New York: Oxford University Press.

Feldman, H. W. (1968). Ideological supports to becoming and remaining a heroin addict. *Journal of Health and Social Behavior, 9,* 131-139.

Ferrence, R. G. (1980). Sex differences in prevalence of problem drinking. In O. J. Kalant (Ed.), *Research advances in alcohol and drug problems: Vol. 5. Alcohol and drug problems in women* (pp. 69-124). New York: Plenum Press.

Ferrence, R. G., & Whitehead, P. C. (1980). Sex differences in psychoactive drug use: Recent epidemiology. In O. J. Kalant (Ed.), *Research advances in alcohol and drug problems: Vol. 5. Alcohol and drug problems in women* (pp. 125-201). New York: Plenum Press.

Fillmore, K. M. (1984). "When angels fall": Women's drinking as cultural preoccupation and as reality. In S. C. Wilsnack & L. J. Beckman (Eds.), *Alcohol problems in women* (pp. 7-36). New York: Guilford.

Galbraith, S. (1991). Women and legal drugs. In P. Roth (Ed.), *Alcohol and drugs are women's issues: Vol. 1. A review of the issues* (pp. 150-154). Metuchen, NJ: Women's Action Alliance and The Scarecrow Press.

Glynn, T., Pearson, H. W., & Sayers, M. (Eds.). (1983). *Women and drugs.* Rockville, MD: National Institute on Drug Abuse.

Goldstein, P. J. (1979). *Prostitution and drugs.* Lexington, MA: Lexington Books.

Greene, M. H. (1974). An epidemiologic assessment of heroin use. *American Journal of Public Health, 64* [Suppl.], 1-10.

Gutierres, S. E., Patton, D. S., Raymond, J. S., & Rhoads, D. L. (1984). Women and drugs: The heroin abuser and the prescription drug abuser. *Psychology of Women Quarterly, 8,* 354–369.

Hendrickson, S. P. (1992). Women's voices: A guide for listening to chemically dependent women. *Women and Therapy, 12,* 73–85.

Hughes, R., & Brewin, R. (1979). *The tranquilizing of America: Pill popping and the American way of life.* New York: Warner Books.

Hunt, L. G., & Chambers, C. D. (1976). *The heroin epidemics.* New York: Spectrum.

Inciardi, J. A., Lockwood, D., & Pottieger, A. E. (1993). *Women and crack-cocaine.* New York: Macmillan.

Inciardi, J. A., & Pottieger, A. E. (1986). Drug use and crime among two cohorts of women narcotics users: An empirical assessment. *Journal of Drug Issues, 16,* 91–106.

Inciardi, J. A., Pottieger, A. E., & Faupel, C. E. (1982). Black women, heroin and crime: Some empirical notes. *Journal of Drug Issues, 12,* 241–250.

James, J. (1976). Prostitution and addiction: An interdisciplinary approach. *Addictive Diseases, 2,* 601–618.

James, J., Gosho, C. T., & Watson, R. (1976). The relationship between female criminality and drug use. In Research Triangle Institute (Ed.), *Report of the panel on drug use and criminal behavior* (pp. 441–445). Springfield, VA: National Technical Information Service.

Johnson, S. (1991). Recent research: Alcohol and women's bodies. In Paula Roth (Ed.), *Alcohol and drugs are women's issues: Vol. 1. A review of the issues* (pp. 32–42). Metuchen, NJ: Women's Action Alliance and The Scarecrow Press.

Jonsen, A. R., & Stryker, J. (Eds.). (1993). *The social impact of AIDS in the United States.* Washington, DC: National Academy Press.

Kilbourne, J. (1991). The spirit of the czar: Selling addictions to women. In P. Roth (Ed.), *Alcohol and drugs are women's issues: Vol. 1. A review of the issues.* Metuchen, NJ: Women's Action Alliance and The Scarecrow Press.

Kimmel, W. A. (1992). *Need, demand and problem assessment for substance abuse services.* Rockville, MD: Office for Treatment Improvement.

Levy, S. J., & Doyle, K. M. (1974). Attitudes toward women in a drug abuse treatment program. *Journal of Drug Issues, 4,* 428–434.

Levy, S. J., & Rutter, E. (1992). *Children of drug abusers.* New York: Lexington Books.

Lex, B. W. (1991). Some gender differences in alcohol and polysubstance users. *Health Psychology, 10,* 121–132.

McCoy, C. B., & Inciardi, J. A. (1994). *Sex, drugs, and the secondary spread of AIDS.* Los Angeles: Roxbury.

Miller, H. G., Turner, C. F., & Moses, L. E. (Eds.). (1990). *AIDS: The second decade.* Washington, DC: National Academy Press.

Mondanaro, J. (1989). *Chemically dependent women: Assessment and treatment.* Lexington, MA: Lexington Books.

Mutch, P. B., McBride, D. C., Amey, M., & Gray, J. (1991). *The status of substance use in Berrien County.* Report to Project SAIL. Institute of Alcoholism and Drug Dependency, Andrews University, Berrien Springs, MI.

Mutch, P. B., McBride, D. C., Kilcher, C. L., Hartmann, A., Gray, J., & Amey, M. (1993). *Women's needs for substance abuse services in Berrien, Cass, and Van Buren counties of southwestern Michigan.* Institute of Alcoholism and Drug Dependency,

A Report to the Southwestern Michigan Commission of the Michigan Public Health Department, Andrews University, Berrien Springs, MI.

National Institute on Drug Abuse (NIDA). (1990). *National household survey on drug abuse.* Rockville, MD.

Novello, A., & Wise, P. H. (1991). Public policy issues. In P. A. Pizzo & C. M. Wilfert (Eds.), *Pediatric AIDS: The challenge of HIV infection in infants, children, and adolescents* (pp. 745–755). Baltimore: Williams and Wilkins.

Nurco, D. N., Wegner, N., Baum, H., & Makotsky, A. (1979). *A case study: Narcotic addiction over a quarter of a century in a major American city 1950–1977.* Rockville, MD: National Institute on Drug Abuse.

Polit, D. F., Nuttall, R. L., & Hunter, J. B. (1976). Women and drugs: A look at some of the issues. *Urban & Social Change Review, 9,* 9–16.

Prather, J. E., & Fidell, L. S. (1978). Drug use and abuse among women: An overview. *International Journal of the Addictions, 13,* 863–885.

Preble, E., & Casey, J. L., Jr. (1969). Taking care of business: The heroin user's life on the street. *International Journal of the Addictions, 4,* 1–24.

Ramer, B. S., Smith, D. E., & Gay, G. R. (1972). Adolescent heroin abuse in San Francisco. *International Journal of the Addictions, 7,* 461–465.

Reed, B. G. (1981). Intervention strategies for drug dependent women. In G. M. Beschner, B. Glover Reed, & J. Mondanaro (Eds.), *Treatment services for drug dependent women* (Vol. 1, pp. 1–24). Rockville, MD: National Institute on Drug Abuse.

Report lists barriers to treatment for women. (1993, November). *The Journal,* Addiction Research Foundation, Toronto, p. 1.

Root, M. P. P. (1989). Treatment failures: The role of sexual victimization in women's addictive behavior. *American Journal of Orthopsychiatry, 59,* 542–549.

Rosenbaum, M. (1981). *Women on heroin.* New Brunswick, NJ: Rutgers University Press.

Schmidt, A. (1994). *The health statistics of Berrien County.* Berrien Springs, MI: Berrien County Health Department.

Sonderegger, T. B. (Ed.). (1992). *Perinatal substance abuse: Research findings and clinical implications.* Baltimore: Johns Hopkins University Press.

Substance Abuse and Mental Health Services Administration (SAMHSA). (1993). *National household survey on drug abuse.* Rockville, MD.

Sutter, A. G. (1966). The world of the righteous dope fiend. *Issues in Criminology, 2,* 177–222.

Toray, D. A. (1993). Gender effects in diagnosing alcohol abuse and dependence. *Journal of Clinical Psychology, 49,* 298–308.

Wallen, L. (1992). A comparison of male and female clients in substance abuse treatment. *Journal of Substance Abuse Treatment, 9,* 2–7.

Chapter 9

WHAT WORKS FOR CRACK COCAINE SMOKERS IN TREATMENT?*

Barbara Wallace

Through a review and analysis of outcome-evaluation research studies, this chapter will attempt to answer the question, "What works for crack smokers in treatment?" What constitutes a state-of-the-art treatment for crack addiction, in this author's opinion, is a treatment that appreciates the role of biological, psychological, and social factors, as in a biopsychosocial model; recognizes the type of patient for whom the treatment works; acknowledges the phase of treatment or recovery when the treatment should be administered; and includes relapse prevention. A treatment that "works" produces, on follow-up, relatively high rates of abstinence from crack or cocaine.

Certain limitations are placed on the discussion and our ability definitively to answer the question of what works with crack smokers because of the dearth of outcome-evaluation research on actual crack-smoking populations. As a result, an analysis of what works with mostly white, middle-class, intranasal cocaine users will direct our attempt to ascertain what should work with crack smokers possessing diverse demographics and characteristics.

COMPREHENSIVE, INTENSIVE, MULTIFACETED OUTPATIENT TREATMENT

An outpatient-treatment program that can be described as providing comprehensive and intensive services, while clinicians use multifaceted clinical interventions, appears to work. A comprehensive treatment addresses the drug problem through a number of interventions, such as education, urine

* Barbara C. Wallace, *Crack cocaine: A practical treatment approach for the chemically dependent.* New York: Brunner/Mazel, 1991. Reprinted by permission.

testing, individual sessions, family/couples sessions, group sessions, and re-lapse prevention. An intensive treatment requires patients to participate at a level that involves contacts several times per week with the treatment pro-gram. Use of a multifaceted clinical technique means that professionals uti-lize educational, cognitive, behavioral, and psychodynamic interventions, or techniques derived from a rationale that involves cognitive, behavioral, or psychodynamic theory. Research studies support this characterization of the kind of outpatient treatment that works.

An Exemplary Treatment Model

Washton, Gold, and Pottash (1986) present treatment outcome data on 63 chronic cocaine abusers consecutively admitted to the Regents Hospital outpa-tient program during a 6-month period. Their largely white, employed sample included a majority of patients who did not have a prior inpatient hospital stay. Another quarter of their patients (25%) did enter outpatient treatment from in-patient treatment. In their sample, a third (33%) engaged in free-base smoking, a minority (5%) presented intravenous use, and the majority (62%) were in-tranasal users. Compulsive use for 6 months preceded treatment. The actual treatment included the use of contracting (an agreement to stay in treatment for six months), drug education, urine monitoring, problem-oriented counseling, cocaine recovery groups, individual psychotherapy mixed with couples and/or family sessions where indicated, and relapse-prevention strategies. The program included flexibility in responding to individual patient needs. Follow-up status was determined by supervised urine testing and clinical assessment interviews. What kind of follow-up results does this kind of comprehensive and intensive outpatient treatment produce?

Washton et al.'s (1986) findings show that of the original 63 patients, nearly all (94%, $n = 59$) completed at least three months of treatment, and the majority (67%, $n = 42$) completed at least six months of treatment. Average time of retention in treatment was 26.5 weeks, with a large proportion (49%) continuing treatment beyond seven months at the time of follow-up investiga-tion. At the seven- to 19-month follow-up, 81% ($n = 51$) of the original 63 pa-tients were still abstinent and 12 patients had dropped out of treatment and relapsed to cocaine use. Among the 51 (81%) who were still abstinent, approx-imately half had experienced at least one or two returns to cocaine use with-out a full-blown relapse to chronic or compulsive use. Success rates were directly related to length of time in treatment. A longer time in treatment re-lated to more successful abstinence (pp. 382–383).

Patient and Program Characteristics as Keys to Outpatient Success.
Washton et al. (1986) attribute their high success rates to patient characteristics (successfully employed in professional or highly skilled jobs, history of good func-tioning before cocaine use, willingness to enter a program that required complete abstinence, motivation out of fear of losing valued rewards—job, marriage).

However, success rates were also attributed to characteristics of their program (addressed drug-abuse problem immediately, held high expectations, and placed a strong emphasis on abstinence, as well as recovery and relapse prevention). The researchers also note their use of a wide range of interventions, including cognitive, behavioral, and supportive techniques (peer support groups).

Good reason exists for speculating that active focus on the drug problem, conveyance of high and positive expectations of a good prognosis, emphasis on relapse prevention, and use of a wide range of interventions (individual, family/couples counseling, recovery groups, urine testing) with a multifaceted clinical technique might produce substantial success rates with crack smokers.

Inpatient Plus Outpatient Treatment for High-Severity Patients. Within the Washton et al. (1986) study, those with the most severe cocaine problems (25%) had inpatient treatment first and experienced a structured environment in which to undergo withdrawal from cocaine. "The hospitalized patients were using larger doses of cocaine and were more likely to show medical and psychiatric complications related to drug use" (Washton et al., 1986, p. 383). Washton and colleagues emphasize that, without initial hospitalization, these patients probably would have had little chance of succeeding in outpatient treatment. They assert that the treatment sequence of inpatient followed by outpatient treatment was an effective intervention strategy for these high-severity patients (pp. 383–384).

Charles P. O'Brien of the University of Pennsylvania in Philadelphia reports that two thirds of crack addicts who have enrolled in his outpatient-treatment program drop out within the first month. Bernard Bihari of Kings County Hospital in Brooklyn, N.Y., reports that only 15% of crack users showed up for the second day of an outpatient-treatment program he administered. The problems noted as accounting for the high failure rates of these outpatient programs relate to the fact that crack users must return to the same surroundings, have few social supports to help them stay in treatment, and usually lack employment. Herbert Kleber suggests that the institution of more programs that house addicts should be considered despite the greater expense (Kolata, 1989, p. B7).

Crack cocaine smokers require the kind of thorough assessment that determines whether they should be matched to inpatient treatment before direct entrance into outpatient treatment. Separation from the environment during a phase of withdrawal may be crucial if crack smokers experiencing intense neurochemically based cravings for more crack are to avoid conditioned stimuli in the environment and easy access to crack. Washton et al. (1986) conclude by emphasizing that no single treatment modality will be optimal for all cocaine abusers, and that research is needed to identify the essential ingredients of the most effective approaches.

The treatment model Washton and colleagues investigated emerges as a state-of-the-art treatment that includes carefully assessing patients for individual needs, matching patients to treatments (either inpatient followed by outpatient or direct entrance into outpatient), and educating for relapse prevention. It can be assumed that the need for biological interventions is inherent in an approach that recognizes that the high-severity, high-dosage cocaine user, or the user with psychiatric complications, requires inpatient interventions that probably include biological or pharmacological interventions. For cocaine users who are screened, assessed, and deemed appropriate for direct entrance into outpatient treatment, such treatment can work when it includes an intense and comprehensive program with the kind of elements Washton et al. include.

The Intensive Outpatient Rehabilitation Program

Washton's treatment approach (Washton, 1987, 1989a; Washton, Stone, & Hendrickson, 1988) has evolved toward an even more intensive and comprehensive outpatient program than the one evaluated by Washton et al. (1986). Washton (1989a) cites crucial elements of an intensive outpatient-rehabilitation program that may be capable of producing substantially higher long-term success rates than traditional inpatient care. The intensive outpatient-rehabilitation program has an intensive component that lasts two months and a relapse-prevention program that lasts six months. In the first intensive program, patients attend group-therapy sessions, educational lectures, and self-help meetings four evenings a week; this program usually lasts three hours each evening. Patients receive, in addition, individual, marital, and family counseling at least once per week, and family members attend an eight-week family education and counseling program. In the relapse-prevention program, patients attend group-therapy meetings, educational lectures, and self-help meetings three evenings a week, and receive individual and/or marital/family counseling once a week. Family members also continue in ongoing family recovery groups (Washton, 1989a, pp. 76–77).

Clearly, this program of interventions constitutes the very best in comprehensive and intensive outpatient treatment. Evaluation of the intensive outpatient-rehabilitation program shows that over 80% of patients admitted to the program successfully complete treatment; long-term follow-up studies have yet to be completed (Washton, 1989a). However, when this kind of nearly daily, intense involvement in a comprehensive treatment program takes place, Washton reports finding referrals to inpatient treatment decreasing. According to Washton, prior to implementing the intensive program, 35% of all treatment applicants were referred to residential care; however, now fewer than 15% require inpatient treatment (p. 77). Hence, Washton anticipates that utilization of an intensive outpatient-rehabilitation treatment model may be capable of producing substantially higher long-term success rates than traditional inpatient care (p. 77).

Still, Washton continues to recognize that some patients will require inpatient care—severely dysfunctional, debilitated patients, those with serious medical and psychiatric complications, and those for whom outpatient treatment has not worked (p. 77). Yet, here, inpatient treatment must serve as a "launching pad" for involvement in continuing treatment posthospitalization (p. 78).

More recent findings support the efficacy of treating employed cocaine and crack addicts in inpatient or outpatient rehabilitation programs that are combined with intensive aftercare treatment emphasizing relapse prevention; at 6-to-18 month followup, according to urine tests and clinical interviews, 68% of outpatients (n = 40) and 64% of inpatients (n = 20) were abstinent. Among these patients, 33% experienced a slip at least once to their drug of choice, 23% used alcohol or marijuana, and 46% experienced no slip or relapse to chemical use (Washton, 1989c). Again, individualized assessment of patients will likely reveal that substantial numbers of crack smokers will require not only some period of hospitalization or separation from the environment, but also the kind of intensive and comprehensive outpatient services following an inpatient stay that Washton (1989a) has refined.

Further Support for Comprehensive Outpatient Treatment

Rawson, Obert, McCann, and Mann (1986) provide further evidence that an outpatient program with certain key elements can indeed work. They examined treatment outcome following inpatient, outpatient, and no treatment among a group of 83 subjects who presented themselves at an information and education session regarding cocaine use and available treatment. Subjects were recruited from those calling a 24-hour cocaine hotline. After the educational session, subjects could choose inpatient hospital treatment, structured outpatient treatment, participation in anonymous self-help groups, or no treatment. Despite the limitations of no random assignment, findings showed there were no differences in subject characteristics prior to entering treatment. Among subjects, free-base smokers accounted for 43% of those who chose no treatment, 40% of those who chose outpatient treatment, and 30% of those who chose hospital treatment. Results showed a return to cocaine use by 13% of those undergoing approximately six months of outpatient treatment, 43% of those completing a 28-day hospital stay and being interviewed some seven months after hospitalization, and 47% of those who received no formal treatment.

It should be noted that those in outpatient treatment in the Rawson et al. (1986) study were questioned fairly soon after completion of outpatient treatment, whereas those in the inpatient group were questioned nearly seven months posttreatment. Wallace (1989a) reports that of those who relapse, 76% do so within three months posttreatment and 94% before six months expire. Hence, for the inpatient group questioned seven months posthospitalization, more time had expired since treatment, and so this group was likely to include more patients who had relapsed. Another criticism of the study is that those who participated in outpatient treatment received the key elements of a state-of-the-art treatment—individual sessions, relapse prevention, family and couples counseling, and urine testing. However, the hospital model lacked relapse prevention, and direct entrance into outpatient treatment did not occur for the majority of patients. The provision of relapse prevention during inpatient treatment and direct entrance into aftercare treatment after an inpatient stay are critical in order to reduce the chances of relapse (Wallace, 1989b). Thus, these factors deserve consideration when analyzing the conclusions of Rawson et al.

Rawson et al. (1986) conclude that their preliminary outcome data suggest that outpatient treatment may result in a lower relapse rate than hospital treatment or no treatment. The limitations of the study's design, however, and of the particular hospital model utilized must not be overlooked. In fact, the researchers acknowledge that the current hospital aftercare program may not be appropriately oriented to the needs of cocaine patients, since most patients did not attend the aftercare-treatment component. The deficits of the hospital program prevented its emergence as a treatment that works. What does emerge as something that works is an outpatient program that includes individual counseling, family and couples counseling, relapse prevention, and urine testing. This study reinforces the notion that outpatient treatment works when it has certain crucial elements that produce, in effect, a comprehensive and intensive treatment model.

Even within the most successful group of outpatients in the Rawson et al. (1986) study, a full 13% relapsed to at least monthly cocaine use. And some may have had just one or two episodes of cocaine use that did not qualify as monthly use. A report of 13% returning to monthly cocaine use highlights the risk of relapse that challenges clinicians and researchers to strive to improve even successful program models to better meet the needs of patients. Since within this study a considerable percentage of patients were free-base-cocaine smokers, it may be assumed that motivated crack smokers who would call a hotline and attend an informational session would probably do as well in recovery as did those patients who received no treatment, inpatient treatment, or outpatient treatment of the kind provided in the Rawson et al. study. Instead of having patients prone to a denial of the severity of their addiction select their own treatment, professional consultation might have better matched patients to treatments of appropriate intensity according to the severity of their addiction, perhaps further reducing relapse rates.

The Neurobehavioral Model of Cocaine Outpatient Treatment

In view of their earlier findings in the Rawson et al. (1986) study, Rawson began in January 1990 a study of 100 cocaine-addict volunteers randomly assigned to either what they now label the neurobehavioral treatment program or to a comparison situation consisting of referral to available community resources. Rawson has further articulated the components of the neurobehavioral model, which, he feels, works with cocaine and crack patients, outlining even more explicitly the elements of an effective outpatient treatment. Treatment focuses on behavioral, cognitive, emotional, and relationship problems that typically characterize different phases of recovery from cocaine addiction. The program lasts 12 months and strives to ensure that clients complete treatment, learn about issues critical to addiction and relapse, receive direction and support from a trained therapist (master's-degree level with 60 hours of specialized training), receive education for family members, and be monitored by urine testing. The actual treatment includes 52 individual 45-minute sessions in the first six months, a 12-week educational group, a four-week group focusing on structuring weekends and leisure time, a 20-week relapse-prevention group, seven conjoint/couples sessions in the first six months, weekly random urine tests, analysis of relapse episodes in individual sessions, and AA meetings. In months 7–12 of recovery, a weekly same-sex group is held, while individual and couples sessions continue for patients desiring to remain in ongoing therapy (Rawson, Obert, McCann, Smith, & Ling, 1990).

Rawson et al (1990) admits that this program is fairly expensive by outpatient standards, ranging in cost from $1,500 to $6,000 (p. 11). His treatment costs "$4,500 for patients whose health insurance covers treatment or who can easily afford it" (p. 12). In one facility, a sliding scale exists, and for those at the bottom of the scale, treatment costs $25 a month (p. 12)

The evolution and refinement of Rawson's neurobehavioral model have benefited from the assistance, recommendations, research, and experience of the best chemical-dependency-treatment professionals across the nation (Kleber, Gawin, O'Brien, McLellan, Washton, Marlatt, Gorski, Smith, Zweben, and Resnick and Resnick; see references). The resulting state-of-the-art treatment provides for the kind of structure, intensive level of participation, and availability of comprehensive services necessary to produce an effective outpatient program. Patients receiving these kind of supportive services "every day in the first weeks and at least several times per week for six months thereafter" (Rawson, 1990, p. 11) are likely to benefit in terms of a successful recovery from cocaine addiction. Rawson views his yearlong outpatient approach as preferable to inpatient treatment, which is "excessively expensive and often unnecessary for recovery" (p. 11). On the other hand, hard-core crack users who have been on a binge in the streets for a long time are placed in the hospital by Rawson for three to five days. He acknowledges that unless they have respite from cocaine, are able to sleep, and receive nutritious food, such patients are not coherent enough "to even hear the therapist" (p. 11). Thus, crack-cocaine smokers may require some period of inpatient care prior to entrance into the kind of quality outpatient treatment Rawson describes.

Individual Psychotherapy in an Inpatient Plus an Outpatient Treatment Model

Although based on a rather small sample size, suggestive findings support the assertion that a well-structured hospital program that includes aftercare treatment with certain crucial elements can also work in producing a successful treatment outcome. Schiffer (1988) reports that he successfully treated nine cocaine abusers with long-term in-depth dynamic psychotherapy that began on an inpatient drug-abuse unit and continued on an outpatient basis as aftercare treatment. After at least a year posthospitalization, Schiffer notes that these mostly white, male, employed patients, who for the most part used intranasal cocaine, were drug-free. Only two patients (22.2%) had a brief relapse a few months after hospitalization, but reestablished their abstinence and have been drug-free for over three years. While in the hospital, patients were seen three times a week in individual psychotherapy, and after discharge were seen as outpatients on a twice-a-week basis for one month. Patients were then seen individually once a week for an average of 22 months. The length of treatment ranged from ten months to 37 months.

Schiffer's rationale for individual psychotherapy rests on the fact that all patients suffered some form of trauma or psychological abuse in childhood that necessitates that the therapist do the following: (1) look for the traumatic or abusive condition; (2) establish empathic emotional contact with the patient involving appreciation of why cocaine abuse occurred; (3) help the patient appreciate the covert trauma (narcissistic injuries, neglect, rejection, humiliation, intimidation) suffered in childhood and its impact on his or her development; and (4) help the patient master traumatic experiences. A result of impaired psychological development may be depression and anxiety, which can be addressed in psychotherapy, according to Schiffer. He feels that supportive therapy aimed at enhancing abstinence is necessary as others have suggested; however, he argues that "supportive therapy without working successfully on the deeper issues would have been insufficient for a good long-term outcome" (p. 136).

Random urine-testing results and signed statements of abstinence by patients and their family contributed to the efficacy of the approach. Schiffer views the hospital environment as facilitating a decathexis from the life of drugs by providing firm limits, structure, and education. While psychotropic medication is often recommended based on clinical assessments, none in the sample received it. Beyond provision of in-depth dynamic individual psychotherapy, the hospital treatment also offered psychotherapy groups, drug-education groups, discussions of stress-coping techniques, and frequent staff talks. All of these elements emerge as important dimensions of a sufficiently intense and comprehensive inpatient program that works in contrast to the inpatient model in the Rawson et al. (1986) study.

Long-Term Individual Psychotherapy as Relapse Prevention. Despite the weakness inherent in Schiffer's (1988) small sample size, the study highlights the role of long-term, in-depth individual psychotherapy as relapse prevention. In the process, the study reinforces the assertion of Washton et al. (1986) that where intensive aftercare treatment follows inpatient treatment, we effectively have a state-of-the-art treatment that works. While some patients attended a combination of group therapy and individual psychotherapy or self-help groups plus individual psychotherapy, aftercare treatment that addresses deeper psychological issues emerges as an element of treatment that may be crucial for successful recovery.

Kleber (1988) points out that cocaine use is extremely compelling in itself and may not require predisposition for abuse to develop (p. 1364). However, evidence that all patients in Schiffer's sample had traumatic childhood experiences and other data showing that 91% of crack smokers similarly experience trauma in dysfunctional families in childhood (Wallace, 1989b) argues for interventions that address this possibly predisposing risk factor for the development of addiction. Treatments that address these underlying emotional and psychological issues may provide an essential kind of relapse prevention or risk reduction for reinvolvement in any kind of addictive behavior and work in the long term as Schiffer's data suggest. Perhaps Schiffer correctly emphasizes that a good long-term outcome may depend on addressing these underlying traumatic events in a cocaine abuser's childhood.

Even though Schiffer's sample included mostly white, employed, intranasal-cocaine users, the fact that they, too, experienced childhood trauma argues strongly for the kind of vulnerabilities cocaine and crack users possess for the development of dependence regardless of race or demographics. It therefore logically follows that crack cocaine smokers may also benefit from long-term individual psychotherapy that addresses the impact of childhood trauma and its relationship to the development of chemical dependency. The distinct advantage of individual psychotherapy that begins on an inpatient unit and continues with the same therapist on an outpatient basis also arises from Schiffer's work.

Outpatient Treatment for Pregnant Crack Smokers and Mothers

Regarding treatments that work for special populations, evidence suggests the efficacy of the treatment provided at the Center for Perinatal Addiction at Northwestern Hospital in Chicago under the initiative of Ira Chasnoff. The components of this "model program" are prenatal medical care, pediatric follow-up, social-service case management, chemical-dependency treatment on site, an interdisciplinary staff, parent education, support groups, and the use of community outreach (Kronstadt, 1989). According to Kronstadt, the importance of these components arises from the fact that pregnant cocaine abusers present a typical profile of a history of physical/sexual/emotional abuse, present with chemical dependency, likely live with a drug-using partner, often come from poor and chaotic environments, feel guilty and responsible for their plight, and have low self-esteem. Kronstadt goes on to explain that once cocaine/crack babies are born, mothers face the challenge of caring for a difficult baby who will be jittery and have tremors; be irritable, overexcitable, and very sensitive to the mildest environmental stimulation; cry a lot; and be unable to calm itself. Even experienced caregivers find it difficult to care for cocaine/crack babies. Thus, treatment and support of mothers for their addiction and parent education are critical components of a model program (Kronstadt, 1989).

In the Northwestern outpatient program for pregnant crack mothers, 79% are still off drugs one year after giving birth (*"Crack's smallest, costliest victims,"* 1989). However, Chandler (1989) concedes that while pregnant women are able to maintain abstinence while pregnant and shortly after giving birth within this outpatient program, they are still plagued by the problem of relapse. This author notes that this program may require a more intensive relapse prevention education component. Chandler reports that a study that was to begin in early 1990 will compare the treatment outcomes of 30 women treated in an inpatient setting and 30 women in an outpatient setting.

Halfon (1989) characterizes the kind of treatment models that need to be created for pregnant crack users and their babies as having to provide a continuum of care. Patients need linked services at every step of the treatment process. Halfon points out that "turf issues" among different social-service agencies must be resolved and that few good models exist. He suggests that the kind of continuity of care utilized with the elderly might provide a model for the kind of services he envisions as critical for pregnant women and cocaine babies.

Kronstadt's (1989) survey of experts across the nation indicates that programs for pregnant crack mothers must be comprehensive, offering as many services as possible at one site, such as prenatal medical care, pediatric care of the infant, chemical-dependency treatment, and coordination of social services. In addition, treatment interventions must be intensive, providing frequent contacts with clients over a long period, even home visits, a drop-in center, and a 24-hour crisis phone line. Upon treatment experts' strong recommendations, Kronstadt highlights the need for residential treatment programs for those most severely dependent, as well as drug-free housing for all other clients, which includes provisions for children to remain with their mothers. Most important, national treatment experts stressed the critical need for more treatment programs to serve the increasing numbers of pregnant women and their children, according to Kronstadt.

Northwestern's program emerges as a model comprehensive and intensive program, while exploration of the efficacy of inpatient care represents an appropriate direction for continuing research efforts. However, the kind of models that provide a continuity of care, and recognize that some mothers require inpatient treatment; others, outpatient treatment alone or after inpatient treatment; and still others, long-term residential treatment, have yet to be created in adequate numbers to meet the critical needs of this special population.

IMPLICATIONS FOR DESIGNING COST-EFFECTIVE TREATMENT

Marlatt (1988) cautions against uniformity myths where the same treatment is recommended for everyone exhibiting signs of the particular addiction problem. In this regard, he suggests that one alternative is the "notion that treatment for addiction problems should be graded in intensity, relevant to the magnitude of the presenting problem" (p. 480). This graded series of interventions would include first asking clients to make efforts to change on their own or with minimal intervention, such as attending a self-help group (AA/NA/CA). If progress is not made, a "more intensive form of treatment (e.g., outpatient professional treatment coupled with a self-help group) can be tried. Finally, if all else fails, the use of long-term inpatient treatment programs can be implemented as a last resort" (p. 481). Marlatt also explains that careful assessment must determine the nature and severity of the addictive behavior and must be carried out at each stage of the graded intervention process to monitor progress and select a matched treatment strategy (p. 481).

The Need for a Graded Series of Interventions

The research reviewed in this chapter suggests that such a graded series of interventions must be applied in the treatment of crack smokers. Individualized assessment of patients remains critical in matching patients to treatments of appropriate intensity. Rawson (1990) states that many "of these cocaine abusers won't be able to get off the drug no matter what treatment they receive. These hard-core abusers may be mentally ill, are often heavily involved in criminal activity, and generally suffer severe societal problems such as chronic unemployment" (p. 10). However, if we consider the wisdom of Marlatt (1988), upon failure in even the best outpatient treatment program, clinical assessment turns toward consideration of placing patients in even more intensive inpatient and long-term residential programs.

The Need for Modifications in Hospital Treatment

Marlatt (1988) notes that too many experts have erred by recommending the ubiquitous 30-day inpatient treatment followed by lifelong participation in AA. Changes in clinicians' strategies of assessing patients and matching them to treatments may be necessary considering the crack epidemic and what is likely to work with crack smokers characterized by diverse demographics and varied crack-smoking patterns. Improvements in hospital programs may be needed to increase their efficacy with crack smokers and ensure that they match patients to appropriate aftercare treatment. Instead of a 28- or 30-day hospital stay, a variable-length inpatient detoxification schedule may be a viable alternative, to be determined by patient assessments. The utility and benefits of a 14-day inpatient detoxification for the cocaine and crack dependent have been described (Wallace, 1987). Special programs should be designed for crack patients or existing programs modified to increase treatment outcome with challenging and difficult populations. Inpatient treatment programs need to include relapse prevention and other elements that make model programs sufficiently intense and comprehensive.

The Need for Funding Cost-Effective Hospital Care

A conclusion that inpatient treatment has no role in the recovery process can have damaging consequences for those crack smokers desperately needing separation from crack-saturated environments during a period of withdrawal or when most vulnerable to relapse to chronic crack use. Policymakers must not conclude that funding need not support inpatient detoxification as a treatment option. On the contrary, they must act to ensure the availability of both comprehensive and intensive inpatient and outpatient treatment programs, as must those who design or modify crack-treatment models.

In view of "the current trend toward developing more cost-effective treatment approaches and the resulting emergence of a new treatment modality, namely, the intensive outpatient rehabilitation program" (Washton, 1989a, p. 75), it is imperative to underscore further the needs of many crack smokers. In further support of the specific importance of inpatient detoxification, policymakers and administrators must understand that the high-dose and high-frequency crack smoker must be separated from a crack-saturated environment during a withdrawal period when neurochemically based cravings (Rosecan & Spitz, 1987) and a compulsion to smoke more crack (Cohen, 1987; Herridge & Gold, 1988) may lead to immediate relapse. The characterization as a hard-core crack abuser (Rawson, 1990) arises from being driven by a pharmacological imperative (Cohen, 1987) to smoke more and more crack. Crack smokers *become,* as a result of this compulsion, unemployed and resort to crime to support daily or nearly daily $100–500 crack habits. These severely debilitated and dysfunctional crack patients must be able to enter inpatient detoxification programs in order to achieve initial abstinence and negotiate outpatient-treatment requirements.

Policymakers must strive to understand the complexities arising from the fact that cocaine and crack smokers have diverse crack-smoking patterns and addictions that vary in severity. The cost-effective option of a variable-length inpatient detoxification stay, perhaps ranging from 5 to 14 days, must be available as a treatment alternative that saves money in comparison with a 28- to 30-day inpatient rehabilitation period. On the other hand, assessment of some patients may still justify some intensive and comprehensive 28- and 30-day inpatient programs.

Toward a Continuum of Care for Crack Patients

Our policymakers must realize the importance of funding comprehensive and intensive outpatient programs into which patients can enter directly upon leaving inpatient detoxification. Without direct entrance into an outpatient phase of treatment, vulnerable crack patients suffering from recurrent cravings and anhedonia, and trying to avoid conditioned stimuli in the environment, will likely relapse to chronic crack use. Hence, policymakers cannot simply ask professionals, "What works?" They must ask, "What works for whom?" In this way, they may acknowledge responses that denote what works for patients with certain characteristics, and during specific phases of recovery (a first period of withdrawal or early abstinence, a second period of prolonging abstinence characterized by cravings and anhedonia, and a third period of one to several years to a lifetime of recovery). A continuum of care is needed that directly links inpatients completing hospital treatment (appropriate for a withdrawal or early abstinence phase) to outpatient services that can permit them to prolong abstinence and avoid relapse.

While the issues are somewhat complex, policymakers must comprehend the dimensions of the crack-treatment challenge and the kind of programs that need to be created and funded. Unless we concentrate efforts on constructing a service-delivery system providing a continuum of quality care, society will have to pay the price of crack smokers further deteriorating because no treatment is available, and relapsing to chronic use after they finally receive treatment.

Deficits in our national treatment strategy, flaws in currently inadequate programs, and errors by clinicians in matching patients to treatment must be examined before we conclude that some cocaine patients, or hard-core crack abusers, may not recover regardless of the treatment they receive. Professionals must analyze how we set patients up for failure when we mismatch them to inappropriate treatment that fails to meet their needs. Policymakers and program administrators collude in preordaining failure when they do not ensure the availability of a range of treatment options that provide a continuity of care. A cost-effective response to the needs of the crack-using population can result in the establishment of an artillery of treatment weaponry sufficiently potent to win the crack war.

CONCLUSION

This chapter has articulated a standard against which crack treatments should be judged. State-of-the-art crack treatments should attend to biological, psychological, and social factors underlying crack dependence, following a biopsychosocial model. In addition, model treatments should recognize the circumscribed population or type of patient for whom the treatment works acknowledge the phase of treatment or recovery when it should be administered, and include relapse prevention. Despite the limitations of the available research, which is lacking random assignment and controls and is marked by a dearth of outcome-evaluation studies specifically with crack-smoking populations, a review of research with mostly white, middle-class intranasal-cocaine, intravenous cocaine, and free-base-cocaine smokers has identified effective crack treatments.

Long-term outpatient treatment (six to 12 months), which is comprehensive and intensive (providing nearly daily contact with patients) and includes urine testing, individual sessions, family/couples sessions, group sessions, and relapse prevention, affords an exemplary treatment model. Moreover, within these outpatient treatments, well-trained or professional therapists typically utilize a multifaceted clinical technique that includes educational, cognitive, behavioral, and psychodynamic interventions, or techniques that derive a rationale from cognitive-behavioral or psychodynamic theory.

The review also highlights how for high-severity patients—perhaps most comparable to compulsive high-frequency and high-dose crack smokers—the intervention of inpatient before outpatient treatment may be critical to patients' recovery. We saw that even where treatment is successful, a brief return to cocaine use often characterizes a pattern of recovery. Although research supports the superiority of outpatient treatment over inpatient treatment, deficits in inpatient programs may explain their higher relapse rates. Inpatient treatment works when well structured (groups, education, stress-coping techniques, staff talks) and when it includes intensive individual psychotherapy (three times per week); moreover, after the inpatient phase, individual psychotherapy continues during outpatient treatment for one to two years, in addition to urine testing and group involvement. Thus, when an inpatient program can be characterized as comprehensive and intensive, and includes an excellent outpatient component, it may also work. Crack patients require a continuum of care that ensures that treatments take place in the early phase of abstinence or withdrawal, a second phase of prolonging abstinence characterized by continued cravings and anhedonia, and a third phase of a one- to several-year or lifetime period of recovery.

REFERENCES

Chandler, J. (1989, December). *Chemical dependency treatment for pregnant addicts.* Paper presented at the Drug-Free Pregnancy Conference, San Mateo, CA.

Cohen, S. (1987). Causes of the cocaine outbreak. In A. Washton and M. Gold (Eds.), *Cocaine: A clinician's handbook* (pp. 3–9). New York: Guilford Press.

Crack's smallest, costliest victims. (1989, August 7). *New York Times,* p. A14.

Gawin, F. (1989, October). Treatment of crack and cocaine abusers. Paper presented at the "What Works" Conference, New York, NY.

Gawin, F. H., & Kleber, H. D. (1984). The spectrum of cocaine abuse and its treatment. *Journal of Clinical Psychiatry, 45,* 18–23.

Gawin, F. H., & Kleber, H. D. (1986). Abstinence symptomatology and psychiatric diagnosis in cocaine abusers. *Archives of General Psychiatry, 43*(2), 107–113.

Gorski, T. (1988a). *The staying sober workbook: A serious solution for the problem of relapse* (instruction manual). Independence, MO: Herald House/Independence Press.

Gorski, T. (1988b). *The staying sober workbook: A serious solution for the problem of relapse* (exercise manual). Independence, MO: Herald House/Independence Press.

Gorski, T., & Miller, M. (1984). *The phases and warning signs of relapse.* Independence, MO: Herald House/Independence Press.

Gorski, T., & Miller, M. (1986). *Staying sober: A guide for relapse prevention.* Independence, MO: Herald House/Independence Press.

Halfon, N. (1989, December). Intervention, treatment, and policy. Paper presented at the Drug-Free Pregnancy Conference, San Mateo, CA.

Herridge, P., & Gold, M. (1988). Pharmacological adjuncts in the treatment of opioid and cocaine addicts. *Journal of Psychoactive Drugs, 20*(3), 233–242.

Kleber, H. (1988). Epidemic cocaine abuse: America's present, Britain's future? *British Journal of Addiction, 83,* 1359–1371.

Kleber, H. D., & Gawin, F. H. (1984a). Cocaine abuse: A review of current and experimental treatments. In J. Grabowski (Ed.), *Cocaine: Pharmacology, effects, and treatment of abuse.* NIDA Research Monograph 50, Department of Health and Human Services. Washington, DC: U.S. Government Printing Office.

Kleber, H. D., & Gawin, F. H. (1984b). The spectrum of cocaine abuse and its treatment. *Journal of Clinical Psychiatry, 45,* 18–23.

Kolata, G. (1989, August 24). Experts finding new hope on treating crack addicts. *New York Times,* pp. A1, B7.

Kronstadt, D. (1989, March). Pregnancy and cocaine addiction: An overview of impact and treatment. Report presented at the Drug-Free Pregnancy Project, Far West Laboratory for Educational Research and Development, San Francisco, CA.

Marlatt, G. A. (1980). Determinants of relapse: Implications for the maintenance of behavior change. In P. O. Davidson and S. M. Davidson (Eds.), *Behavioral Medicine: Changing health lifestyles.* New York: Brunner/Mazel.

Marlatt, G. A. (1982). Relapse prevention: A self control program for the treatment of addictive behaviors. In R. B. Stuart (Ed.), *Adherence, compliance, and generalization in behavioral medicine.* New York: Brunner/Mazel.

Marlatt, G. A. (1985). Relapse prevention: Theoretical rationale and overview of the model. In G. A. Marlatt and J. R. Gordon (Eds.), *Relapse prevention.* New York: Guilford Press.

Marlatt, G. A. (1988). Matching client to treatment: Treatment models and stages of change. In D. M. Donovan & G. A. Marlatt (Eds.), *Assessment of addictive behaviors.* New York: Guilford Press.

Marlatt, G. A., Curry, S., & Gordon, J. R. (1986). A comparison of treatment approaches in smoking cessation (unpublished manuscript).

Marlatt, G. A., & Gordon, J. (1989). Relapse prevention: Future directions. In M. Gossop (Ed.), *Relapse and addictive behavior.* New York: Routledge.

Marlatt, G. A., & Gordon, J. R. (1985). *Relapse prevention.* New York: Guilford Press.

McLellan, A. T. (1986). "Psychiatric severity" as a predictor of outcome from substance abuse treatments. In R. E. Meyers (Ed.), *Psychopathology and addictive disorders.* New York: Guilford Press.

O'Brien, C., Childress, A., McLellan, A., Ehrman, R., & Ternes, J. (1988). Progress in understanding the conditioning aspects of drug dependence. NIDA Research Monograph 81. Rockville, MD: NIDA.

O'Brien, C. P. (1976). Experimental analysis of conditioning factors in human narcotic addiction. *Pharmacology Review, 227,* 533–543.

O'Brien, C. P., Nace, E. P., Mintz, J., Meyers, A. L., & Ream, N. (1980). Follow-up of Vietnam veterans: 1. Relapse to drug use after Vietnam service. *Drug and Alcohol Dependence, 5,* 333–340.

Rawson, R. (1990, Winter). Cut the crack: The policymaker's guide to cocaine treatment. *Policy Review,* 10–19.

Rawson, R. A., Obert, J. L, McCann, M. J., & Mann, A. J. (1986). Cocaine treatment out-come: Cocaine use following inpatient, outpatient, and no treatment. NIDA Research Monograph 67. Rockville, MD: NIDA.

Rawson, R. A., Obert, J. L, McCann, M. J., Smith, M. S., & Ling, W. (1990). Neurobehav-ioral treatment for cocaine dependency. *Journal of Psychoactive Drugs, 22,* (2).

Resnick, R. B., & Resnick, E. (1986). Psychological issues in the treatment of cocaine abuse. NIDA Research Monograph 67. Rockville, MD: NIDA.

Rosecan, J. J., & Spitz, H. I. (Eds.). (1987). *Cocaine abuse: New directions in treatment and research.* New York: Brunner/Mazel.

Schiffer, F. (1988). Psychotherapy of nine successfully treated cocaine abusers: Tech-niques and dynamics. *Journal of Substance Abuse Treatment, 5,* 131–137.

Smith, M. (1989a, July 25). The Lincoln Hospital acupuncture drug abuse program. Tes-timony presented to the Select Committee on Narcotics of the House of Represen-tatives.

Smith, M. (1989b, August). Interview by author at Lincoln Hospital Acupuncture Clinic, South Bronx, NY.

Wallace, B. C (1987). Cocaine dependence treatment on an inpatient detoxification unit. *Journal of Substance Abuse Treatment, 4,* 85–92.

Wallace, B. C (1989a). Psychological and environmental determinants of relapse in crack cocaine smokers. *Journal of Substance Abuse Treatment, 6*(2), 95–106.

Wallace, B. C (1989b). Relapse prevention in psychoeducational groups for crack co-caine smokers. *Journal of Substance Abuse Treatment, 6*(4), 229–239.

Washton, A. M. (1986). Treatment of cocaine abuse. In NIDA Research Monograph 67. Rockville, MD: NIDA.

Washton, A. M. (1987). Outpatient treatment techniques. In A. M. Washton and M. S. Gold (Eds.), *Cocaine: A clinicians' handbook.* New York: Guilford Press.

Washton, A. M. (1989a). *Cocaine addiction: Treatment, recovery, and relapse preven-tion.* New York: W. W. Norton.

Washton, A. M. (1989b) Cocaine abuse and compulsive sexuality. In *Medical Aspects of Human Sexuality,* pp. 32–39.

Washton, A. M. (1989c). Outpatient works, too. *The U.S. Journal of Drug and Alcohol Dependence, 13*(12), 1.

Washton, A. M., and Gold, M. S. (Eds.). (1987). *A clinician's handbook.* New York: Guilford Press.

Washton, A. M., Gold, M. S., & Pottash, A. C. (1986). Treatment outcome in cocaine abusers. In NIDA Research Monograph 67. Rockville, MD: NIDA.

Washton, A. M., Stone, N. S., & Hendrickson, E. C. (1988). Cocaine abuse. In D. M. Donovan and G. A. Marlatt (Eds.), *Assessment of addictive behaviors.* New York: Guilford Press.

Zweben, J. E. (1986). Treating cocaine dependence: New challenges for the therapeutic community. *Journal of Psychoactive Drugs, 18*(3).

ABOUT THE AUTHORS

Robert S. Anwyl, M.A., is professor of sociology in the Department of Behavioral Studies at Miami Dade Community College, Florida. His research interests include the epidemiology of drug abuse, AIDS, and cancer.

Dale D. Chitwood, Ph.D., is professor of medical sociology within the Departments of Sociology, Psychiatry, and Epidemiology and Public Health and a member of the Comprehensive AIDS Center and Comprehensive Drug Research Center at the University of Miami, Florida. His research interests include the epidemiology of HIV/AIDS, cocaine use, evaluation, and health services research.

Mary Comerford, M.S.P.H., is senior research associate within the Department of Sociology at the University of Miami. She has been engaged in research in the areas of HIV and drug use for the past nine years.

David K. Griffin, Ed.D., is research assistant professor in the Department of Sociology and a member of the Comprehensive Drug Research Center at the University of Miami. He is a psychologist whose research interests include the evaluation of behavioral change models.

James A. Inciardi, Ph.D., is professor and director of the Center for Drug and Alcohol Studies at the University of Delaware, Newark, and an adjunct professor in the Department of Epidemiology and Public Health at the University of Miami School of Medicine. His research interests include substance abuse and public policy, treatment evaluation, and AIDS prevention.

Carole Luke Kilcher, Ph.D., is assistant professor of communications at Andrews University, Berrien Springs, Michigan. She conducts applied research in the areas of women's issues, substance abuse, interpersonal skills, team building, and the baby boomer generation.

Duane C. McBride, Ph.D., is professor and chairperson of the Department of Behaviorial Sciences at Andrews University, Berrien Springs, Michigan, and an adjunct professor at the Comprehensive Drug Research Center at the University of Miami. His research interests are in the areas of crime and drugs, community needs assessments, HIV/AIDS, and health-care services.

Clyde B. McCoy, Ph.D., is director of the Comprehensive Drug Research Center and professor within the Department of Epidemiology and Public Health at the University of Miami. He currently is conducting national and international AIDS research projects and his research interests include epidemiology, drug abuse, HIV/AIDS prevention among drug users, and cancer prevention.

H. Virginia McCoy, Ph.D., is associate professor and chairperson of the Department of Public Health at Florida International University, Miami, and an adjunct professor at the University of Miami Comprehensive Drug Research Center. Her research interests are in migration and health, minorities and women in community-based settings, and program evaluations of interventions to prevent HIV risk behavior among drug users.

Lisa R. Metsch, Ph.D., is research assistant professor in the Department of Epidemiology and Public Health and a member of the Comprehensive Drug Research Center at the University of Miami. She is project director of two studies that evaluate HIV risk reduction intervention programs, and her research interests center on women who use drugs, and the children of those women.

Patricia B. Mutch, Ph.D., is professor and director of the Institute of Alcoholism and Drug Dependency at Andrews University, Berrien Springs, Michigan. Her research interests include substance abuse among women, needs assessment, the prevention of substance abuse, and nutrition.

J. Bryan Page, Ph.D., is professor in the Department of Anthropology and the Department of Psychiatry of the University of Miami. He has spent 23 years studying patterns of drug use, usually in street settings. In-depth interviews and direct observations of behavior have served as Dr. Page's primary research methods in these investigations.

Anne E. Pottieger, Ph.D., is a scientist with the Center for Drug and Alcohol Studies at the University of Delaware. She currently directs a study funded by the National Institute on Drug Abuse entitled "Barriers to Treatment for Cocaine-Dependent Women." Her publications are in the areas of crime, delinquency, and drug use.

James E. Rivers, Ph.D., is research associate professor in the Department of Epidemiology and Public Health and deputy director of the Comprehensive Drug Research Center at the University of Miami. He recently completed an analysis of drug courts and currently is conducting several substance abuse prevention and treatment program evaluation projects.

Prince C. Smith, Ph.D., is assistant professor in the Department of Psychiatry at the University of Miami. He has worked for 10 years with street-based populations of drug users, both as an interventionist and as a researcher. During his career, Dr. Smith has conducted hundreds of interviews with homeless people who use drugs.

Hilary L. Surratt, M.A., is research associate at the Comprehensive Drug Research Center of the University of Miami and project director of an HIV/AIDS seroprevalence and prevention project in Rio de Janeiro, Brazil. Her research interests include HIV prevention and drug abuse treatment evaluation.

Barbara C. Wallace, Ph.D., is a faculty member in the Department of Health Education, Teachers College, Columbia University. She has published numerous books and articles in the area of drug-abuse treatment.

Norman L. Weatherby, Ph.D., is research associate professor within the Department of Epidemiology and Public Health and Department of Sociology and is a member of the Comprehensive Drug Research Center of the University of Miami. A demographer and methodologist, he has conducted research in maternal and child health in Africa and the United States. He currently is studying drug abuse and HIV in Miami and in rural migrant farm-worker populations.

GLOSSARY

after-hours club Place where alcohol was illegally sold after club closing time and cocaine was snorted or sold. These 1970s and 1980s clubs were the forerunners of crack houses.

austere house Place where crack is manufactured and sold but not used for drug/crack use.

backs Single hit on a crack pipe.

backup Second hit on a crack pipe, generally described as far less potent than the first.

bandominiums Abandoned buildings that have been taken over by addicts and serve as crack houses.

base Any form of cocaine base including crack and freebase; basic alkaloidal level of cocaine.

base house Crack house.

base whores Women who exchange sex for crack in crack houses.

basuco South American term for coca paste.

beam Single hit of crack as in "Beam me up, Scotty," from TV's *Star Trek*.

bernice Cocaine.

binge Extended period of crack or freebase use.

biscayne babe Epithet for prostitutes who stroll Miami's Biscayne Boulevard.

bloop house Place where any type of sexual activity can occur. See *freak room*.

blowup Chemical additives used to increase the size of crack rocks.

bogey Term for crack, derived from Key Largo fame.

bomb bag Large white plastic bag in which drugs are delivered to a crack house.

bond man Crack dealer.

boost To shoplift.

boulder Large rock or slab of crack.

brick Large rock or slab of crack.

brothel Type of crack house where the prostitutes are not involved in the payment process. They receive their payment, usually crack and boarding, from the owner after services have been rendered. These prostitutes also live in the crack house. In other crack houses, the bartering for sex occurs between the prostitute and customer.

bubb Hit of crack or snort of cocaine.

bush Term for crack named after the former president, who escalated a war on drugs in Miami.

buy-bust operation Similar to a sting: Undercover cops act as drug customers, and then arrest the dealer.

brains Oral sex, specifically fellatio.

castle Fortified structures in which large amounts of crack are manufactured, packaged, and sold.

charlie Cocaine.

chasing ghosts Compulsively searching every inch of a room over and over again looking for bits of crack. See *tweaking.*

chicken head Woman in a crack house who will perform sexually for a hit or piece of crack. Term comes from the motion of the head when performing fellatio, which is similar to that of a chicken when it is walking or pecking the ground.

cigarette Term for crack, named for the high-performance racing boat.

cocaine Cocaine hydrochloride as a white powder or rock crystal.

coca paste Intermediate product in the processing of the coca leaf into street cocaine.

cokey Cocaine user.

comeback Chemical additives used to increase the size of crack rocks. See *blowup.*

conan Term for crack.

cookie Large quantity of crack, approximately 90 rocks.

cop To purchase drugs.

cop house House used for the sale of drugs and/or crack.

corrine Cocaine.

crack Crack has a variety of meanings: (1) crack cocaine: mixture consisting usually of cocaine, lidocaine, and baking soda, but often containing other unknown chemicals; (2) a vagina; (3) vaginal intercourse; (4) a prostitute; (5) a woman who exchanges sex for crack in crack houses.

crackhead Compulsive user of crack or freebase.

crack house Place where crack is bought, sold, and/or smoked.

crack pipe Makeshift smoking devices fabricated from beer and soda cans, jars, bottles, and other containers.

cracks More than one crack rock.

crack smoking Inhalation of vapors produced as a result of crack being heated. Technically, crack is not really smoked. Smoking implies combustion, burning, and the inhalation of smoke. Tobacco and marijuana are smoked; crack is actually inhaled. The small pebbles or rocks, having a relatively low melting point, are placed in a special glass pipe or other smoking device and heated. Rather than burning, crack vaporizes and the fumes are inhaled.

crack whore Woman who exchanges sex for crack in a crack house.

crash Feeling of depression following mood elevation brought about by drugs; often characterized by acute malaise and intense craving for more drugs.

crumbs Small crack rocks.

dead zone Area of the city or community that has been taken over by drugs and drug dealers.

deal Sell drugs.

devil's dick Crack pipe.

dime rock $10 piece of crack.

doctor Person who injects drugs into someone else's arm for a small fee.

doo-wap Two crack rocks.

dope Drugs.

dope house Place where injection equipment is rented and drugs are injected. See *shooting gallery.*

dope man Person who sells crack.

draw a hard one Inhale deeply.

drug house III House where drugs/crack are produced.

drug house IV House where crack and/or money is stored.

dumped people Homeless people whose families and friends have abandoned them usually because of drug or alcohol use.

eight ball Large quantity of crack, generally an eighth of an ounce, sold in a block form.

flavor Term for crack.

freak, freaking A freak was originally a crack whore who would engage in oral sex with another woman. However, it now refers to anyone who trades any type of sex for crack.

freak room Separate room in a crack house where sexual activity occurs.

freebase   Cocaine in its base form after all the impurities have been removed.

freebasing   Smoking any form of cocaine base (crack or freebase).

geek joint   Marijuana cigarette laced with crack.

get-off house   Shooting gallery.

gut bucket   Woman who exchanges sex for crack in crack houses.

handball   Term for crack.

hard white   Term for crack.

hash house   Place where opium could be smoked.

high   Euphoria.

hit   Puff on a pipe.

hit house   Crack house that caters to members of the so-called poverty class where order is not well maintained.

holders   Juveniles used by drug dealers to carry drugs/money in an attempt to reduce personal risk of arrest.

house girl   Woman who literally lives in a crack house and who provides sex to the customers smoking there.

house man (woman)   Owner of a crack house.

hustler   Person who lives by his or her wits.

hustling   Getting drugs/money from someone using any means possible.

hypersexuality   High-frequency, usually unprotected sex with numerous partners.

kibbles and bits   Small pieces of crack.

john   Male customer of a prostitute or a person who purchases sex in a crack house.

juggle   Selling crack, or any drug, for double what it is worth.

junkie   Drug addict.

lace joint   Marijuana cigarette laced with crack. Same as a *geek joint.*

lookout man   A man, woman, or child working in or for a crack house who watches for the police.

losers   Homeless adults who do not work, but wait around for opportunities to make money by petty thievery, begging, or scavenging.

metal rock $5 piece of crack.

milk brothers   Sexual behavior where large numbers of men engage in vaginal intercourse with the same woman and in rapid succession.

mission   Crack-smoking binge, lasting several days, during which users do not eat or sleep.

Montana   Cuban drug dealer.

Noriega's holiday   Term for crack, named after the former Panamanian dictator.

Olympus   Term for crack derived from Greek mythology.

on the boards   Used to buy crack. For example, "My rent money went on the boards."

open house   Crack house in which "anything goes," with considerable social interaction among the users including sex and violence.

ouzie   Crack-smoking device, usually-made from a small liquor bottle, pill bottle, soda can, or baby food jar.

Pablo   Term for crack, after the late head of the Medellin cartel, Pablo Escobar.

party house   Crack house that is the home of an addict and caters to "working-class men."

pasta   South American term for coca paste.

pasta basica de cocaina   South American term for coca paste.

PCP   Phencyclidine, a psychedelic drug.

pin joint   Small geek joint.

residence house   Apartments or houses where numerous people gather regularly to smoke crack. Many owners are reluctant to call these places crack houses; however, the primary activities are the same as those in the crack house. The major differences are that crack is not sold in these houses (only smoked), and there is a social relationship between crack users because they usually knew the owner of the house prior to smoking crack there.

resort   Crack house in which crack is prepared, bought, sold, and smoked, and in which sex is traded for crack.

ripping and running Stealing drugs/money from someone, and running away.

rock (1) Crack; (2) "Rock cocaine": a cocaine hydrochloride product for intranasal snorting.

rocking up The preparation of crack cocaine.

rock monster Any person who exchanges sex for crack in crack houses.

roller/high roller Person who takes risks.

runner Messenger who takes cocaine from the dealer to the buyer. He (or she) may also help in the cooking of crack and help maintain order.

rush Intense flood of pleasure that is felt soon after drug intake.

schoolboy Cocaine.

shake Shavings from crack rocks when they are broken to be sold in smaller quantities. Shake is often smoked in geek joints.

shooting gallery Place where injection equipment is rented and drugs are injected. In some instances, crack may be smoked in a shooting gallery.

shotgun Smoke inhaled from a crack pipe and blown into someone else's mouth so the person can get high from the same hit.

skeezer Woman who exchanges sex for crack in a crack house.

skillet Pipe used to smoke crack.

smoke houses Crack houses where the operator has little or no control over the activities that take place. Smoke houses are often filthy with no running water.

speakeasies Gathering places for the consumption of illegal alcohol, and in many cases, for cocaine as well.

spotter Person who warns dealers of police presence. See *lookout man*.

STDs Sexually transmitted diseases.

steerer One who directs customers to crack spots in copping zones.

stem Pipe used to smoke crack.

straight shooter Long metal or glass stem (about 8 inches long) used to smoke crack.

strawberry Young girl who exchanges sex for crack in a crack house.

sting Police operation in which an undercover cop acts as a drug dealer/buyer.

stroll Major streets where prostitutes solicit customers.

swell-up Chemical additives used to increase the size of crack rocks.

tavern culture house Crack house where "anything goes." See *open house*.

tool Any type of crack-smoking paraphernalia.

toss (tossup) Woman who exchanges sex for crack in a crack house.

tweaking While high on crack, imagining that evey speck of dirt on the floor is a piece of crack, and hence picking up and examining these specks.

white Crack.

white boy Heroin.

white cloud Crack.

wild thing Sexual activity.

workers Homeless people who spend their wages on drugs.

INDEX